IMAGES
of America

DALHART

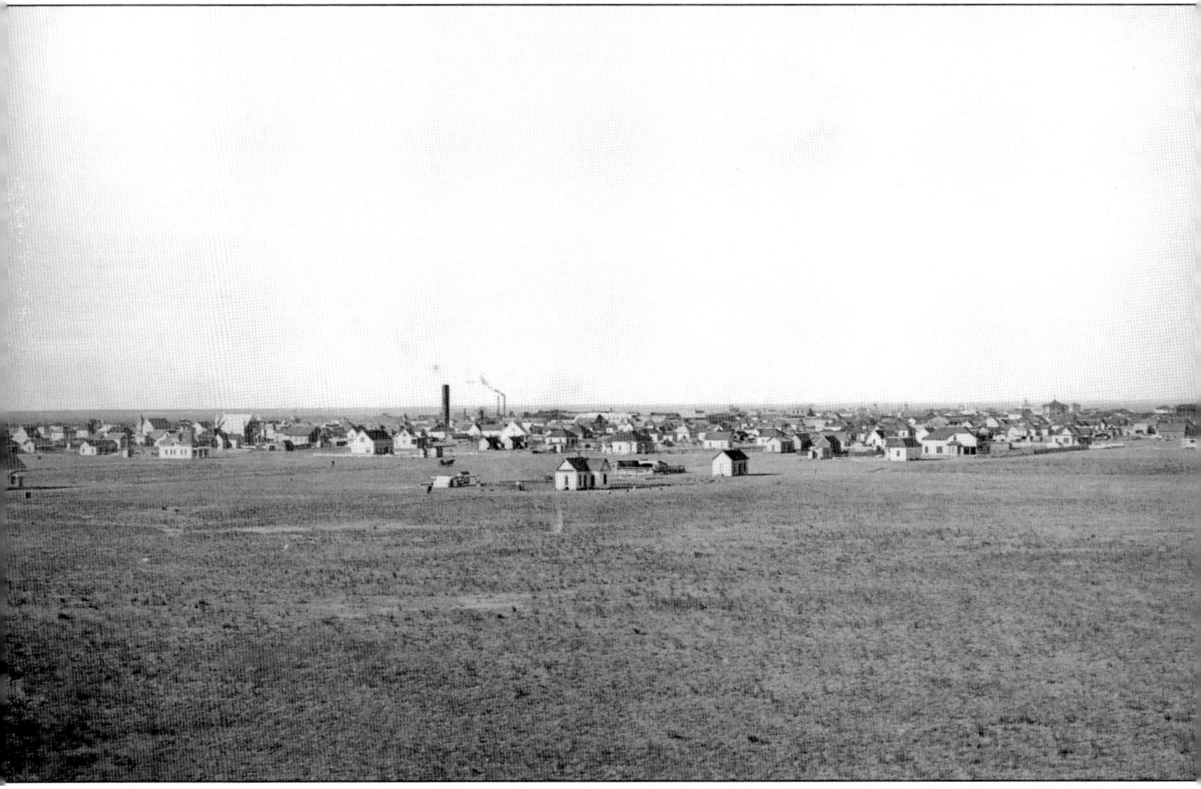

This pre-1908 image was one of the earliest photographs of the entire town of Dalhart. From left to right are Dalhart's first school on Conlen Street, the Presbyterian church on Denver Avenue, C.E. Williams's Water Works at 502 Denver Avenue, the North Side Dallam County Courthouse with jail, and the railroad depot. (Courtesy of the XIT Museum and Jimmy Newby.)

ON THE COVER: In 1906, Dalhart residents posed for this photograph on Denrock Avenue, Dalhart's main street. They are seen here in the 300 block, gathered with their vehicles and wearing their Sunday best. The buildings shown no longer exist, but just out of view to the right is the Felton building, which remains today and was once home to Dalhart's opera house. Today, in this same location sits the First National Bank in Dalhart.

IMAGES
of America

DALHART

Robin Scott

ARCADIA
PUBLISHING

ISBN 978-0-7385-8466-9

Published by Arcadia Publishing
Charleston, South Carolina

Printed in the United States of America

Library of Congress Control Number: 2010940831

For all general information, please contact Arcadia Publishing:
Telephone 843-853-2070
Fax 843-853-0044
E-mail sales@arcadiapublishing.com
For customer service and orders:
Toll-Free 1-888-313-2665

Visit us on the Internet at www.arcadiapublishing.com

To the XIT Museum and the Dalhart Texan *for inspiring my love for the people and places of Dalhart*

Contents

Acknowledgments

When the prospect of writing this book first presented itself, I wasn't quite sure that I was the right person. I hadn't lived in Dalhart very long and had no family ties to Dalhart that might provide a particular connection or source of history and information.

What I had done was spend the two years prior to beginning writing this book writing for the *Dalhart Texan*, the three-days-a-week newspaper in Dalhart. Writing for the paper put me in contact with many people in Dalhart and provided an opportunity to hear about its history and what makes it special.

I had also been working part time at the XIT Museum and sitting as a director on its board. Working with Nick Olson at the museum was like getting paid to learn about Dalhart's history, as he is a wealth of information. The time I have spent on the board of directors for the Dalhart Area Chamber of Commerce provided a third key link in my growing knowledge of Dalhart. Between those three endeavors, the book began to write itself.

I've often referred to myself as Dalhart's cheerleader, and writing Images of America: *Dalhart* has strengthened my love for this city that sits at the top of the Texas Panhandle. The people of Dalhart are like no others that I've ever known and they have welcomed me as one of them.

Writing this book was only possible through the help and encouragement of the XIT Museum, and especially its curator, Nick Olson; the *Dalhart Texan*; the Dalhart Area Chamber of Commerce; and the people of Dalhart who need to have their story told and shared. My connection to all four has grown immensely in the process; it has made me a better Dalhartan, and has made me proud to call Dalhart my home.

Unless otherwise noted, all photographs in this book are courtesy of the XIT Museum in Dalhart, Texas.

Introduction

Dalhart, Texas, is uniquely situated in the northwest corner of the Texas Panhandle and is closer to the state capitals of six other states than to its own in Austin. Five highways lead in and out of Dalhart, and travelers may easily visit New Mexico, Colorado, Oklahoma, Kansas, Nebraska, and Wyoming. Dalhart is also situated within the two counties of Dallam and Hartley, and derived its name by joining the first few letters of each county.

Dalhart got its start as a town in 1882 when the Fort Worth and Denver Railroad first laid tracks. In 1901, the Chicago and Rock Island Railroad made it to the area, giving rise to Dalhart's first name, Twist Junction. Dalhart's main street, Denrock Avenue, derived its name by joining the names of the two railroads. Today, the Burlington Northern Santa Fe and Union Pacific Railroad occupies the tracks that bring industry in and out of Dalhart. The railroads quickly made Dalhart a center of commerce at the turn of the century, and rail remains a major business in the area.

Dalhart sits within two counties. The north side lies in the middle of the lower edge of Dallam County, and the south side sits in the upper stretches of Hartley County. Its location ties together the communities of Dalhart, Channing, Hartley, and Texline, and the community leaders of each city work well together to meet the needs of area citizens.

The infamous XIT Ranch was operated within 10 Texas counties, including Dallam and Hartley counties, in the far-northwest corner of the Texas Panhandle. The XIT was the largest working ranch and largest fenced ranch in the world until it closed in 1912. The ranch was created as the result of a deal made by two businessmen, Charles and John Farwell, who built the $5 million red granite state capitol building in Austin in exchange for 3 million acres of high plains real estate that became the ranch.

Although the ranch quit its operations just after the turn of the century, its rich history is still a part of Dalhart's history. In 2011, Dalhart will host the 75th XIT Rodeo and Reunion, an annual tradition filled with rodeo events, the largest free feeds in Texas, a parade, fiddle contest, and just good, clean fun. The XIT Rodeo and Reunion is Dalhart's largest annual event, and travelers fill hotel and motel rooms each year. The annual event occurs during the first weekend of August each year and includes a professional rodeo. The reunion allows former XIT directors to meet with new directors and plan for the future as well as reminisce. The XIT directors are some of the most well-respected men in Dallam and Hartley Counties, each serving for a three-year term, and bringing their own personal skills and talents to the group.

Dalhart was not only created because the railroads merged here, but also because of the efforts of the publisher of the *Dalhart Texan*, the city's local newspaper. Robert B. Edgell briefly named his newspaper the *Denrock Sun*, but when the town took its official name in 1902, the paper's name changed as well. The *Dalhart Texan* was instrumental in promoting settlement in Dalhart and in keeping people in Dalhart during the Dust Bowl years. It continues today as the community's sole source for local written news.

The *Dalhart Texan* was one of many Panhandle newspapers that promoted growth in the Texas Panhandle. Reports in the newspaper included illustrations meant to bring the area to life. By 1912, Dalhart had a population of 3,500 and grew steadily until the Dust Bowl years, when many residents fled to California. Many of those families later returned to Dalhart.

The newspaperman was joined by bankers and land developers in growing and expanding Dalhart. A tradition began wherein the town's men gathered each morning to discuss Dalhart's progress. Today, the town's men continue to gather at one of the local banks.

Dalhart has had many celebrated community leaders who helped shape the town and bring it into the 20th century. Among the well known was Dr. G.W. Dawson, who founded the Trans-Canadian Sanitarium, a clinic that provided medical care for area residents before the first hospital was built. The larger-than-life doctor, with his Colonel Sanders good looks, helped to modernize Dalhart and put it on the map.

Dalhart's success was a culmination of luck, skill, and talent. Had the Fort Worth and Denver City Railway and the Chicago and Rock Island Railway crossed paths in some other town, Dalhart might have been no more than a blip on history's radar. The railroads' location amidst the XIT Ranch gave Dalhart its impressive beginning. Range ranching was replaced by irrigation farming and feed lots, and now the inclusion of dairies solidifies Dalhart as a leading agricultural community and one that will remain for another 100 years.

One

Twist Junction

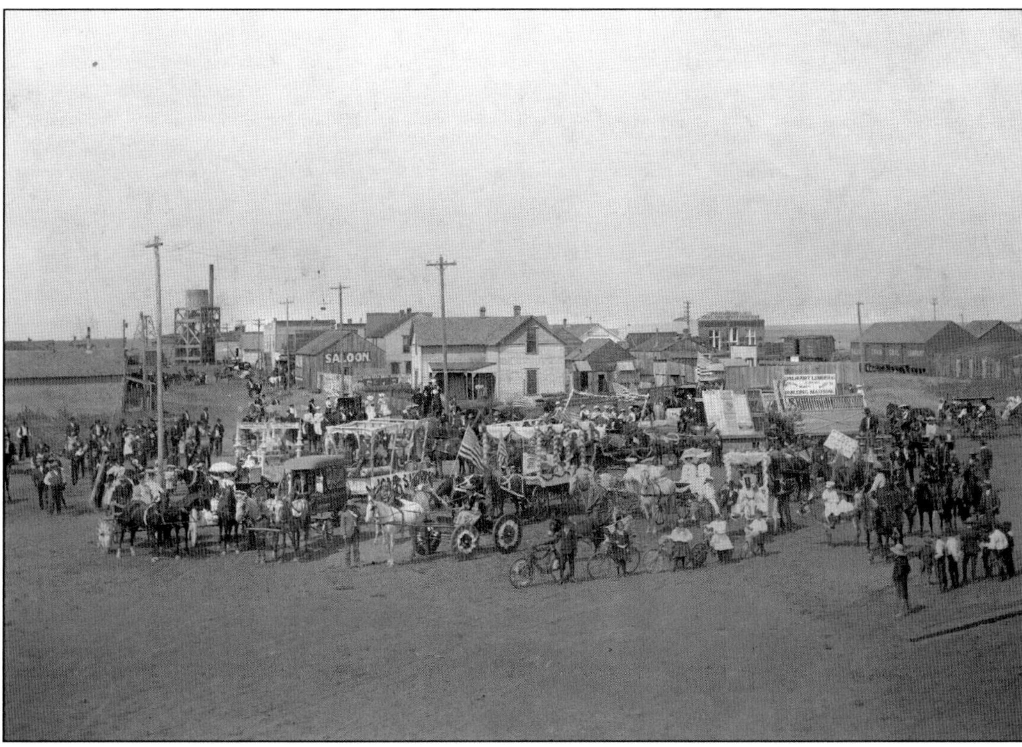

Dalhart began to flourish in the late 1880s when the first railroad, the Fort Worth and Denver City Railway, laid tracks. Another reason for Dalhart's success was the creation of the XIT Ranch, also in the 1880s. The ranch operated until 1912. These two major business endeavors allowed Dalhart to grow rapidly and led to the emergence of many more businesses including banks, saloons, hotels, and groceries; by 1903, Dalhart was fully established as a city that linked the rest of the United States to the great state of Texas. (Courtesy of the XIT Museum and J.W. Harton.)

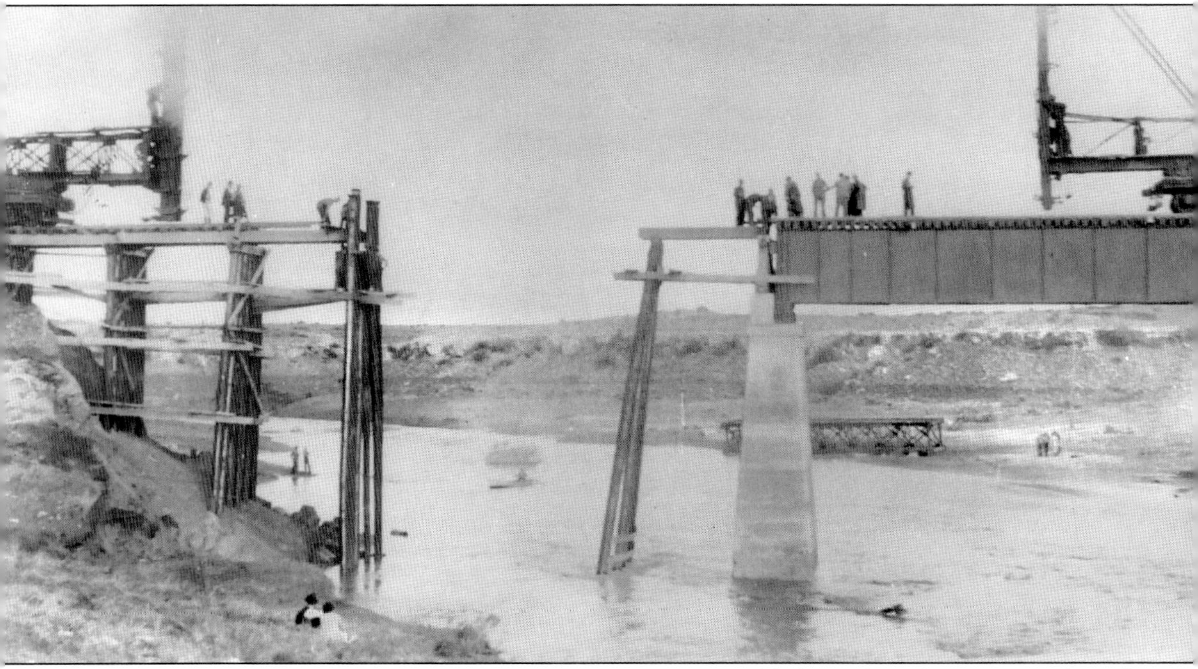

The first railroad tracks were laid on February 27, 1882, and belonged to the Fort Worth and Denver City Railway Company. Tracks were laid in Fort Worth, Texas; and Denver, Colorado, and grew toward one another until they met in the middle. Another railroad, the Chicago and Rock Island Railway, established in 1847 to connect the Mississippi River port of Rock Island with the new Illinois and Michigan Canal in LaSalle, made its way to Dalhart and across the path of the Fort Worth and Denver City Railway Company. The two railroads finally crossed tracks on May 31, 1901.

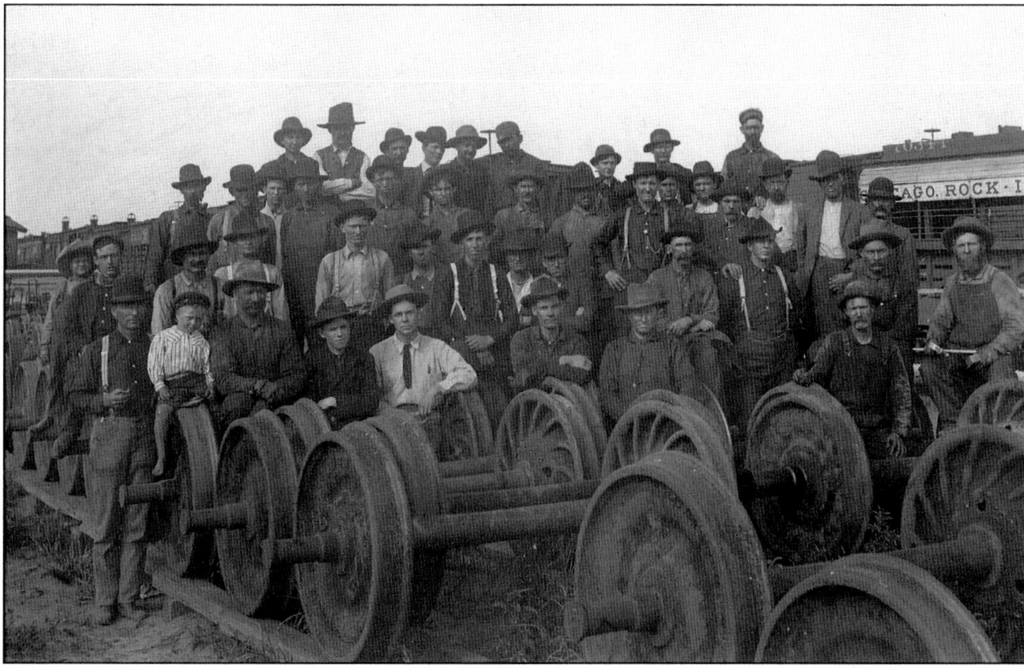

Working for the railroad became a way of life for many men at the turn of the century. The crew of the Chicago and Rock Island Railway are seen here in the railroad yard in 1901. Early freight carried by rail included coal and cattle. By 1903, fresh produce such as fruits and vegetables were carried.

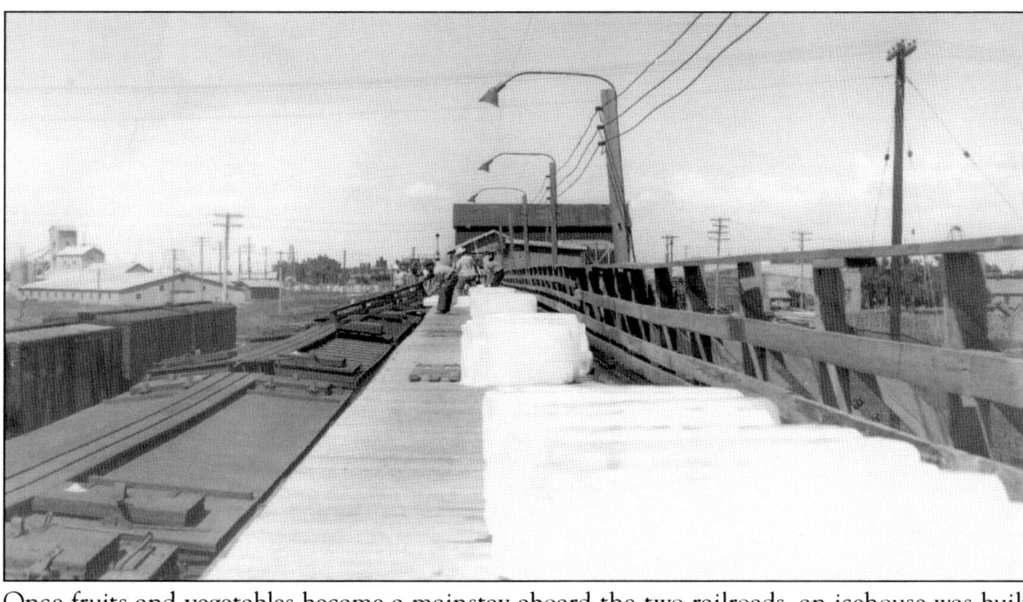

Once fruits and vegetables became a mainstay aboard the two railroads, an icehouse was built in Dalhart to accommodate the need to keep the items fresh. Men from the ice plant iced down the railcars beginning in 1907 and continued through 1959, when refrigerated railcars took over. The ice plant made it possible for the successful shipment of perishables by rail.

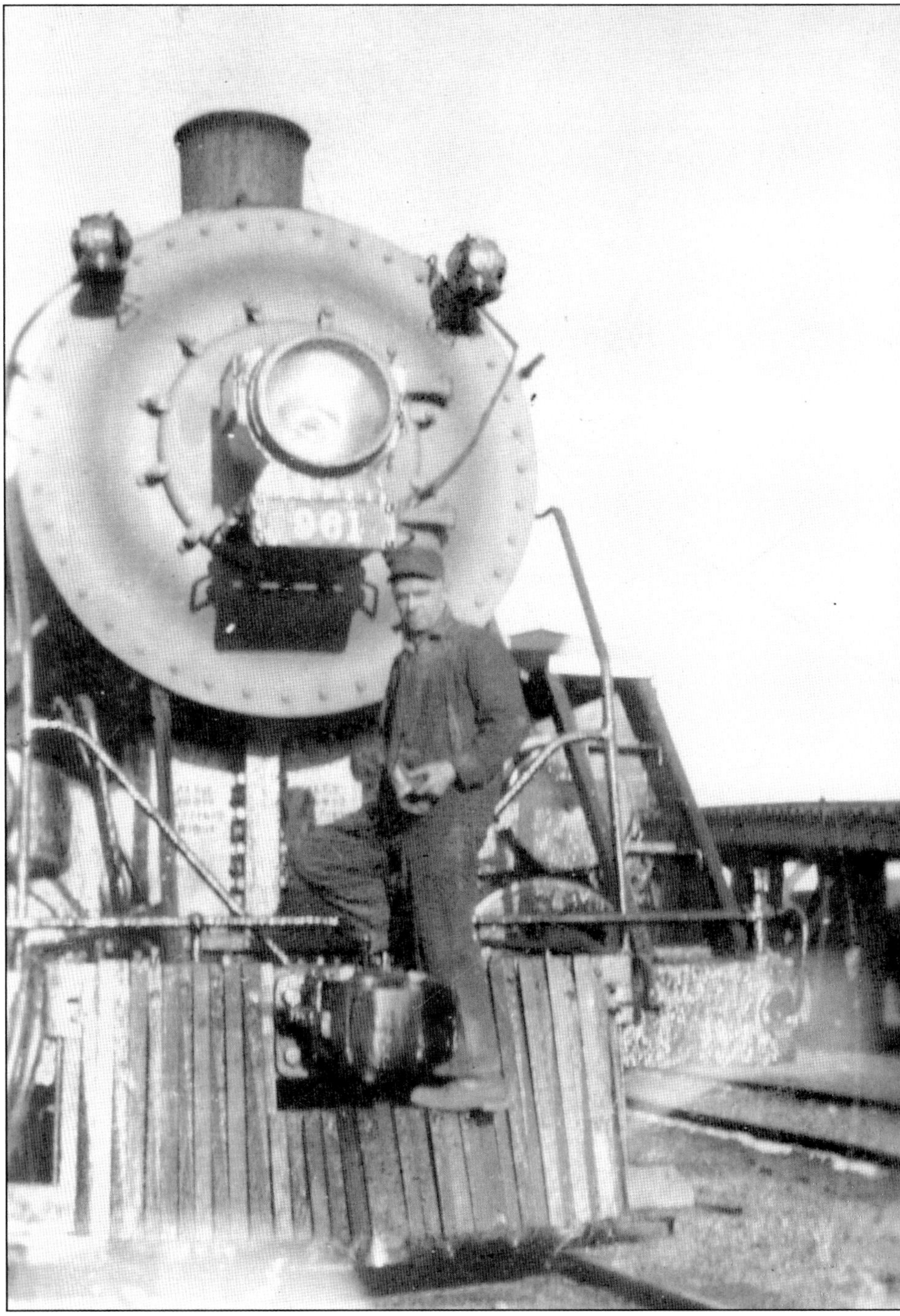

The railroad was something to be proud of, as it brought the world to undeveloped, barren areas. Men often posed in front of the engines, as this man did in the late 1800s. By 1902, the Rock Island reached its final destination in Los Angeles. In Dalhart, a cooler was set up in the railroad's division office for bottles of beer for the men when they quit work for the day. A bucket was also filled with beer from a saloon across the street. The men would pitch in to purchase the bucket of beer.

Railroad workers are seen with an engine on the tracks near Dalhart in the late 1800s. An outbreak of smallpox traveled down the Rock Island line, causing the railroad to create a hospital train. A doctor lived in one car; three cars were for patients. By 1902, city residents from Dalhart, Channing, and nearby communities reported cases of smallpox.

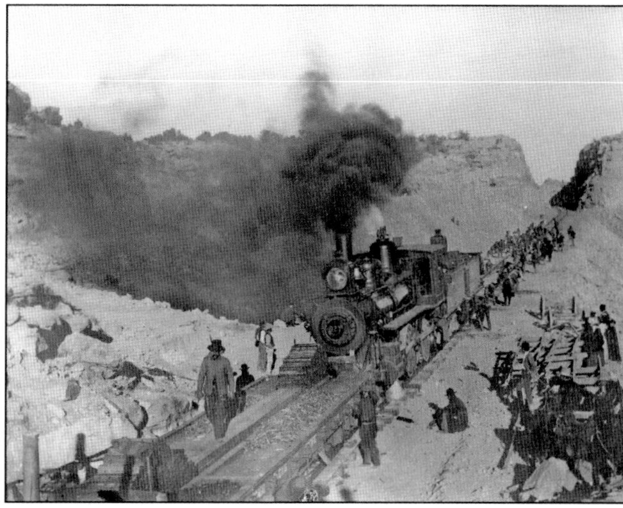

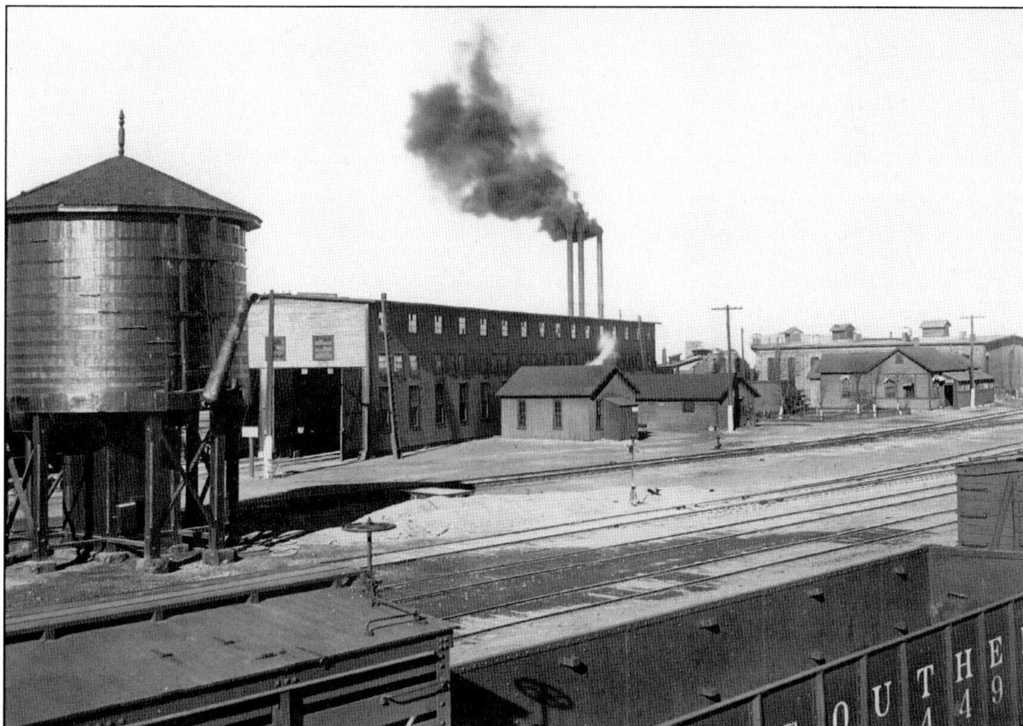

The materials to construct the roadhouse and depot arrived on the Fort Worth and Denver before the Rock Island made it to Dalhart. Capt. J.H. "Jim" Conlen made a deal with the men constructing the railroad to lay 2.5 miles of track each day. The deal allowed the men to get back to camp by 4:00 p.m. each day rather than 6:00 p.m. This photograph shows the Rock Island roundhouse and service yards in Dalhart in 1905. The Chicago and Rock Island Railway operated in Dalhart until 1954, when it went through a decade-long battle with the Interstate Commerce Commission over a merger with Union Pacific Railway. The Rock Island suffered many financial losses as people quit traveling by rail, and its traffic was diminished. When some of the Rock Island's routes finally merged with Union Pacific, Dalhart was one of the areas that Union Pacific took over. The Union Pacific remains in Dalhart today.

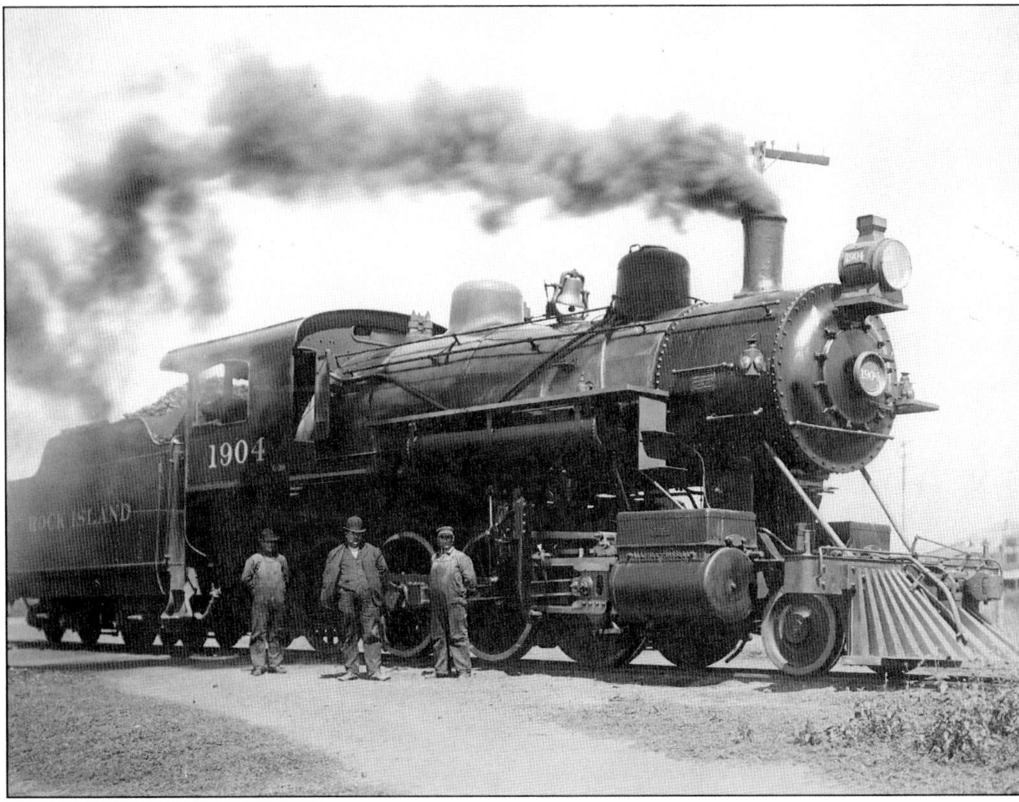

An engine for the Rock Island was often the backdrop for photographs, including this one taken in Dalhart in 1905. The Rock Island suffered many problems with its engineers and railroad men. Capt. J.H. "Jim" Conlen was responsible for the construction of more than 260 miles of track that ran from Liberal, Kansas, to Santa Rosa, New Mexico, bringing the tracks through Sherman, Dallam, and Hartley counties. He was described as a tough but fair boss. The railroad men still participated in a strike, however, because Conlen often had trouble paying the men on time.

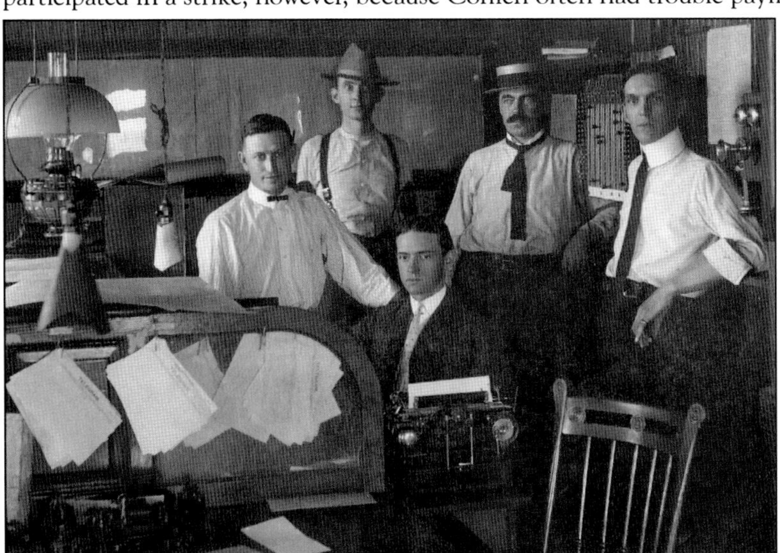

Capt. J.H. "Jim" Conlen sits inside the railroad superintendent's office in Dalhart in 1903. Pictured are Charles Edwards (left), Harry McMullens, Capt. J.H. "Jim" Conlen (in hat), Gene Brewer (seated), and an unidentified man. (Courtesy of the XIT Museum and the Thomas family collection.)

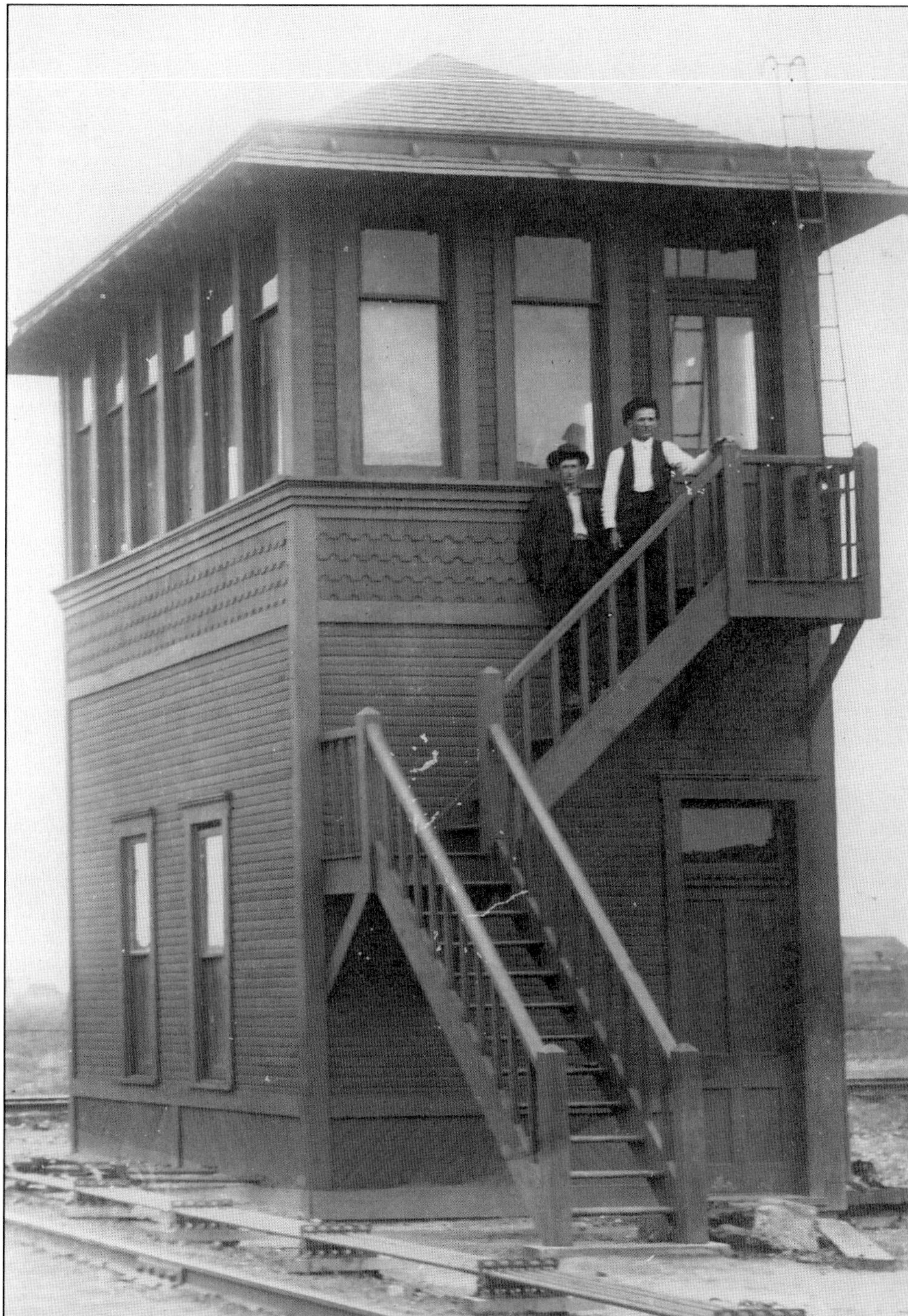

Two men stand on the stairs of the switch tower of the railroad in 1901 when Dalhart was first formed. In the early days, women were never allowed near the camps where the men lived when not working. Most of the railroad men laying tracks were Irish immigrants. Tracklayers had a strict policy of not drinking on the job, while the men who graded the land ahead of the tracks were known for their heavy drinking.

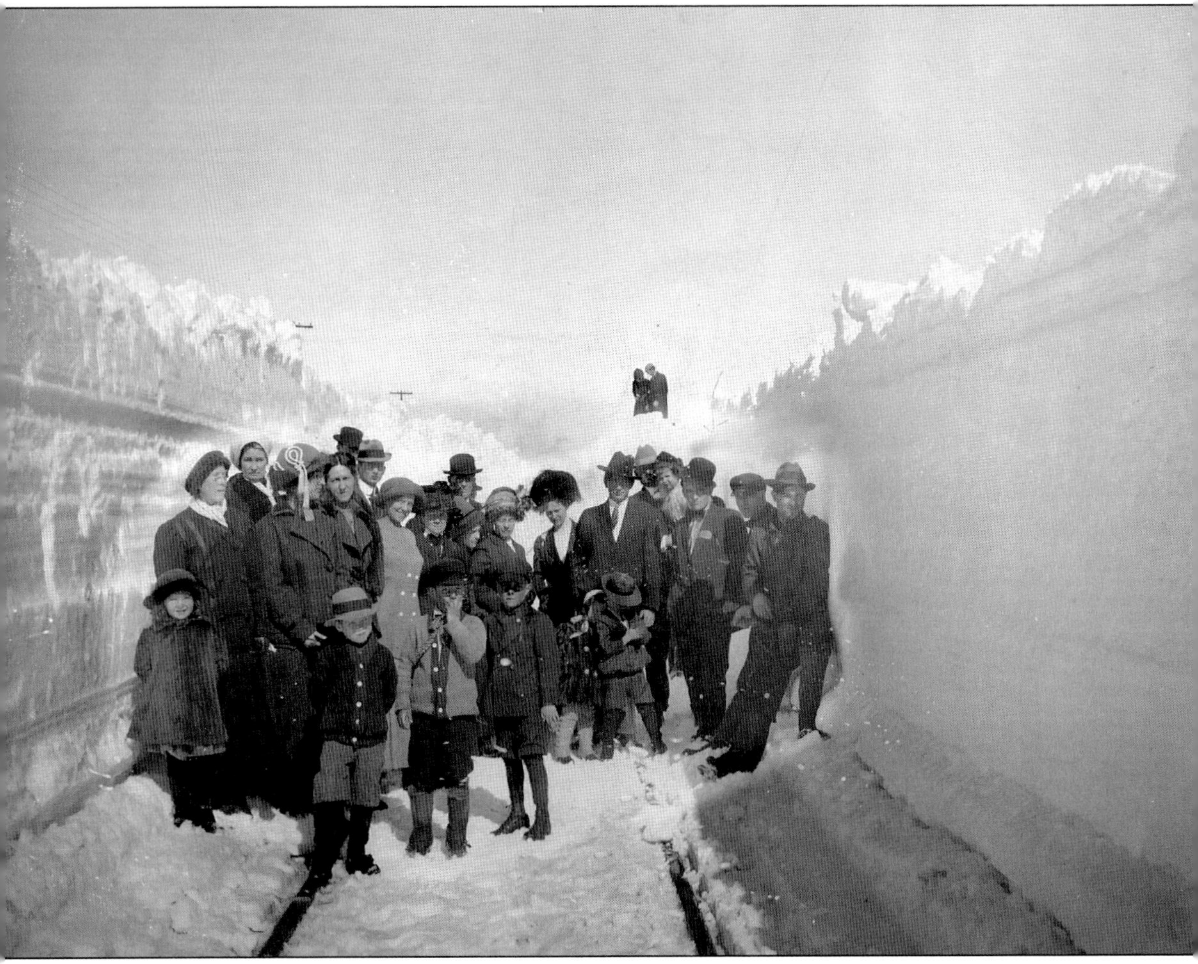

A great snowstorm in Dalhart in 1912 left the railroad tracks a sight to see. A crowd gathers after a train engine's plow has cleared the tracks. The walls of snow on either side of the tracks reached upwards of 10 feet. Although Texas does not conjure up visions of snowfall in most people's minds, Dalhart, resting at an altitude of nearly 4,000 feet, sees an average of 10 to 12 inches annually. Snowdrifts may reach as high as 30 feet due to Dalhart's high winds. (Courtesy of the XIT Museum and the Walup family collection.)

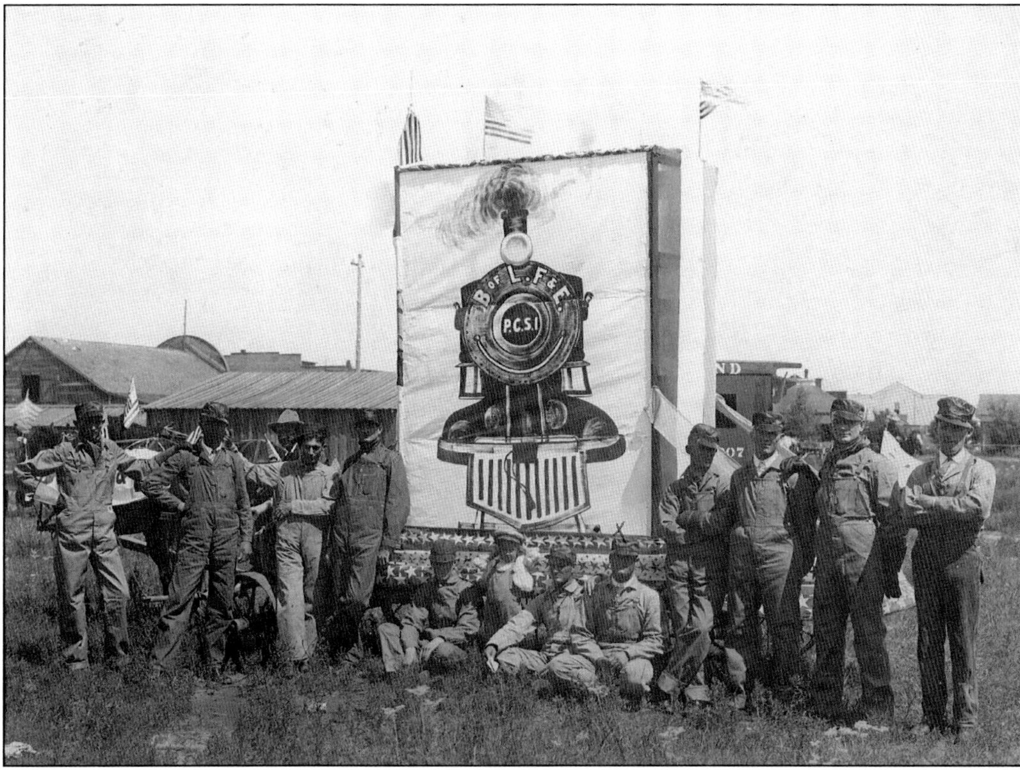

Organized on December 3, 1867, and incorporated on March 1, 1894, Dalhart's Brotherhood of Locomotive Firemen and Engineers is shown here in 1905. Initially established to provide insurance benefits to members, by the late 1800s, the brotherhood had branched out into labor-management relations. After engineers were invited to join, the name of the group changed to the Brotherhood of Locomotive Firemen and Engineers. (Courtesy of the XIT Museum and the Reeves family collection.)

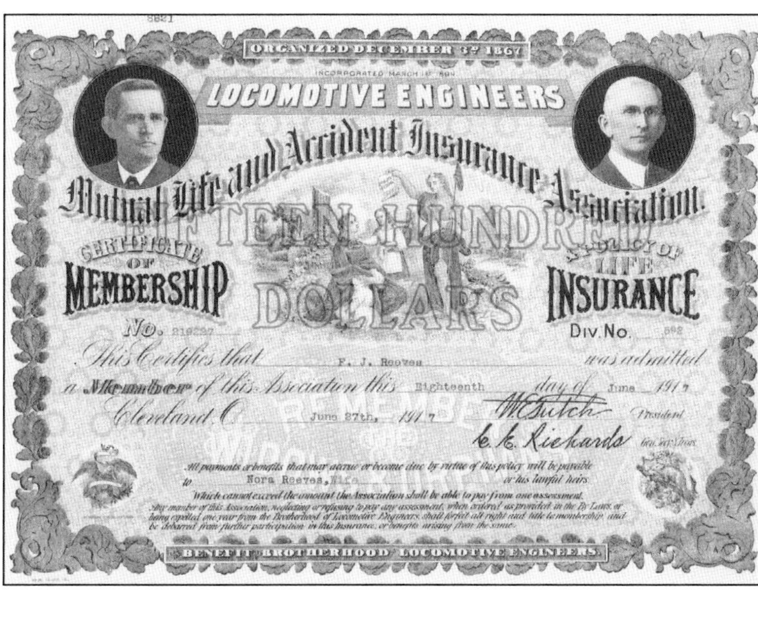

ORGANIZED DECEMBER 3rd 1867

LOCOMOTIVE ENGINEERS

Mutual Life and Accident Insurance Association.

FIFTEEN HUNDRED DOLLARS

CERTIFICATE OF MEMBERSHIP

POLICY OF LIFE INSURANCE

No. 219297 Div. No. 592

This Certifies that F. J. Reeves was admitted a Member of this Association this Eighteenth day of June 1917

Cleveland O. June 27th, 1917

W. Futch President

C. E. Richards Gen. Sec. & Treas.

All payments or benefits that may accrue or become due by virtue of this policy will be payable to Nora Reeves, Wife or his lawful heirs

Which cannot exceed the amount the Association shall be able to pay from one assessment.

Any member of this Association, neglecting or refusing to pay any assessment, when ordered as provided in the By Laws, or being expelled one year from the Brotherhood of Locomotive Engineers shall forfeit all right and title to membership, and be debarred from further participation in this Insurance, or benefits arising from the same.

BENEFIT BROTHERHOOD LOCOMOTIVE ENGINEERS

Locomotive Engineers purchased insurance from the Mutual Life and Accident Insurance Association. In 1917, F.J. Reeves purchased $1,500 worth of insurance, naming his wife, Nora Reeves, as beneficiary. (Courtesy of XIT Museum and Reeves collection/Bess Lott.)

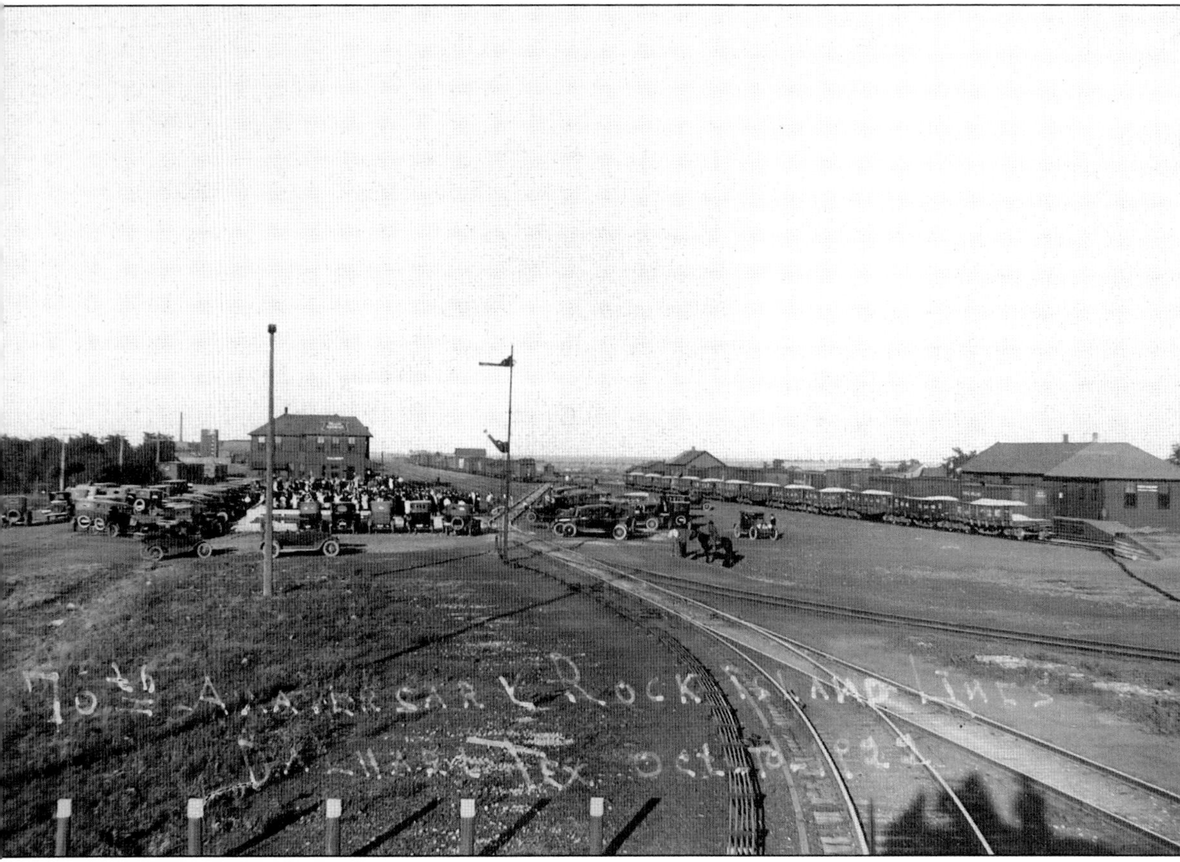

This photograph of the depot and roundhouse in Dalhart was taken on the 70th anniversary of the Rock Island Lines in 1922. At the time of the anniversary, the Rock Island had been in Dalhart for 21 years, but city residents enjoyed any reason to gather for a celebration. The *Dalhart Texan's* banner headline on December 14, 1928, read, "Two Denver Trains Wrecked at Dalhart: Three Dead; Three injured in Head-On. Investigation as to cause is being held by Officials." The southbound Fort Worth and Denver No. 2, a passenger train, had collided with the northbound Fort Worth and Denver freight No. 19 at 2:30 a.m., three miles south of Dalhart. (Courtesy of the XIT Museum and H.R. Parkey.)

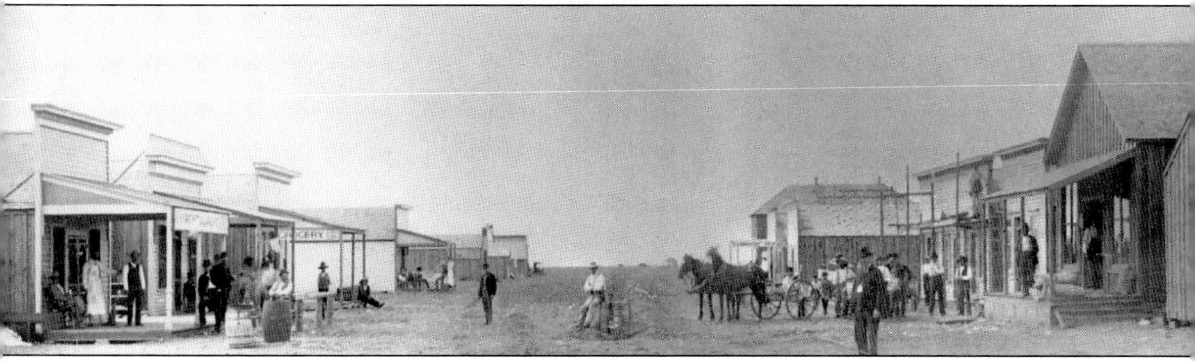

Taken in 1901, one of Dalhart's earliest photographs depicts its downtown and features Noble Brothers Grocery, Dalhart's first non-wooden structure, on the left. Noble Brothers Grocery operated from 1901 until 1918. George W. Ely, August H. Hesse, Ed Kirk, and Scott Kretz incorporated the Ely-Hesse Company, a wholesale grocery firm. They opened Noble Brothers Grocery, which Ely bought out in 1938. The two-story building on the right is McMurry's Lumber Company, home to Bartlett's Lumber today.

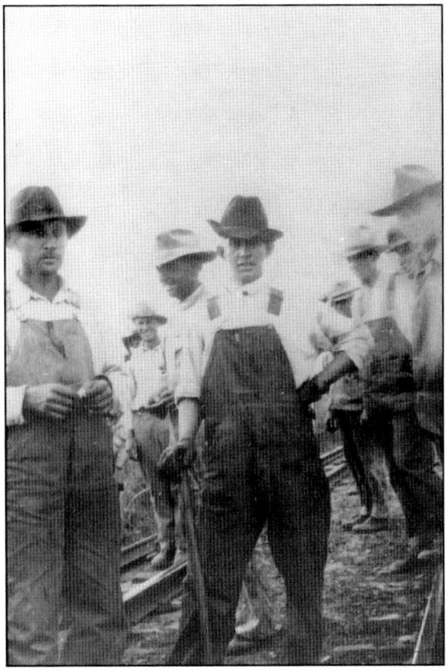

Everything that came in or out of Dalhart after the railroad tracks were laid traveled by rail. Freight trains and passenger trains both traversed the United States, passing through Dalhart. Working for the railroad was a revered profession, and railroad men were well respected. Interestingly, the men who laid the tracks were well respected, while the men who graded the land ahead of the tracks were considered heathen and barbaric. In this photograph, well-respected railroad men stop and stand on the tracks for a photograph in 1901.

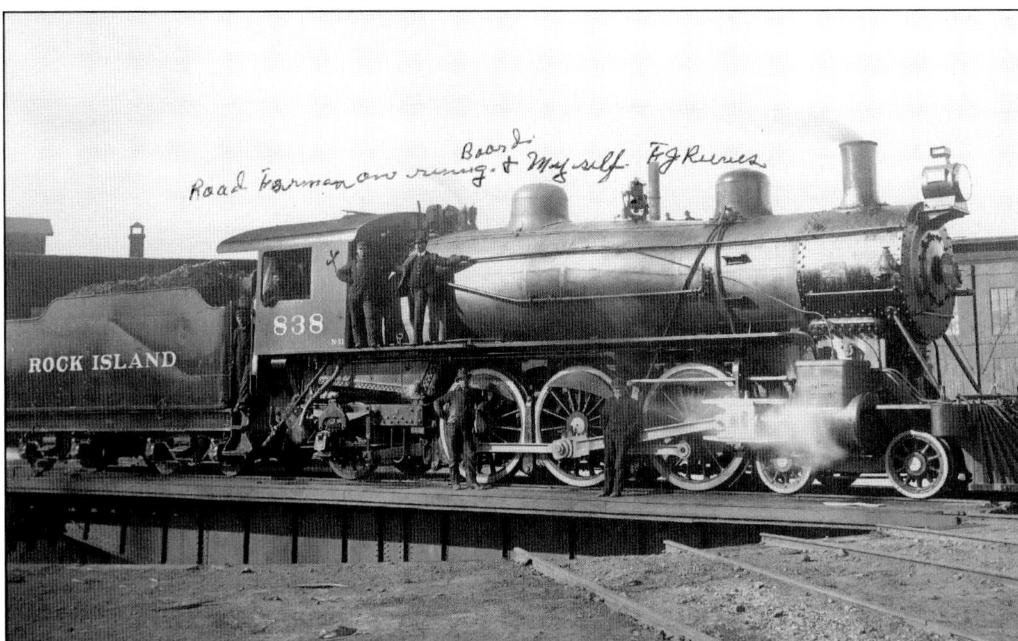

The old steam locomotives have long since left the railroad tracks, but the mark they left on the community is indelible. In the middle of the night, when a train travels through town and blows its horn, one can almost hear the whistle of the old Rock Island steam engines. The steam engine in the photograph belonged to the Chicago and Rock Island Railway Company Railroad and made regular appearances through town. It sits at the railroad turntable. The tracks were rotated until they lined up in the right direction. Engine 838, shown in this photograph, pulled a small freight train. Each engine's number designation signified whether it was used for freight or passenger cars. (Courtesy of the XIT Museum and the Reeves family.)

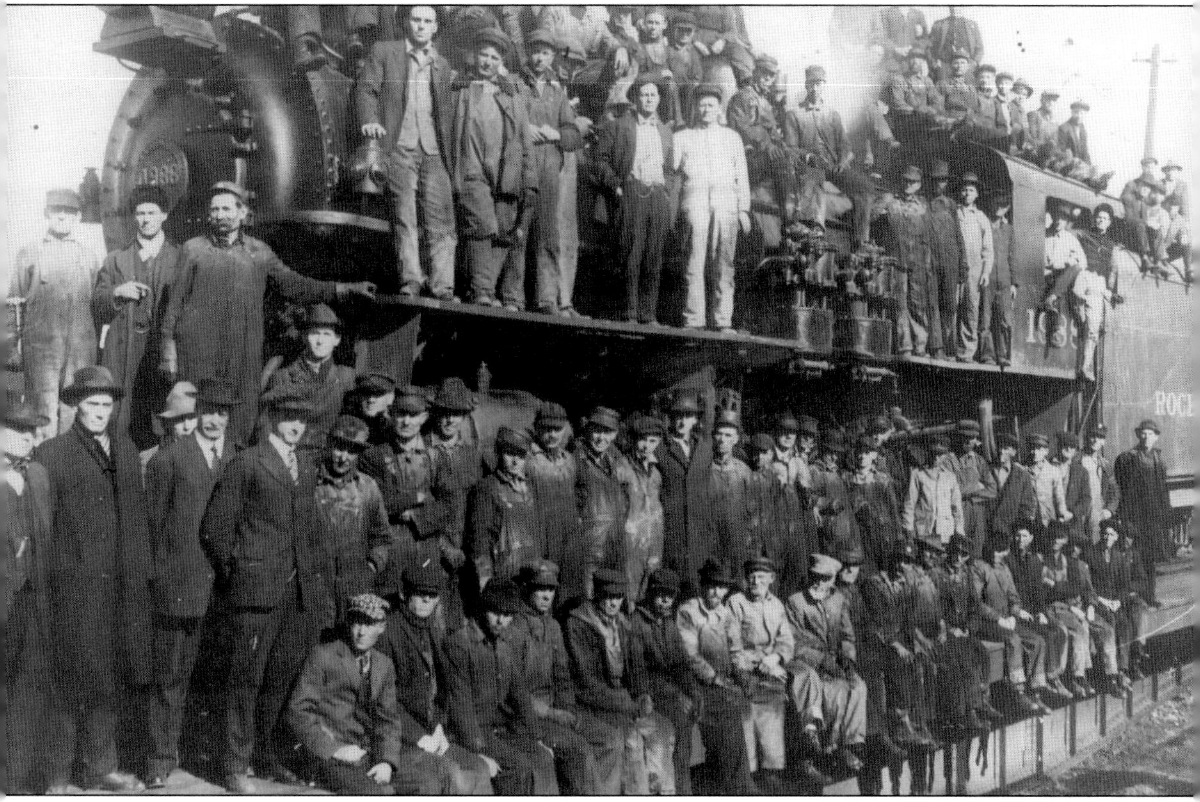

By 1918, the Chicago and Rock Island Railway was a thriving business and key to Dalhart's continued success. Several of the men seen here posing with an engine in Dalhart worked on the XIT Ranch. The Rock Island tried its best to avoid Dalhart altogether because the company did not approve of Texas laws regarding building railroads. The alternative route, however, had too steep a grade, so the rail came through Texas. (Courtesy of the XIT Museum and Bob Wilcoxson.)

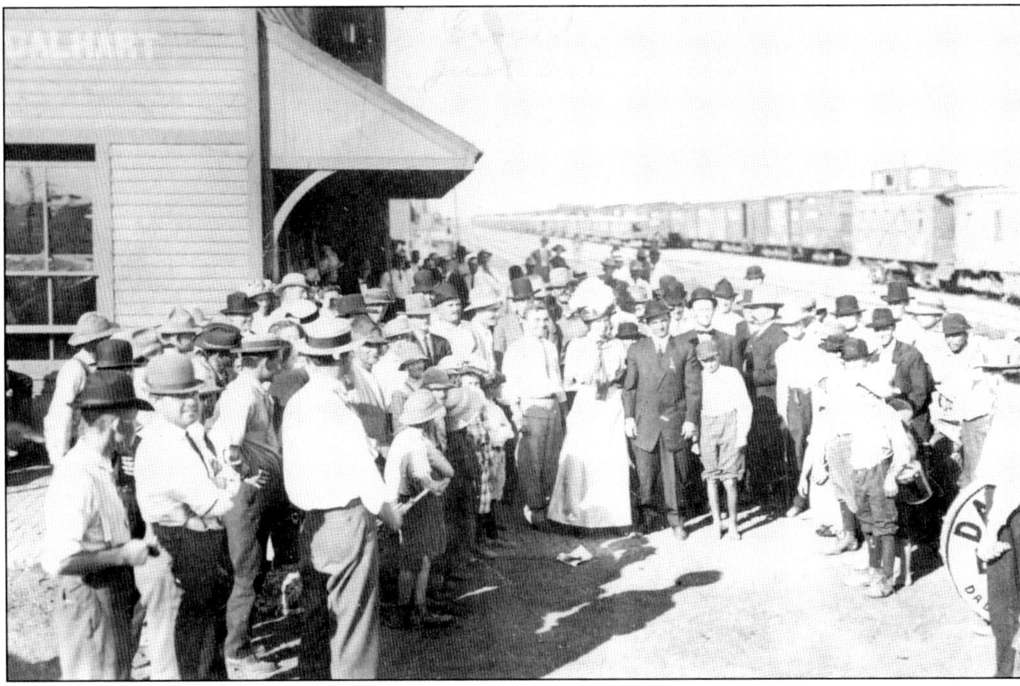

Most Dalhart residents showed up for a big event like the wedding depicted here. This early 1900s wedding took place next to the railroad depot. The bride and groom are seen in the middle. The location of the photograph was the center of commerce in Dalhart, and the people shown all likely worked either for the railroad or within a few yards of the depot. Although the couple's identity is not known, it is likely that the groom worked for the railroad.

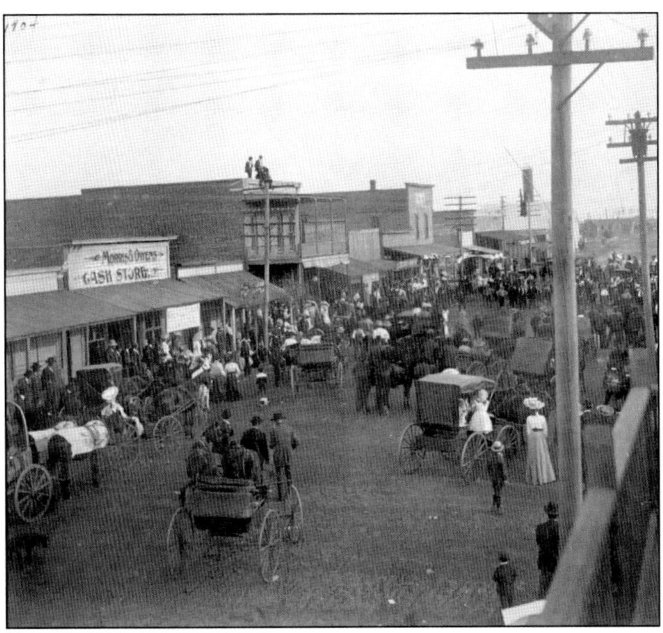

This 1908 photograph of a parade along Denrock Avenue provides a northward look up Dalhart's main street. Parades always brought the people of Dalhart out onto Denrock Avenue. The town continues to host two annual parades: one during the XIT Rodeo and Reunion weekend in August, and the Veterans Day Parade in November. Just as in the early 1900s, area residents line the streets to cheer on the businesses and people who pass by. The bricks on the right of the photograph were used to build the DeSoto Hotel after this photograph was taken. (Courtesy of the XIT Museum and Mr. E.L. Fairchild.)

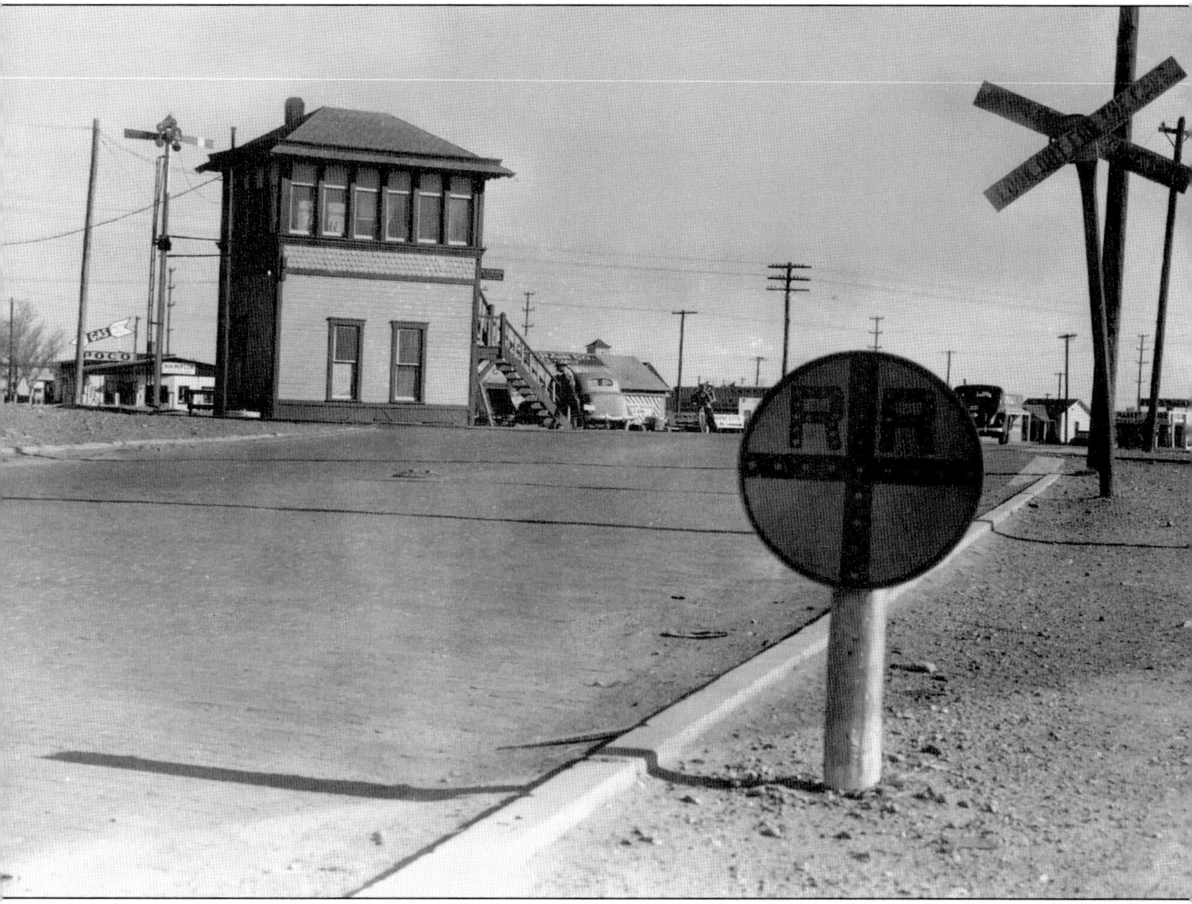

Dalhart was originally named Twist Junction, because the tracks of the Fort Worth and Denver City Railway and the Chicago and Rock Island Railway crossed at what is now the junction of Highways 87 and 54. Dalhart was also briefly known as Denrock, taking parts of each railroad's name. The city was platted in 1901 by W.J. Blair and Charles W. Thornton of the Rock Island Line. Blair was working in a restaurant in Channing when the Rock Island came to town. He bought two sections of land in Dalhart, including what is now North Dalhart, which he purchased from Thornton. Railroad supervisor and civil engineer J.H. "Jim" Conlen, known as "the Captain," turned an old boxcar into a section house at the junction of the two railroads, and a small settlement grew up around it.

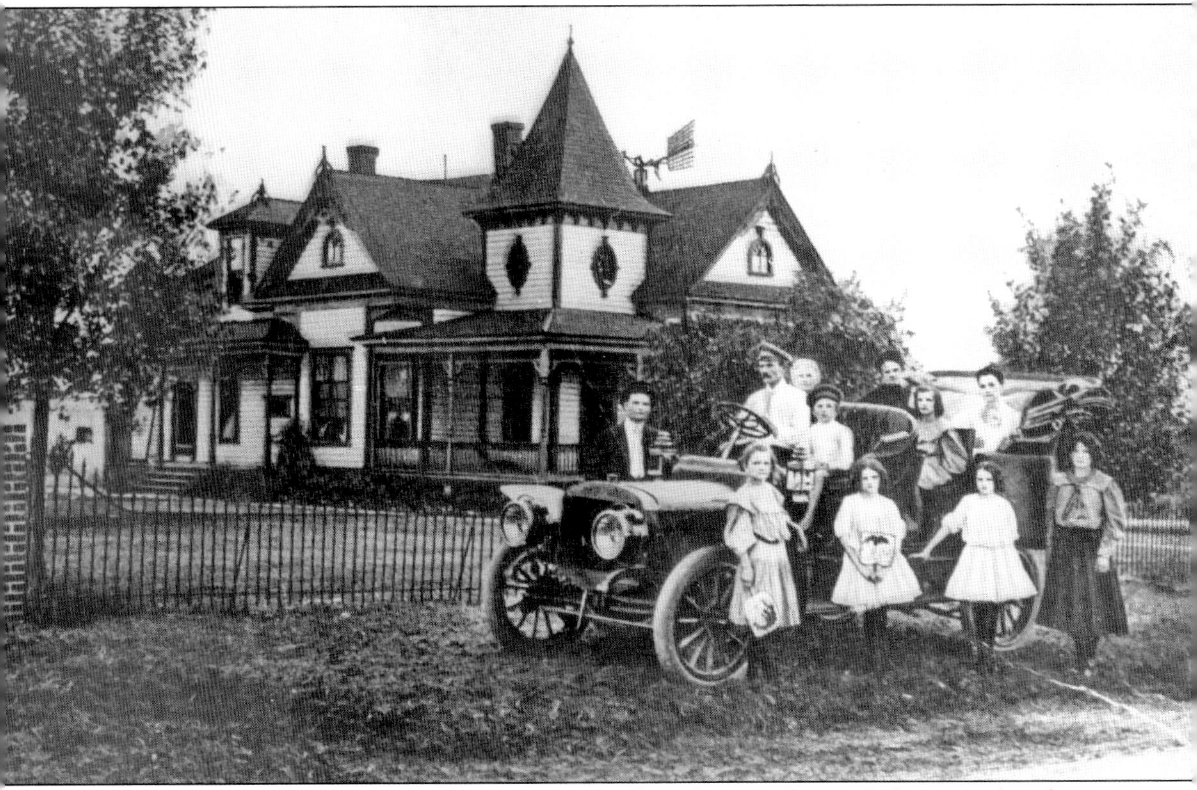

After being called Twist Junction for a time, Dalhart became Denrock, but postal authorities rejected that name. Dalhart took on its formal name by combining the first few letters of the two counties that the town straddles: Dallam and Hartley. Dalhart is also nicknamed "XIT City," as homage to the great XIT Ranch that ran through Dallam and Hartley Counties as well as eight other Texas high plains counties. Dalhart's founder, W.J. Blair, built a beautiful two-story home on Trinidad Street. He and his wife lived there, and she ran a boardinghouse. Outside in the yard, Blair created a zoo with deer and other animals. Blair is pictured here with his wife and children in front of their grand home. Note that they have a driver for their motorcar.

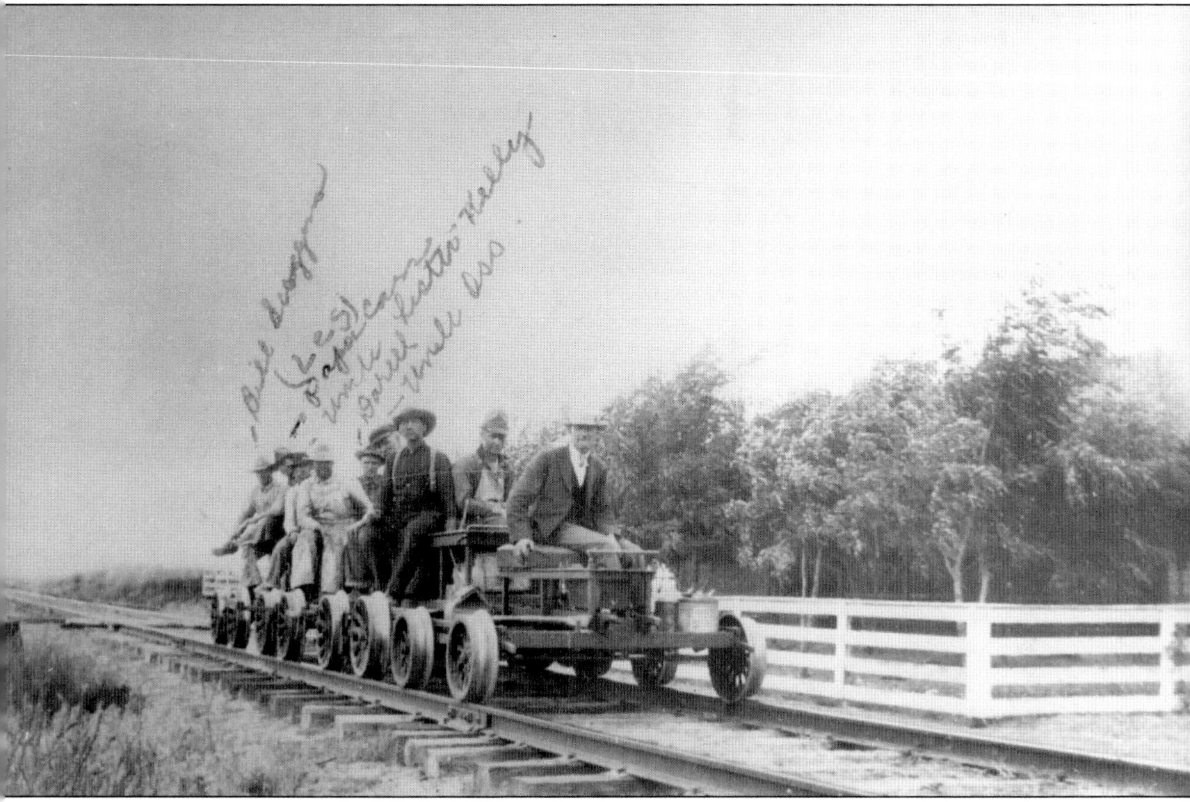

The Dalhart Town Company was formed on June 11, 1901, by Ora D. Atkinson and others and incorporated as a town on May 6, 1902, and as a city on April 6, 1904. On February 21, 1903, Dalhart became the county seat of Dallam County, in place of Texline, a city 38 miles to the northwest.

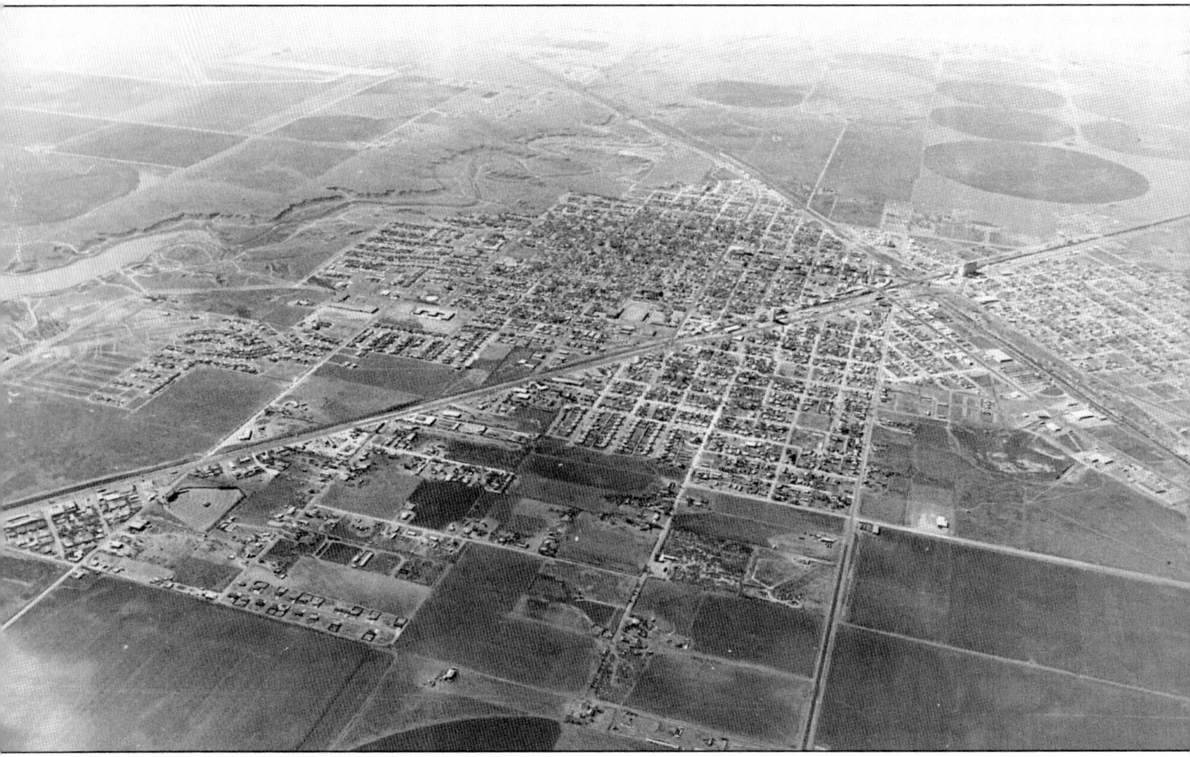

Today, Dalhart has a population near 9,000, stretches across a land area of 5.77 square miles, and rests 3,985 feet above sea level. The Texas state capital at Austin is 580 miles from Dalhart; six other state capitals are closer: Denver, Colorado (249 miles); Santa Fe, New Mexico (270 miles); Oklahoma City, Oklahoma (311 miles); Topeka, Kansas (481 miles), Cheyenne, Wyoming (488 miles); and Lincoln, Nebraska (558 miles).

Two

The XIT Ranch

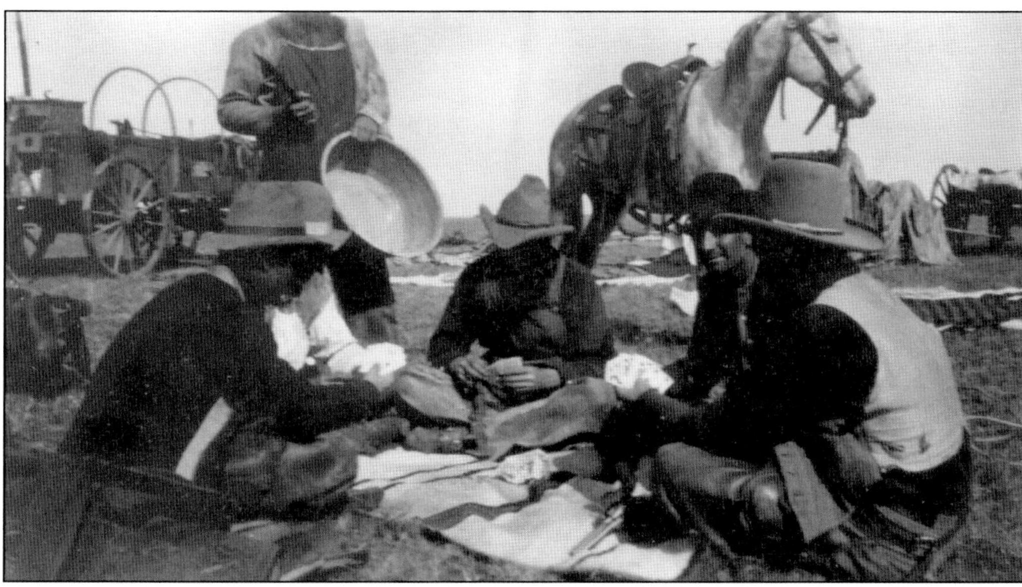

Brothers Charles and John Farwell of Chicago joined with Abner Taylor and A.C. Babcock of Taylor, Babcock, and Company to rebuild the Texas State Capitol building in Austin in red granite in exchange for 3 million acres of land situated in 10 High Plains counties, including Dallam and Hartley Counties in the northwest corner of the Texas Panhandle. The acreage became the XIT Ranch, which operated from the late 1880s until 1912. The estimated cost for rebuilding the capitol was $3 million and time was of the essence as the original building burned on November 9, 1881. The XIT cowboys became living legends as they drove hundreds of thousands of head of cattle across the vast ranch and as far north as Montana. When not moving or branding cattle, the cowboys found time to relax, play a hand of cards, and eat.

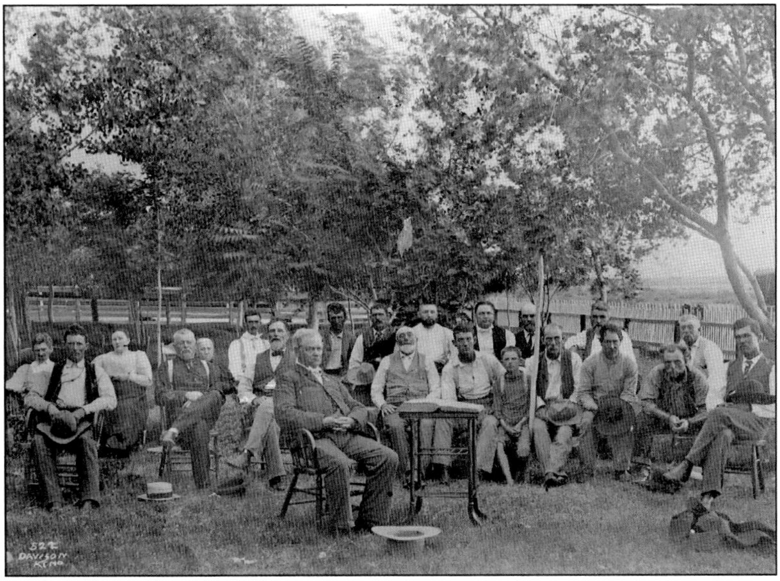

The XIT Ranch quickly ran 150,000 head of cattle and was the largest ranch in the United States. The great success of the railroads through Dalhart changed the way that the ranch ran cattle, and shipping cattle by rail ended the need for big cattle drives. On Sundays, John Farwell held services for the XIT cowboys.

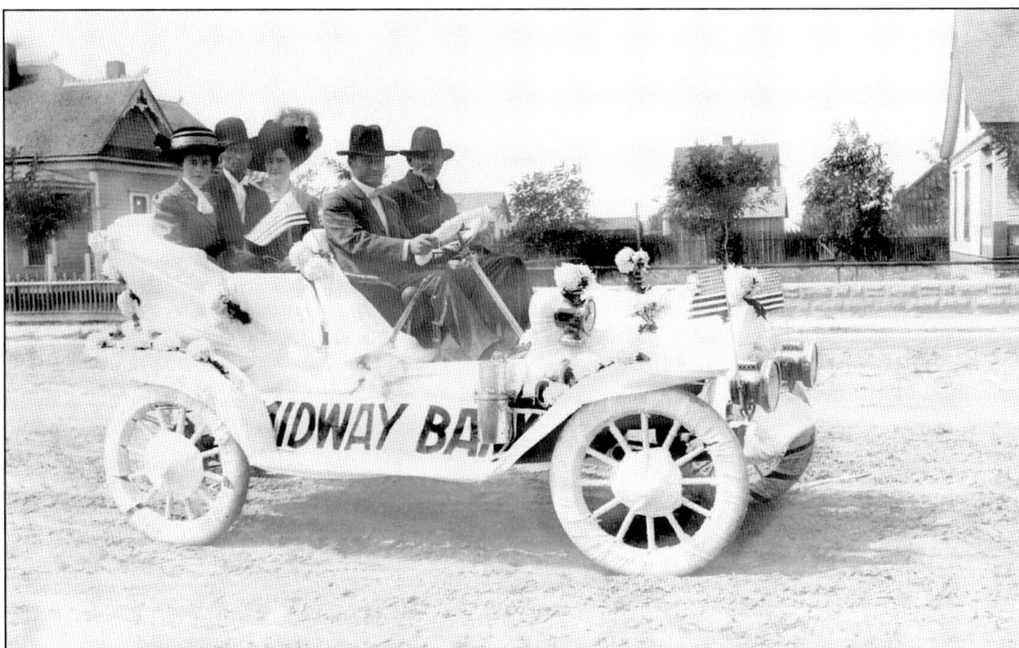

Known as the "Colonel," Albert Gallatin Boyce managed the XIT Ranch for 18 years. Born in 1842, Boyce was considered the greatest civilizing influence in the region. He is credited with issuing an order for the prohibition of six-shooters and playing cards on the ranch, and issued an order declaring that the XIT Ranch would observe Sunday as a Sabbath day. Ironically, his tenure as ranch manager ended with his murder on January 13, 1912. In this photograph, Colonel Boyce drives a car, the Midway Bank & Trust Co. float, in a Dalhart parade. Mrs. Henry Boyce rides in the back seat on the right. (Courtesy of XIT Museum and the Boyce/Bassett collection.)

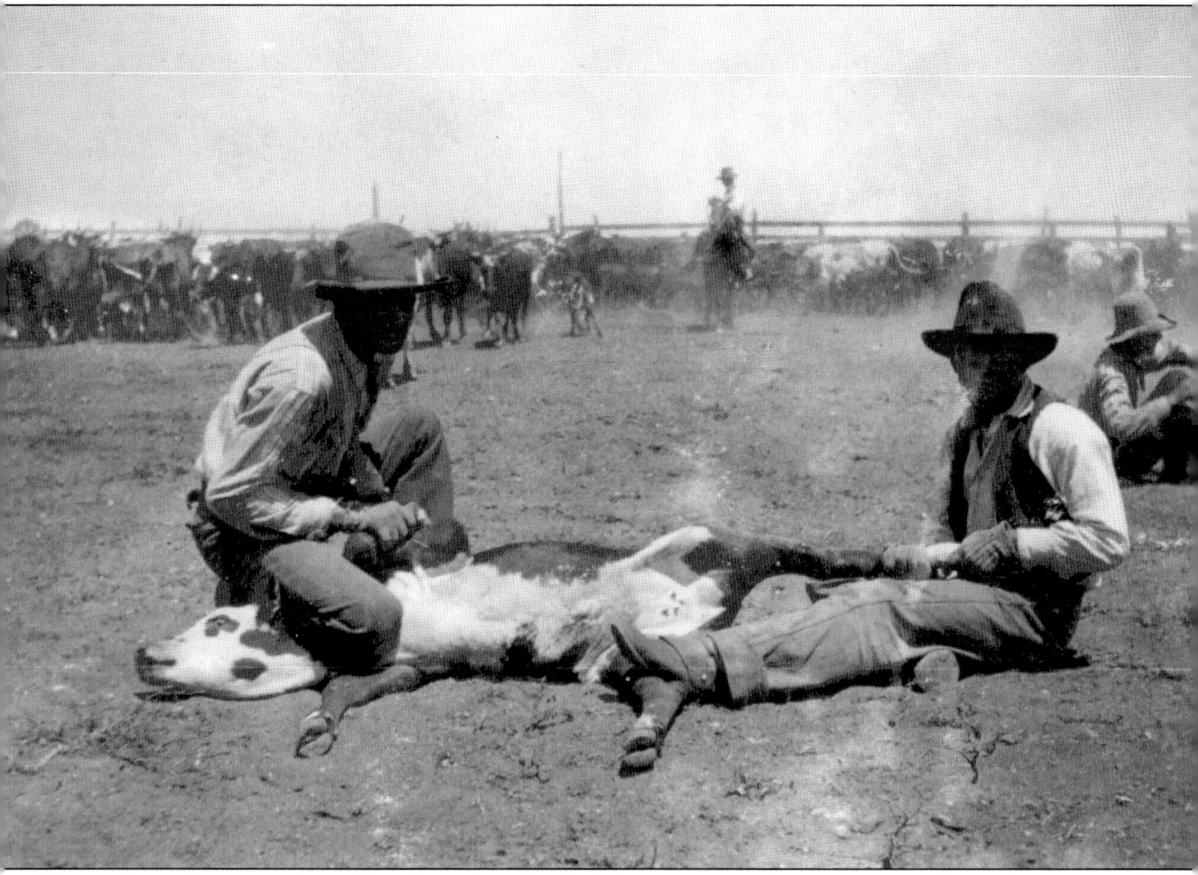

The XIT Ranch was located within 10 Texas counties. It weaved here and there from Dallam County in the north all the way to Hockley County in the south. The eight counties in between included, running north to south, Hartley, Oldham, Deaf Smith, Parmer, Castro, Bailey, Lamb, and Cochran. The "XIT" brand was never recorded, but the "X" brand belonging to the Capitol Freehold Land Trust was the second registered brand in Dallam County. Ab Blocker branded the first XIT cow in 1885.

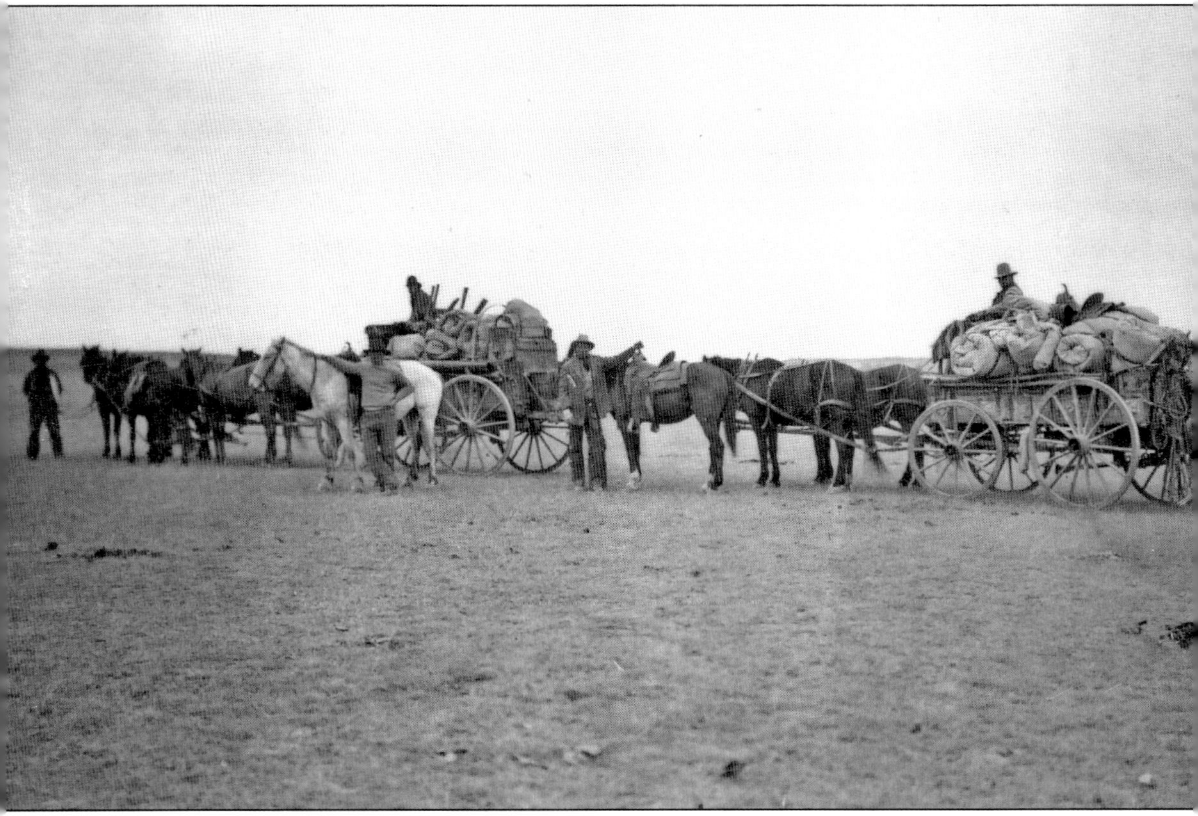

Wagons loaded with gear are shown here headed back to Texas from the Montana XIT Ranch in 1880. Supplies were bought in large amounts and stockpiled to last for several months. At that time, the land was only used for cattle. The XIT Ranch was one of the first to experiment with growing crops, including corn, millet, and sorghum. By the 1890s, crops also included prairie hay, alfalfa, Johnson grass, Kafir corn, rye, wheat, cotton, and garden vegetables. (Courtesy of XIT Museum and the Boyce/Bassett collection.)

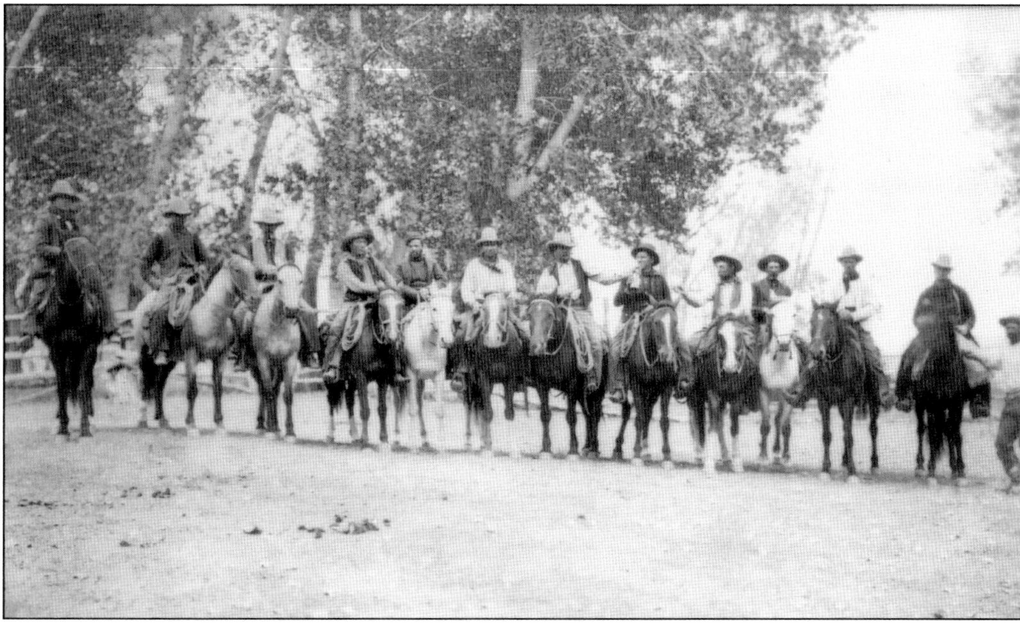

A group of XIT cowboys is shown on horseback in an 1880 cattle drive across the vast acreage of the XIT and out of Texas as far as Montana. An experiment conducted on the ranch by Dr. Hardy Campbell used dry land techniques for farming and was involved with the Farm Land Development Company. (Courtesy of the XIT Museum and the Boyce/Bassett collection.)

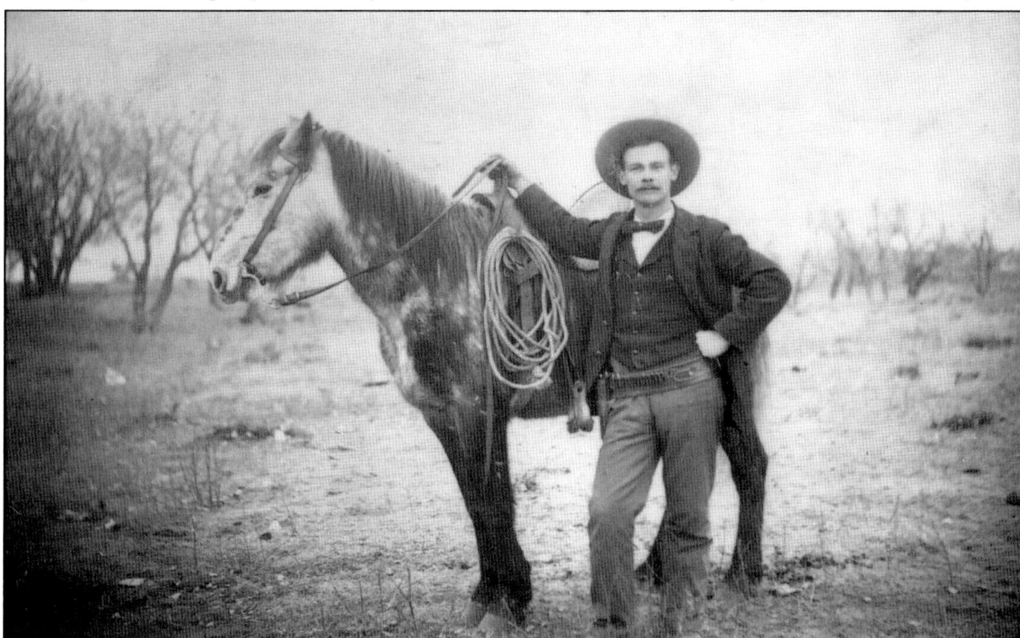

Dalhart provided cowboys with many amenities when they came in from the range. Almost immediately, Dalhart had three saloons to choose from, several hotels and restaurants, and a number of general stores. Cowboys like Marsh Price from the XIT Ranch, shown with his horse in this 1880s photograph, came into Dalhart in their "going-to-town clothes" and helped to grow the local economy. (Courtesy of the XIT Museum and the Boyce/Bassett collection.)

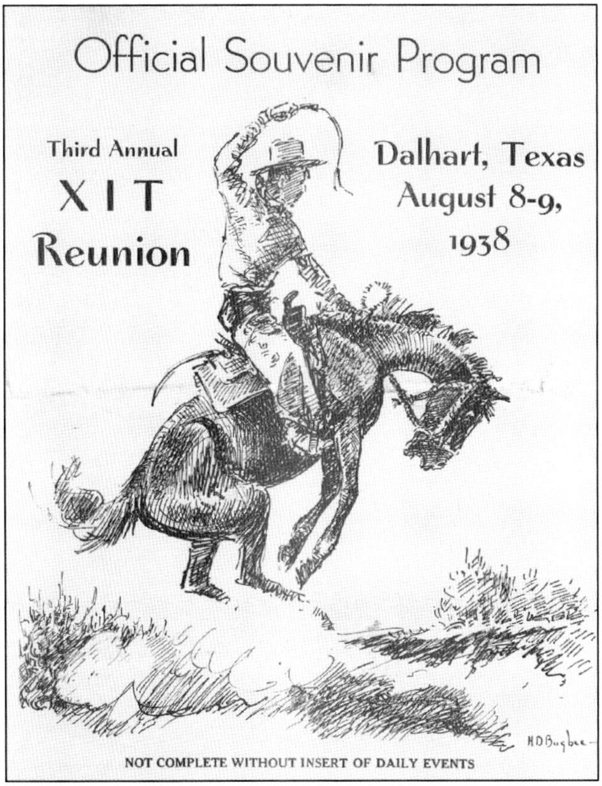

The XIT cattle brand became known throughout the country. Many speculated that "XIT" stood for "Ten In Texas," because of the 10 Texas counties that encompassed the ranch, but that appears to be purely speculation. In truth, the brand was apparently one already in use, and its continued use simply meant that the ranch did not need to create a new brand. This photograph shows XIT cowboys branding cattle in the 1880s. The XIT brand became the nickname for the city of Dalhart, and the name for the popular rodeo and reunion event that celebrates the ranch's history each year in Dalhart. (Courtesy of the XIT Museum and the Boyce/Bassett collection.)

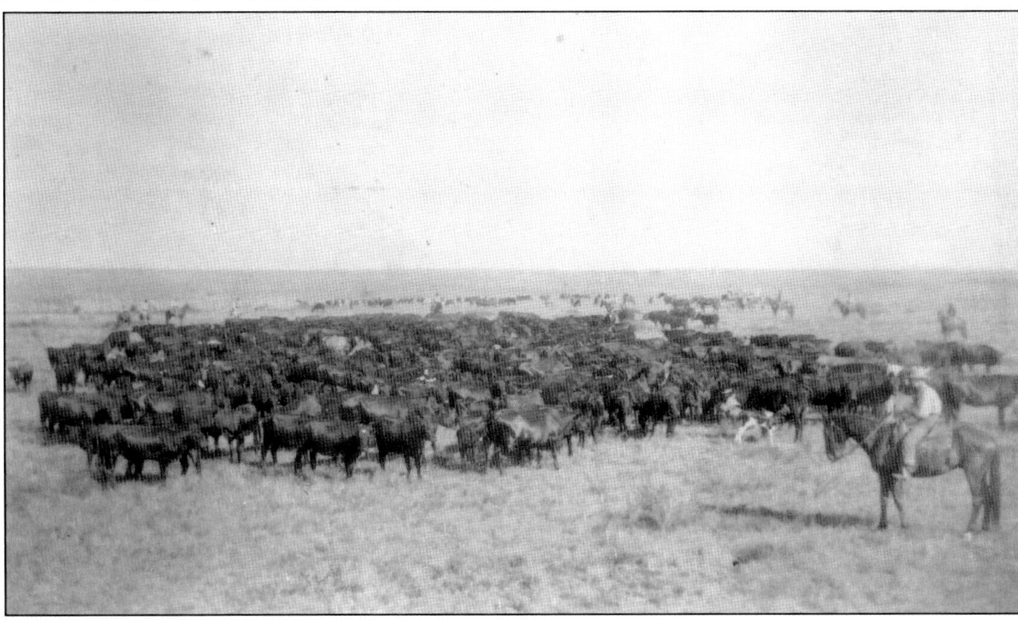

A herd of Angus cattle meanders across the XIT Ranch in the 1880s. By 1906, Dalhart had nine different land development companies working toward the colonization of the area. In the years that followed, when the ranch was broken up and sold beginning in 1912, it was common for a rancher to run cattle on as many as 100,000 acres of land. (Courtesy of the XIT Museum and the Boyce/Bassett collection.)

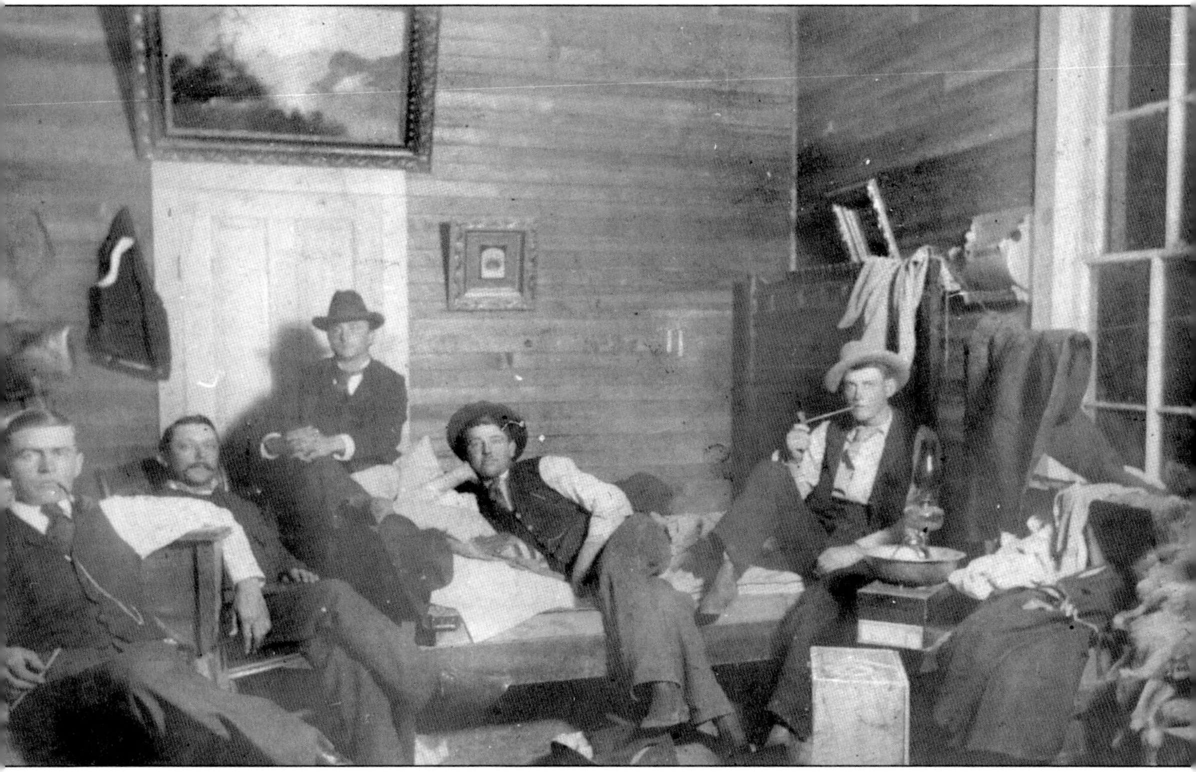

The many cowhands who worked on the XIT Ranch spent the sunset to sunlight hours in bunkhouses like the one pictured here. The Texas Panhandle is prone to powerful winds, dust storms, thunderstorms, and snowstorms, making moving cattle nearly impossible at times. When the weather was unforgiving, the men had to wait it out. The back of this photograph reads, "Having a bull session in the bunkhouse." Note that the kerosene lamp was kept in the wash pan, a precaution against fire. (Courtesy of XIT Museum and the Boyce/Bassett collection.)

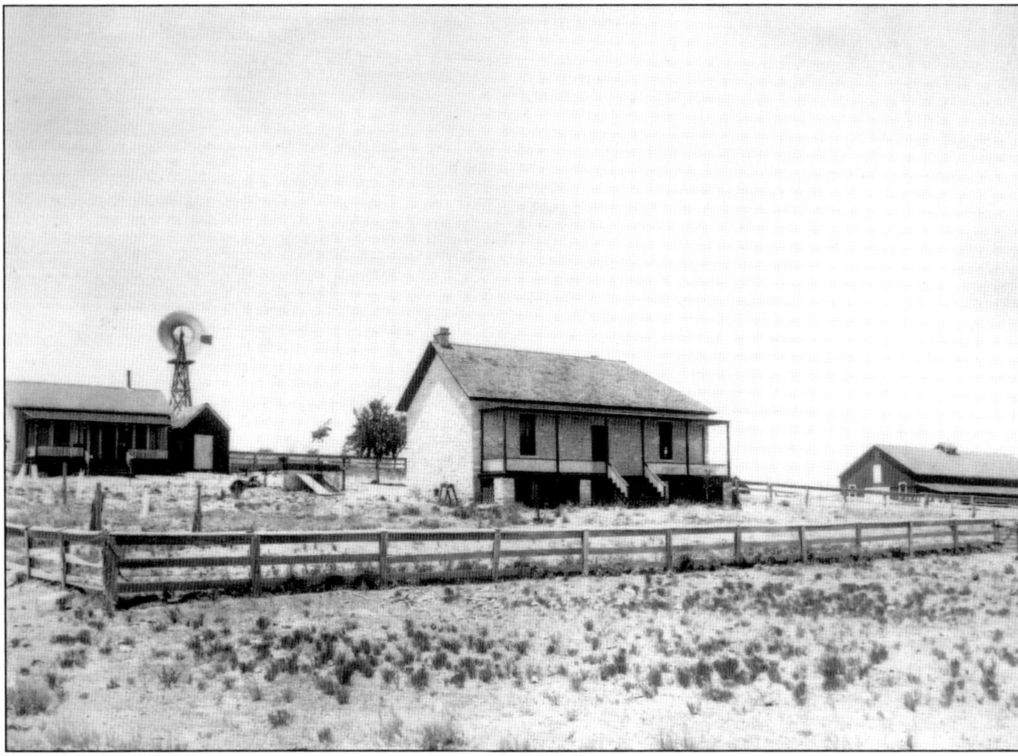

By 1900, ranch houses such as this one were popping up in and all around Dalhart. The typical ranch included a barn and windmill. Trees were rare, as the Panhandle was mostly flat and barren due to high winds and low average rainfall. When people built homes, they often planted trees around them. Thus, the trees, like the people, were immigrants to the area.

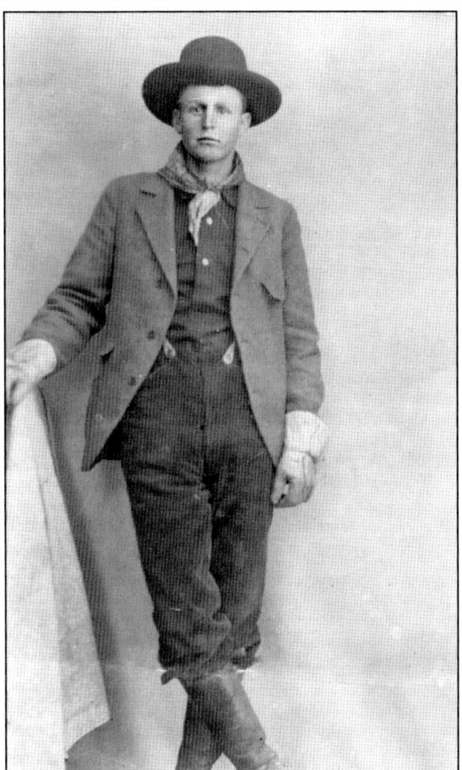

One of the ranch's better-known cowhands was John Childress, pictured here in 1898. Most of the cowhands had their photograph taken at some point, as promoting the ranch was big business. Along with the surveyor, a photographer traveled throughout the vast ranch taking photographs of the cowhands doing their jobs, sitting around the chuck wagon to eat, or living within the bunkhouses.

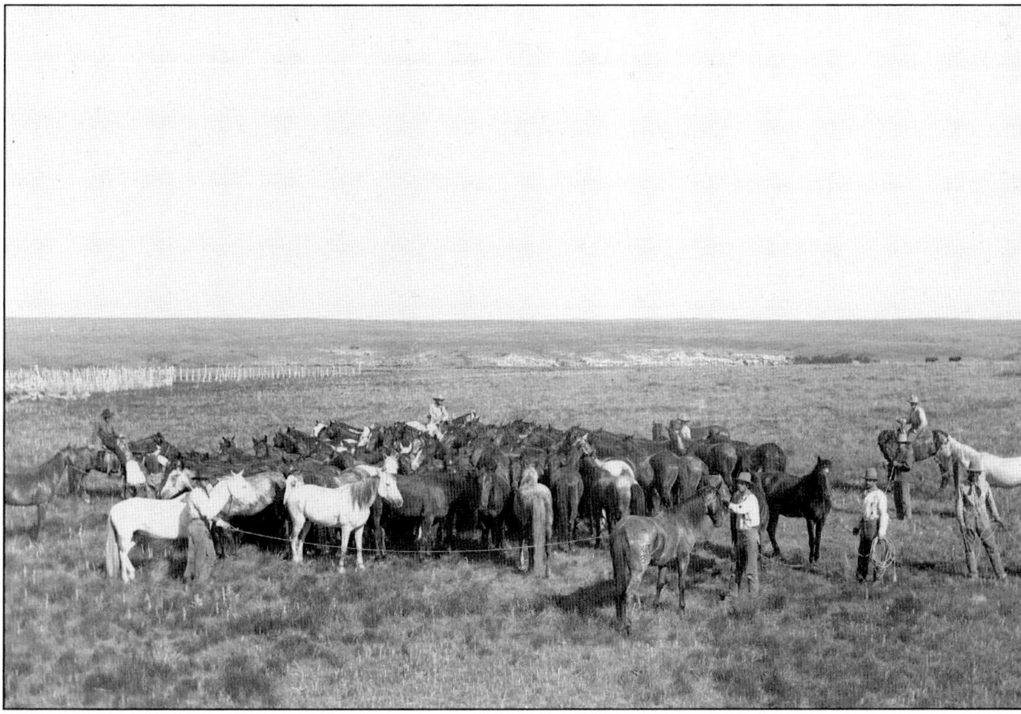

XIT cowhands from the Rita Blanca outfit of the XIT Ranch catch horses in 1899. The cowhands in the photograph are Lee Landers, Ham Hill, Ed Gusin, Lynn Boyce, Charles Ridgley, Steve Newberry, Mark Bean, Bob Duke, Ealy Moore, and Florence Moore. The Rita Blanca was just one of the XIT Ranch's 16 divisions.

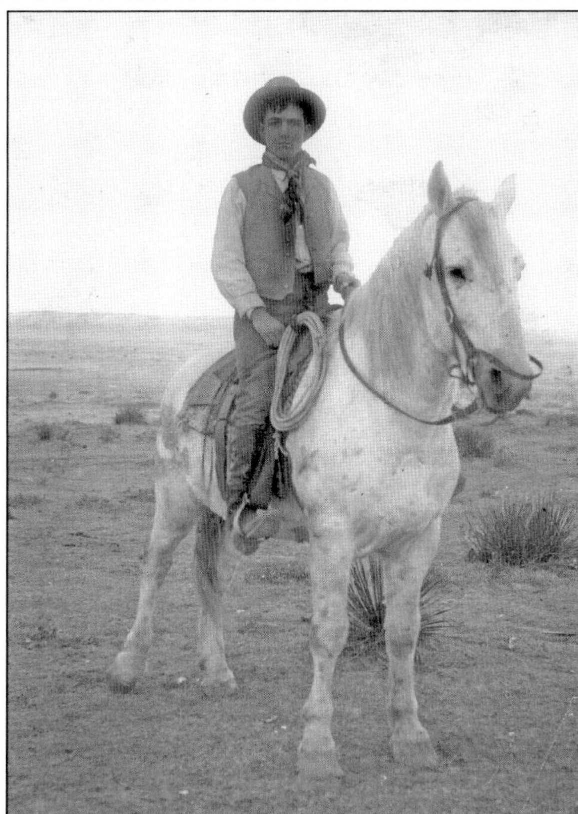

XIT Ranch cowboy Poly Carpenter is pictured on his horse in the Rita Blanca Division in 1911, just before the breakup of the ranch occurred in 1912. The need for one large ranch changed when the railroad made cattle drives all but obsolete. By 1912, cattle were regular passengers aboard railcars, and a change from moving the cattle across rangeland to raising them on feedlots emerged. (Courtesy of XIT Museum and J.E. Thomas.)

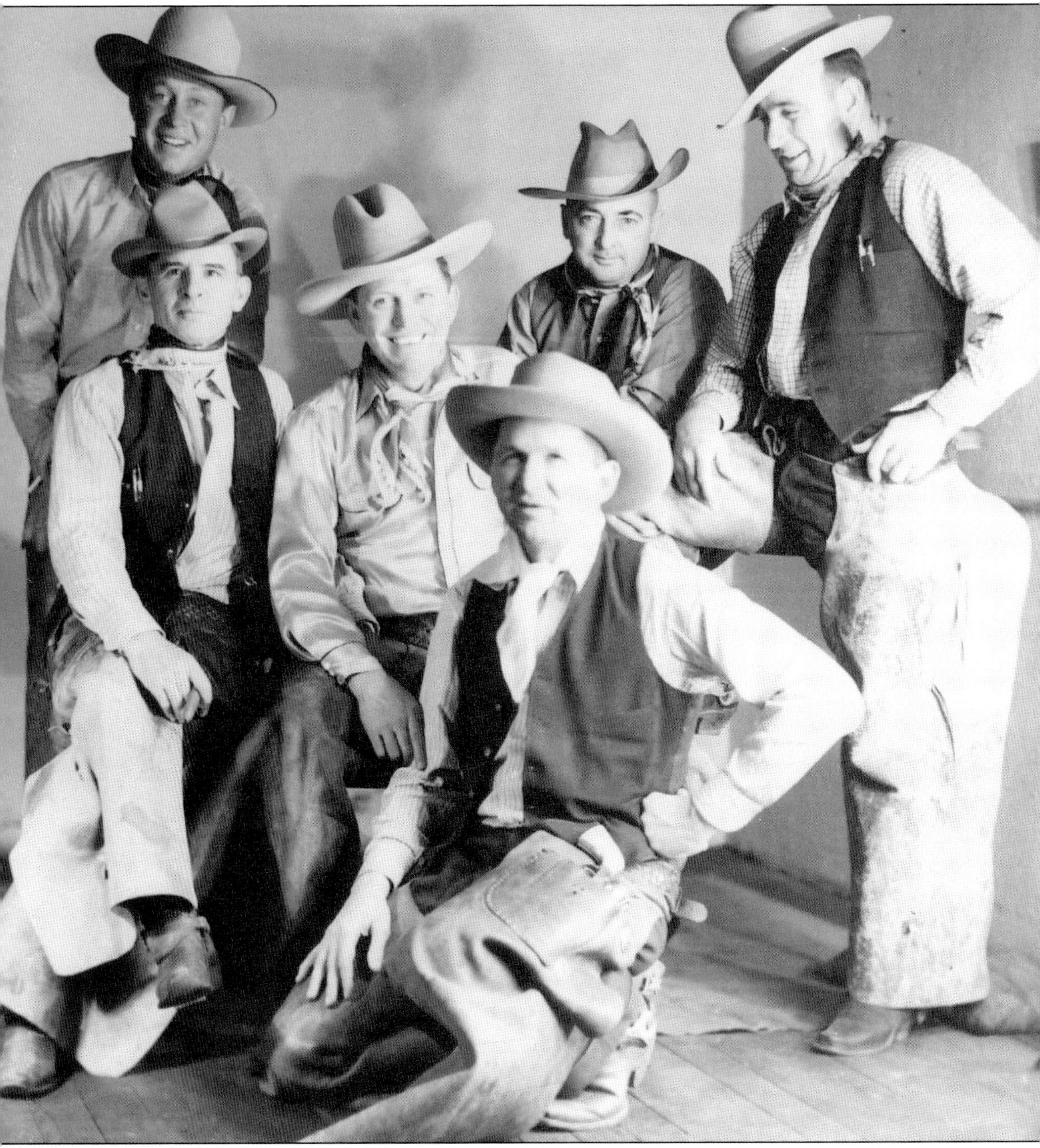

Shown here are the first directors of the XIT Rodeo and Reunion in 1937. They are Allyn Finch, Frank Farwell, John Colquitt Sr., R.S. Chatelain, Charles E. Combs Jr., and S.E. "Eck" Brown. Frank Farwell was the son of John Farwell, one of the brothers who made the land deal that created the XIT Ranch. Allyn Finch was the son of O.H. Finch, and older brother of Orville H. Finch. Jr. Allyn died at the age of 40. He was quite a bit older than Orville, who continues to reside on the family ranch. The XIT Rodeo and Reunion celebrated its 75th anniversary in 2011.

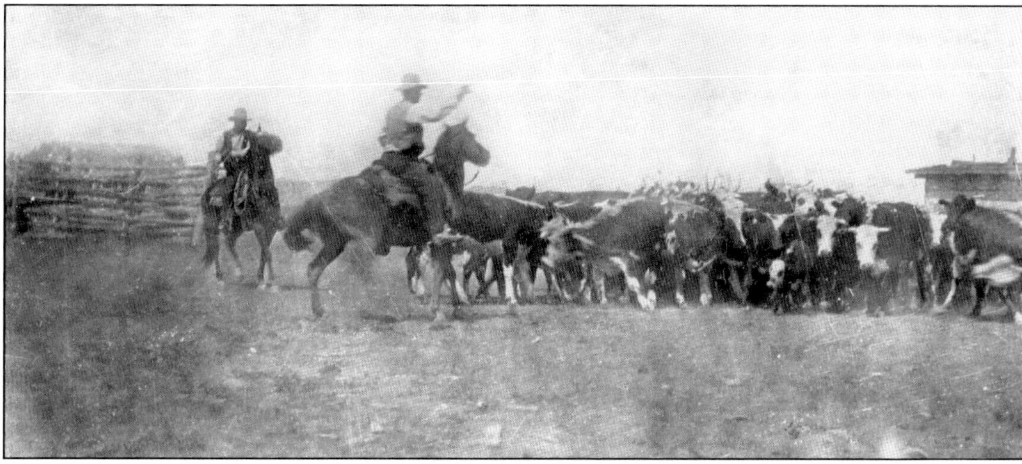

Jeff Meiks (center, with arm raised, riding Timberline) and other cowboys are shown rounding up cattle on the XIT Ranch in the late 1800s. The cattle roundup was a large part of what cowboys did on the ranch. Massive cattle drives were a regular sight. By the time Dalhart began its routes, the cattle drives were dwindling, and cattle were transported by rail. In the early days of the railroad, hauling cattle in and out of Dalhart was common.

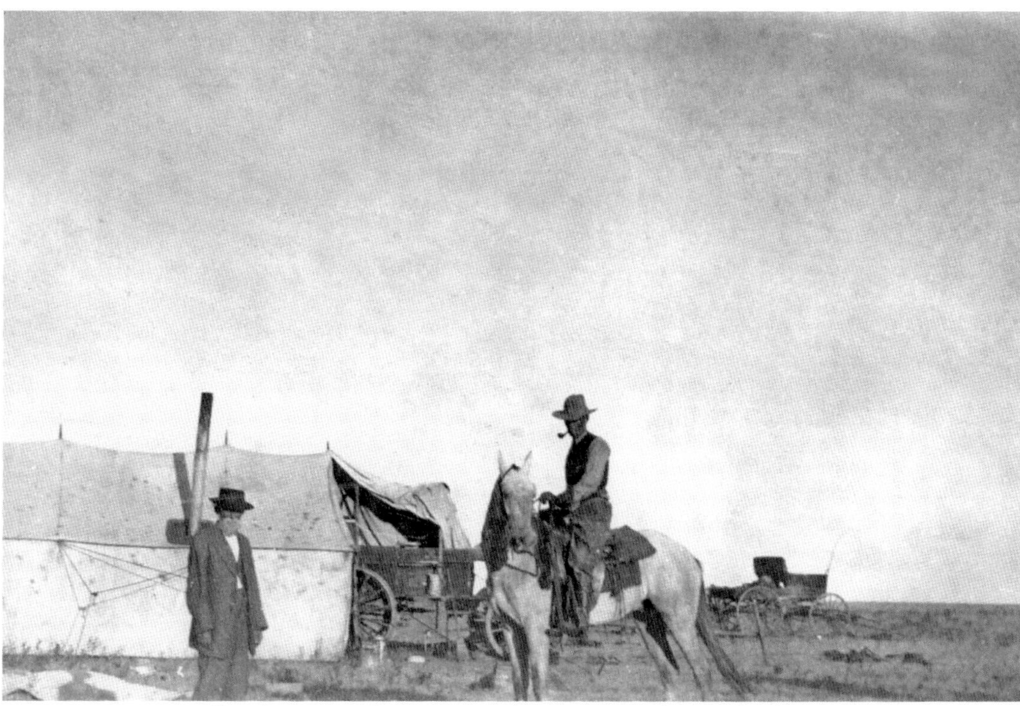

Surveyors spent endless hours on the XIT Ranch, surveying the land. This image shows an XIT surveyor's camp in the 1880s. Although the land was initially surveyed by one company, the surveys continued for many years. The XIT Museum in Dalhart houses surveying items and equipment used in the late 1800s and early 1900s.

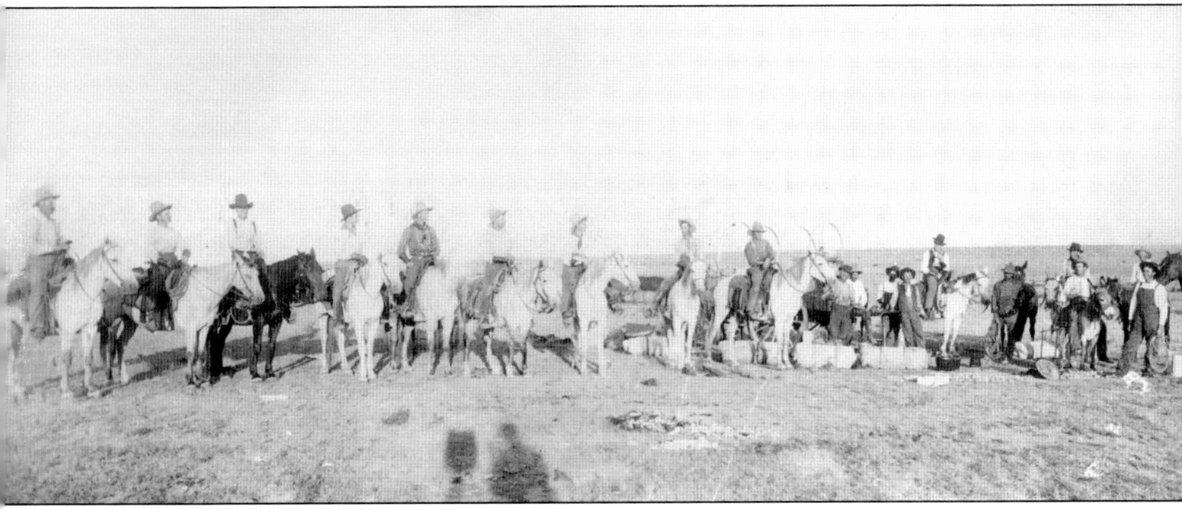

The vast XIT Ranch was divided into many sections, with regional headquarters located in each. The most notable were the Channing headquarters and the headquarters in the Buffalo Springs Division. Seen here are 10 men from the XIT's Yellow House outfit, mounted on horseback with bedrolls and a wagon in the background. Note the shadow of the photographer and his large square box camera.

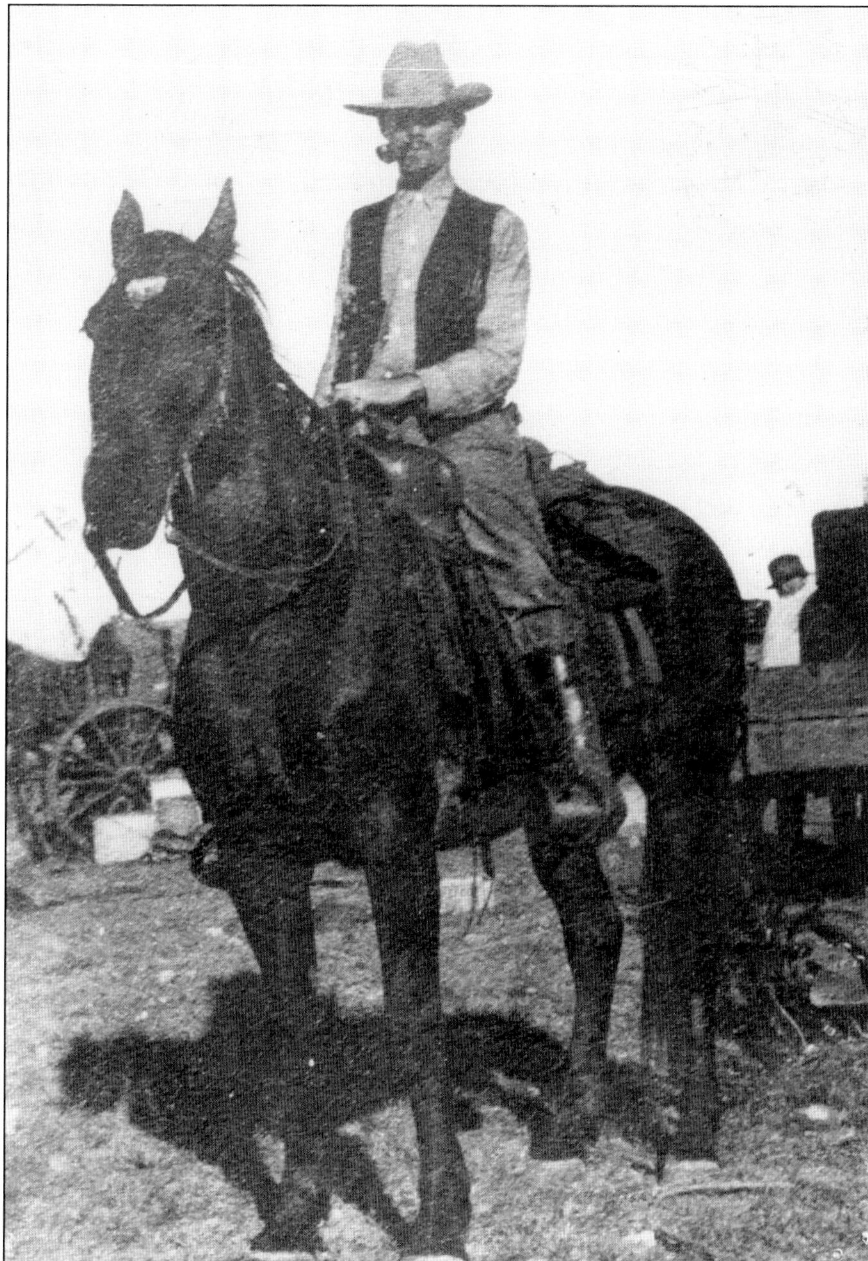

Surveyor William D. Howren, seen here on horseback in the late 1880s, was the son of Aaron S. "A.S." Howren of Amarillo. A.S. Howren was considered one of the XIT Ranch's greatest individuals. He began work for the ranch in 1900, using his skills as a schoolteacher to survey. After his surveying was completed, he spent 17 years as the ranch's tax commissioner. The state of Texas initially advertised for bids from surveyors to survey the XIT's acreage back in the 1870s. On July 17, 1879, the contract was awarded to Joseph Theodore Munson. Though severe drought, followed by severe cold weather, delayed the work, the initial survey was finally completed in 1880. Later, the Capitol Freehold and Investment Company hired Aaron and William to resurvey the XIT Ranch lands.

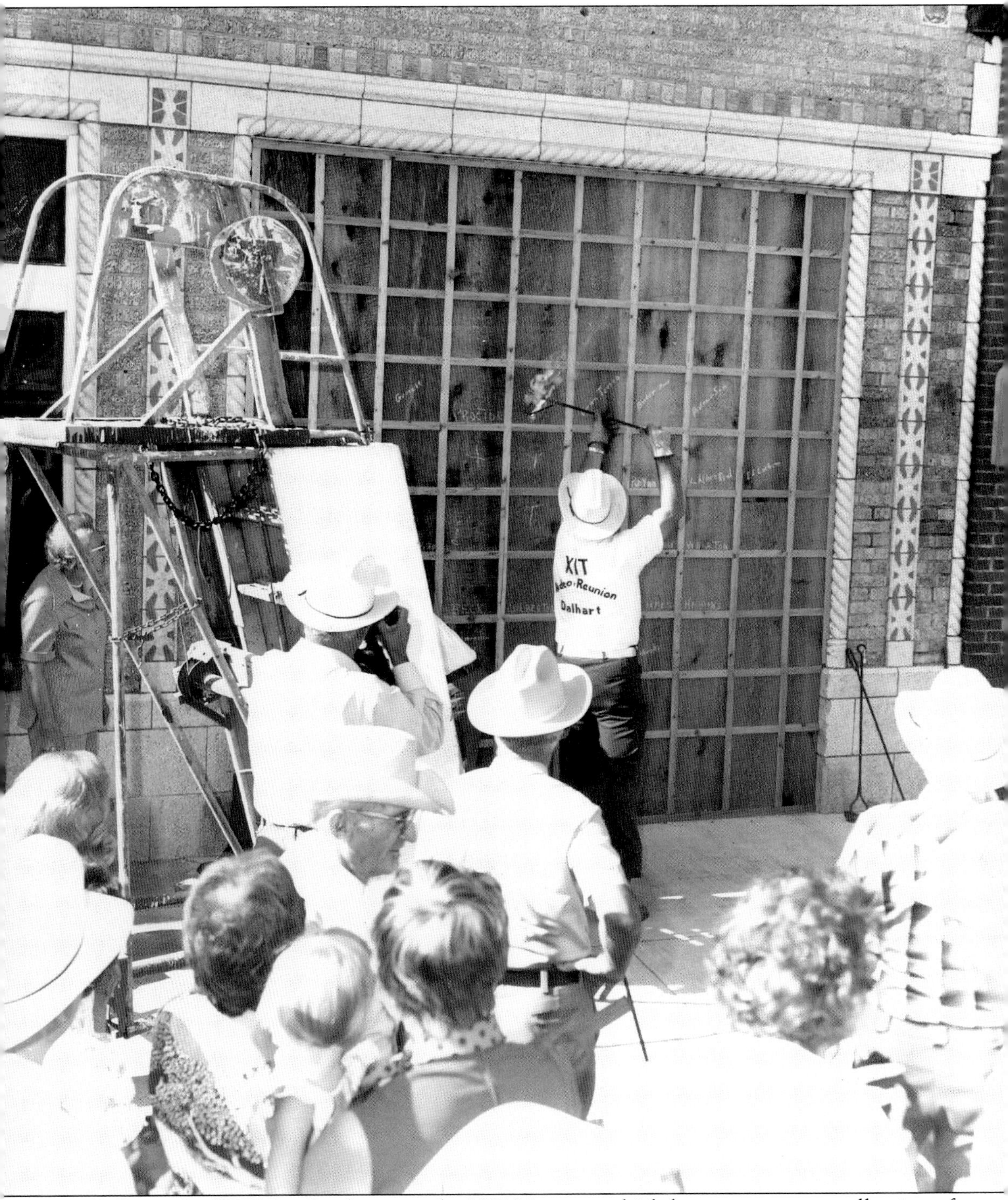

Dalhart, the "XIT City," is home to the XIT Museum, which has a permanent collection of photographs and artifacts dedicated to the XIT Ranch. In 1975, the year the museum opened, the XIT director made the first brand on the wall outside of the museum. The Branding Wall contains brands from area ranches, past and present, added to the collection over several years.

Three

People of Dalhart

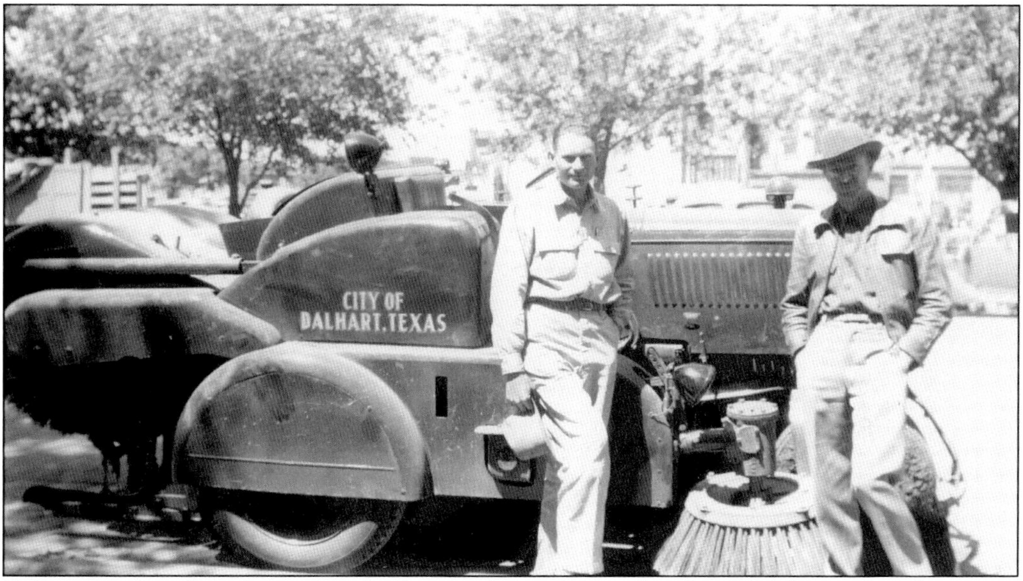

Dalhart may have been located in the flat, dry plains of Texas, but that didn't keep it from becoming the crossroads for trade that ran both north and south, and east and west, right through town on the railroad and eventually the highway. Several families became quite wealthy, including the Farwells, who were known for having the best of everything—from nice homes to the first automobiles and even a grand piano, now on permanent display in the XIT Museum in Dalhart. Family businesses took root all along Denrock Avenue, and the people who ran them became the first Dalhartans. Dalhart has been home to many people since 1901, including doctors, lawyers, and mayors. Pictured here are Dalhart city councilman Burton Hogue (right) and mayor Harold Hogue (left) with Dalhart's new street sweeper. (Courtesy of the XIT Museum.)

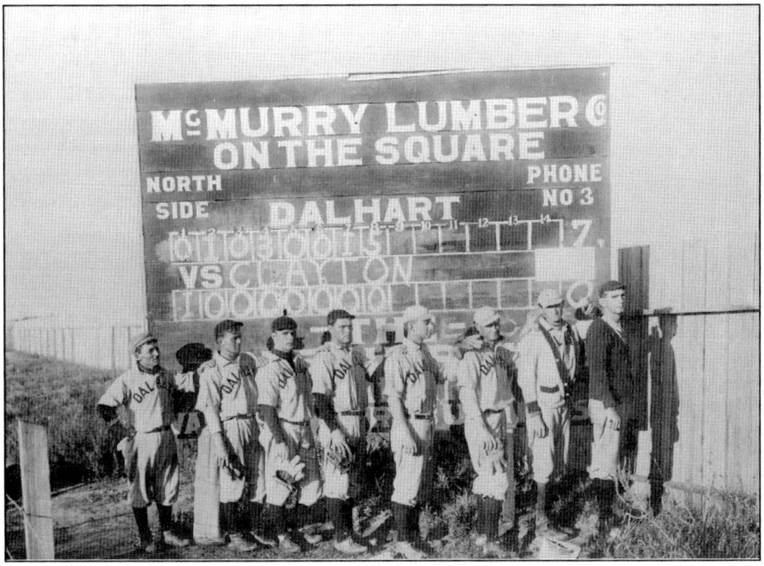

In 1908, Dalhart's first baseball team poses for a photograph in front of the scoreboard provided by McMurry Lumber Company. Dalhart beat a team from neighboring Clayton, New Mexico, 5-0. Note that the lumber company's phone number is "3." (Courtesy of the XIT Museum and Mrs. C. P. Brown.)

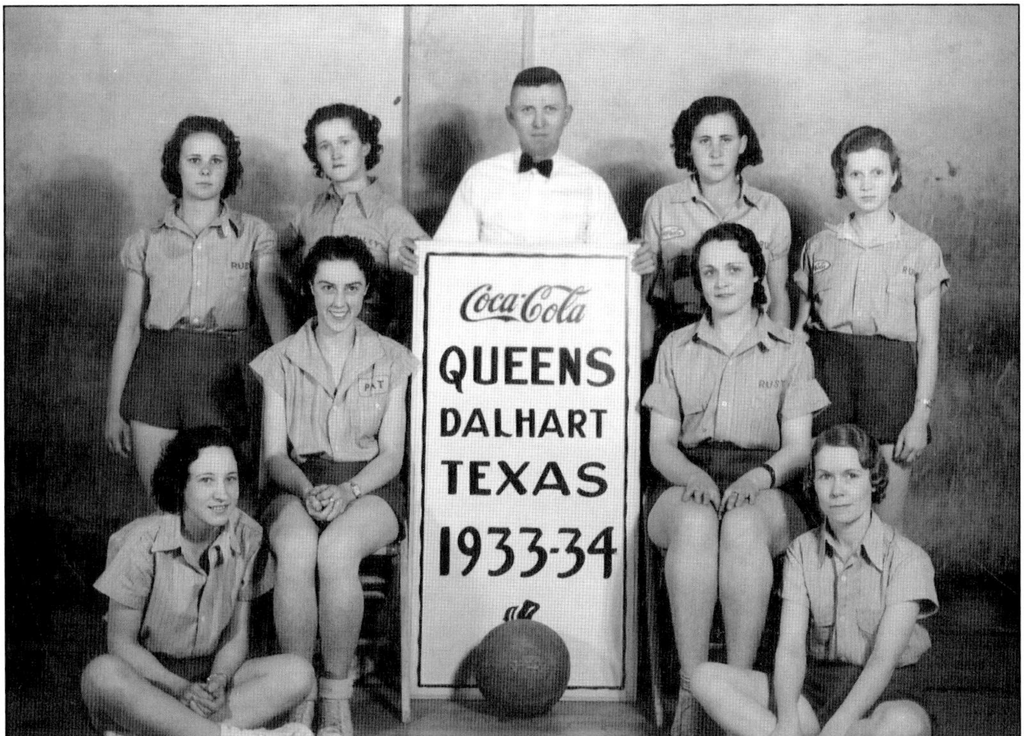

The Dalhart Queens women's basketball team was sponsored by Coca-Cola in the 1933–1934 season. Interesting to note is that the "short" shorts of the women were replaced by longer, gaucho-style shorts in the 1950s. Pictured here from left to right are (floor) Altheta Stead and Elsie Ribble; (seated) Virginia Patterson and Mary Ross; (back row) Nellie Mitchell, Elaine Delli Long, John O. Colquitt, Beatrice Graham, and Catherine Cumins.

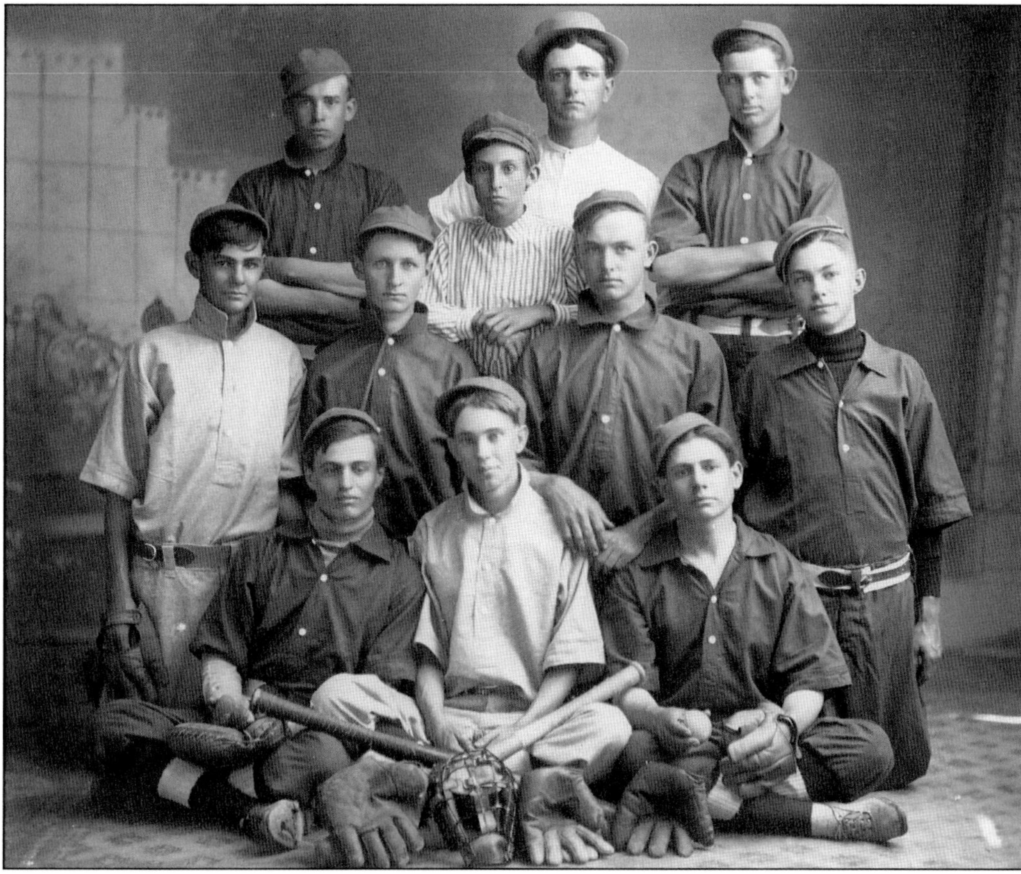

Activities such as baseball, parades down Denrock Avenue, and ballet became commonplace soon after Dalhart was incorporated. Seen below are BeBe Byrd, Earlene Damron Caddell, Betty Jo Hodges Green, Isabell Childers, Winifred Jones Allender, and Bonnie Counts. Earlene Caddell continues to reside in Dalhart and owns one of Dalhart's furniture and appliance stores, Furniture Fashions, along with her son and Dalhart mayor, Kevin Caddell.

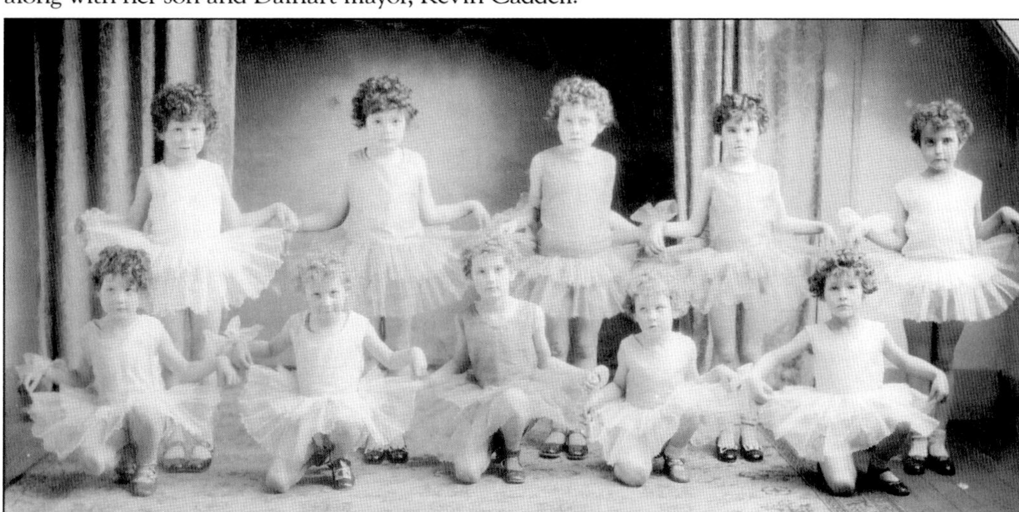

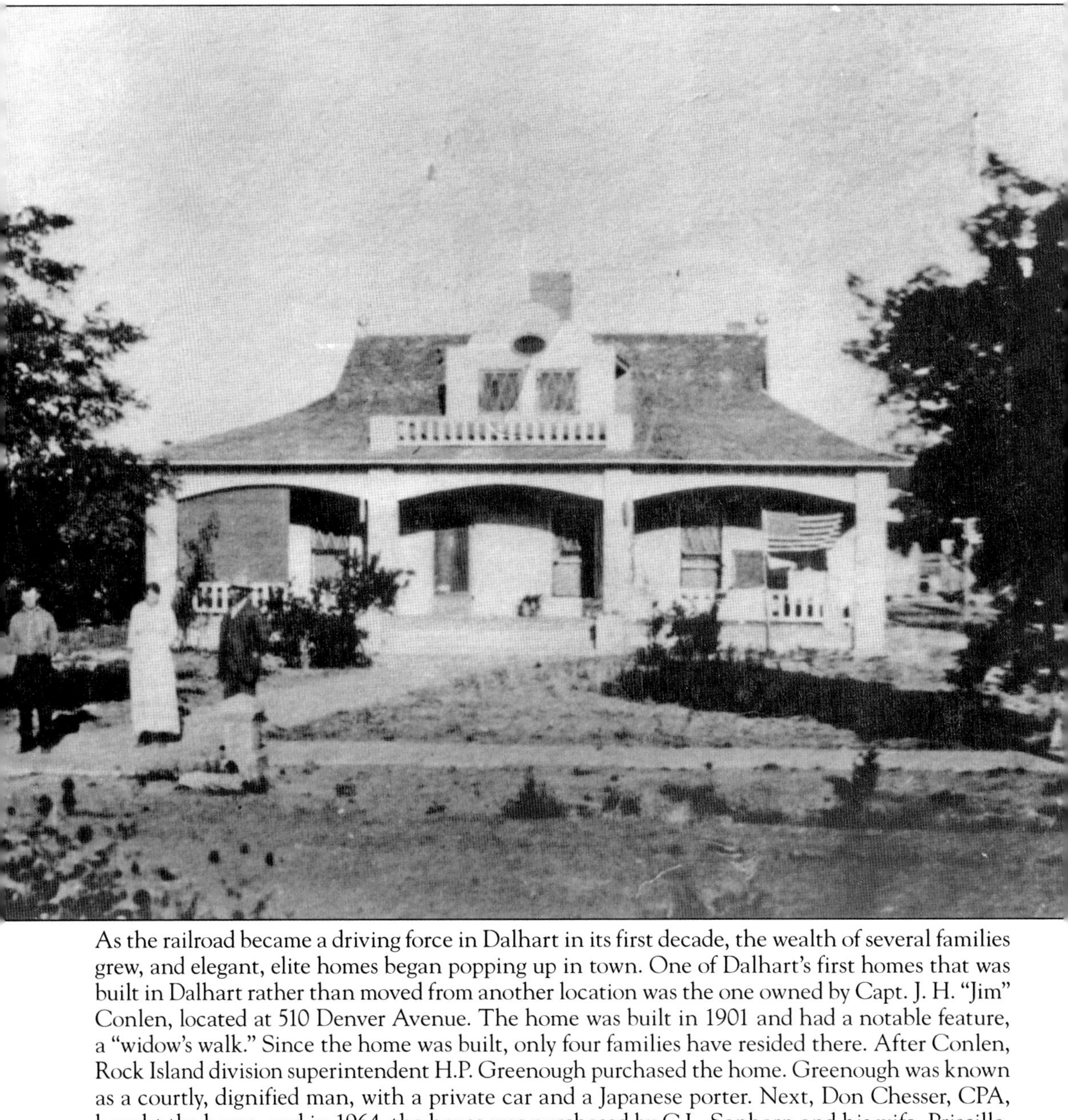

As the railroad became a driving force in Dalhart in its first decade, the wealth of several families grew, and elegant, elite homes began popping up in town. One of Dalhart's first homes that was built in Dalhart rather than moved from another location was the one owned by Capt. J. H. "Jim" Conlen, located at 510 Denver Avenue. The home was built in 1901 and had a notable feature, a "widow's walk." Since the home was built, only four families have resided there. After Conlen, Rock Island division superintendent H.P. Greenough purchased the home. Greenough was known as a courtly, dignified man, with a private car and a Japanese porter. Next, Don Chesser, CPA, bought the home, and in 1964, the house was purchased by C.L. Sanborn and his wife, Priscilla, who continue to reside there today. At one time, the home had a carriage house, but it has since been enclosed. The widow's walk remains, but its access has been closed.

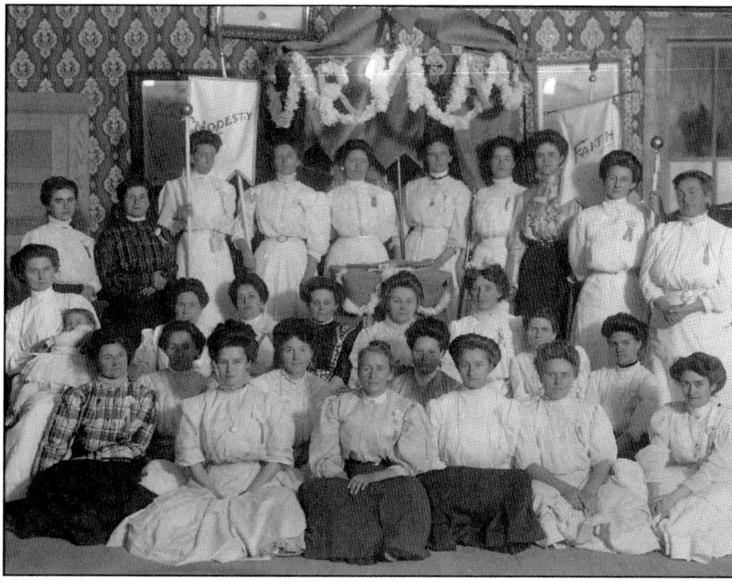

Dalhart's first women's club is pictured here in 1900. The women's clubs offered benevolent services in the area including raising money for important causes, cooking, and rolling bandages in wartime. Notice the banners in the background that read "Modesty" and "Faith;" all of the women are wearing long dresses, and they wear their hair in turn-of-the-century buns. (Courtesy of the XIT Museum and E.L. Fairchild.)

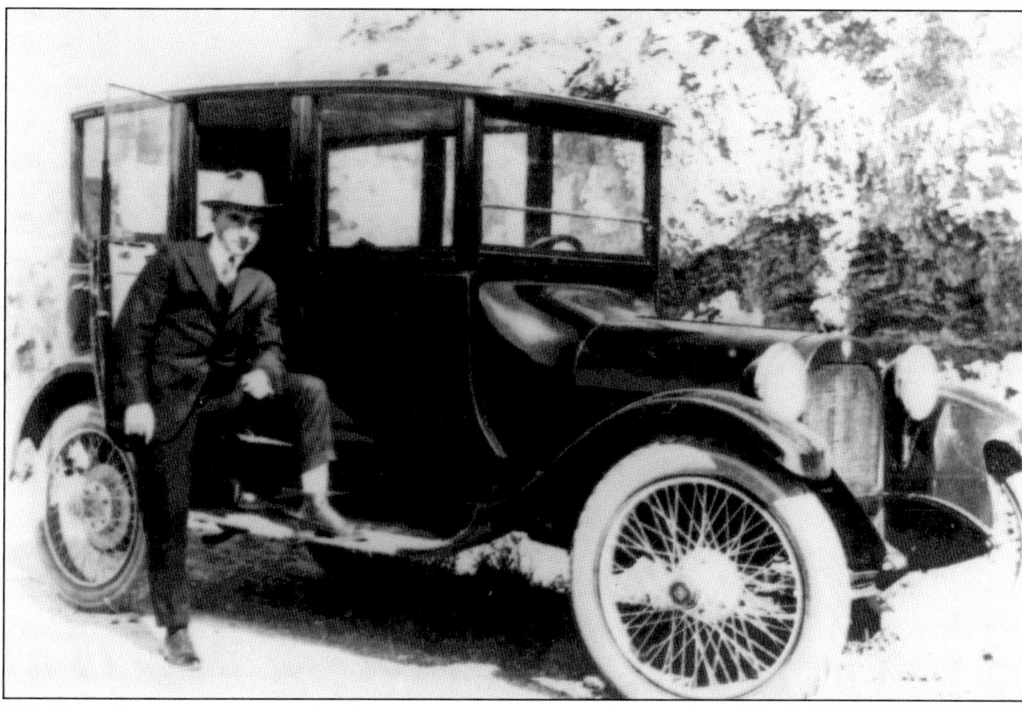

J.W. 'Jim" Pigman arrived in Dalhart from Chicago in 1906, at just 17 years of age. He quickly became one of Dalhart's greatest boosters. His early career was with Rogers Insurance Company, but he later founded Dalhart Federal Savings and Loan Company, which continues as a prominent business in Dalhart today. During his early years, Pigman chauffeured for the Williams brothers and enjoyed driving their vehicles. He is pictured here in 1921 with one of the Williams cars. Pigman married Irene Hazelton, who came to Dalhart with her family in 1910. The Pigmans had a son, Jimmy Pigman, who ran the savings and loan, and two daughters, Betty Jean and Patricia. The Pigmans built one of Dalhart's finest homes at 822 Denrock Avenue after living on Ninth Street for 13 years.

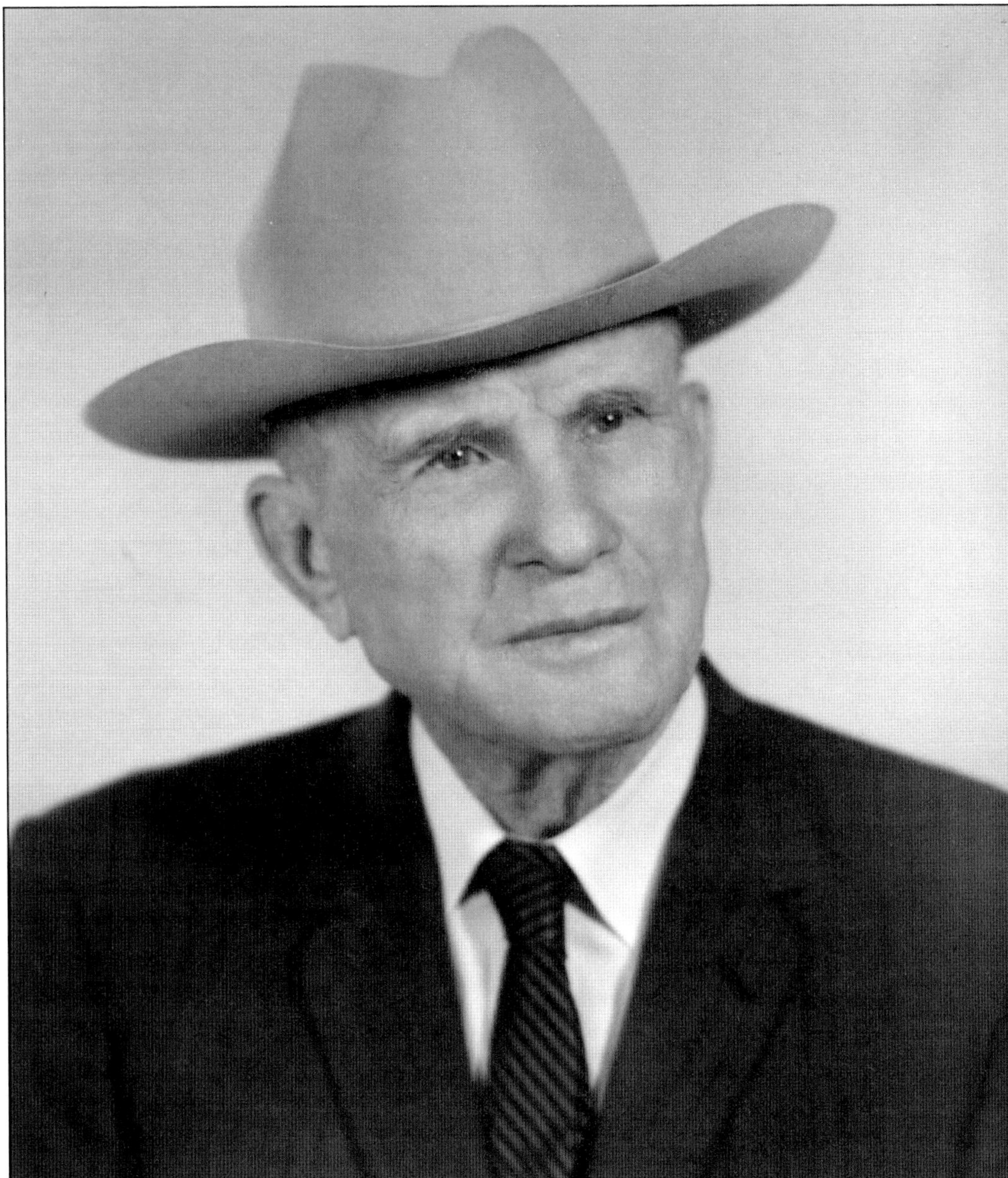

Born in 1880, Orville H. Finch Sr. married Alice Boone. The two had a son, Allyn D. Finch, born in 1909. After Alice's death in 1920, Orville remarried to Olive Pendleton, and Orville H. Finch Jr., was born in 1924. Orville Jr. married Leabelle Sluder. Orville and Leabelle's son Carl D. Finch and Allyn's son Gary C. Finch continue to ranch just southwest of Dalhart. Orville Sr.'s brother, Howard A. Finch, published a book of poetry in 1965, which he dedicated to his brother, Orville, "Who encouraged me to have these verses printed in booklet form." Orville Sr., a pillar of the Dalhart community, is pictured here in 1961 at the age of 81.

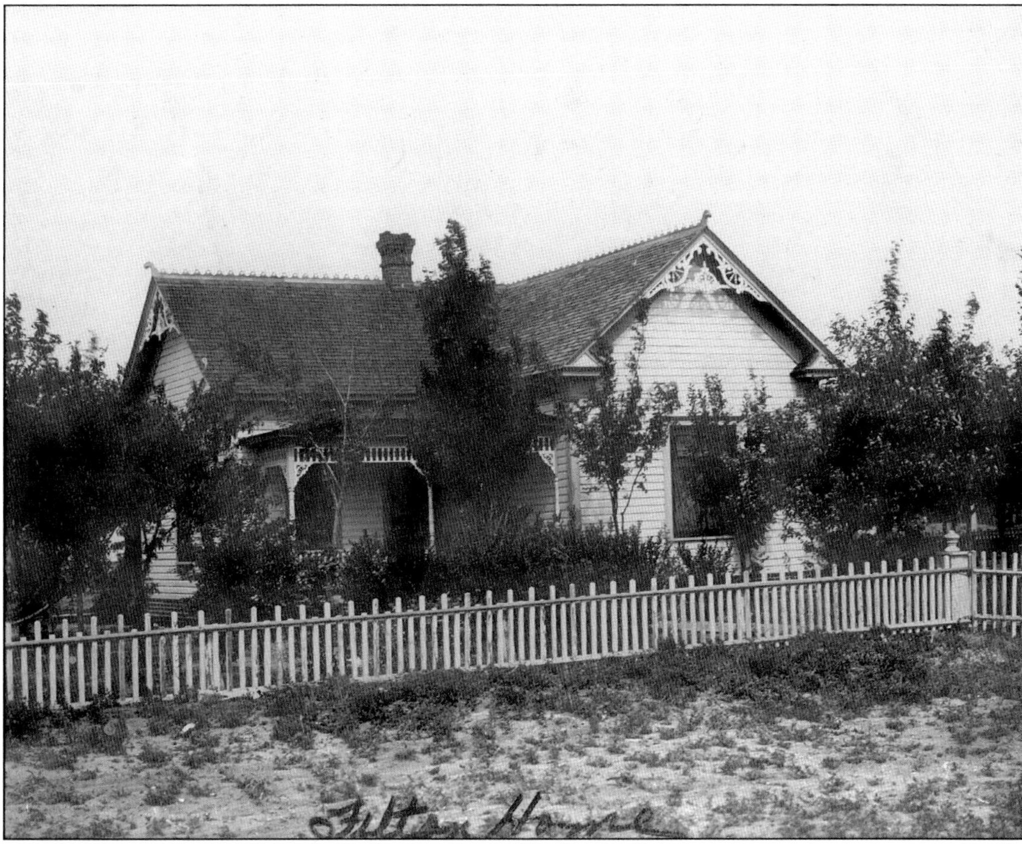

The Feltons were one of the first families to settle in Dalhart. Their home was located at the corner of Sixth Street and Denver Avenue and was photographed in 1900. The Felton building was and is located at the corner of Denrock Avenue and Third Street. The two-story structure has seen many businesses come and go, including the Dalhart Opera House. (Courtesy of the XIT Museum and E.L. Fairchild.)

The Warnocks lived at 523 Rock Island Avenue. B.F. "Bob" Warnock and his wife, Beth, are pictured in this 1909 photograph with Bob in the automobile, and Mr. and Mrs. Homer Wise of Dalhart. (Courtesy of the XIT Museum and E.L. Fairchild.)

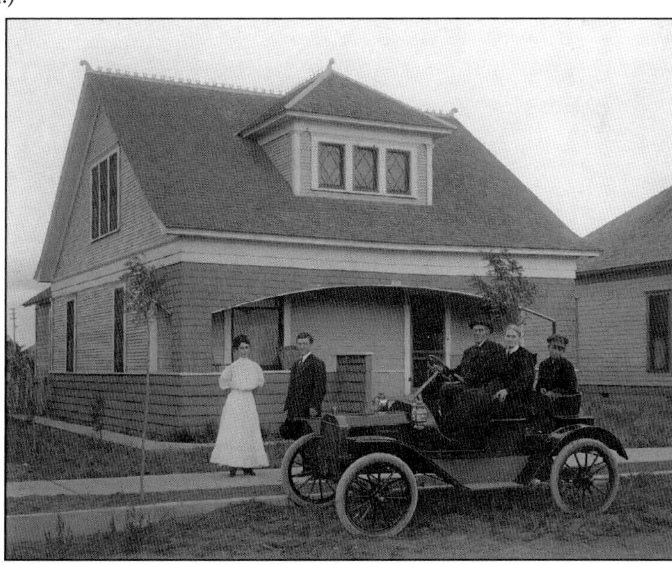

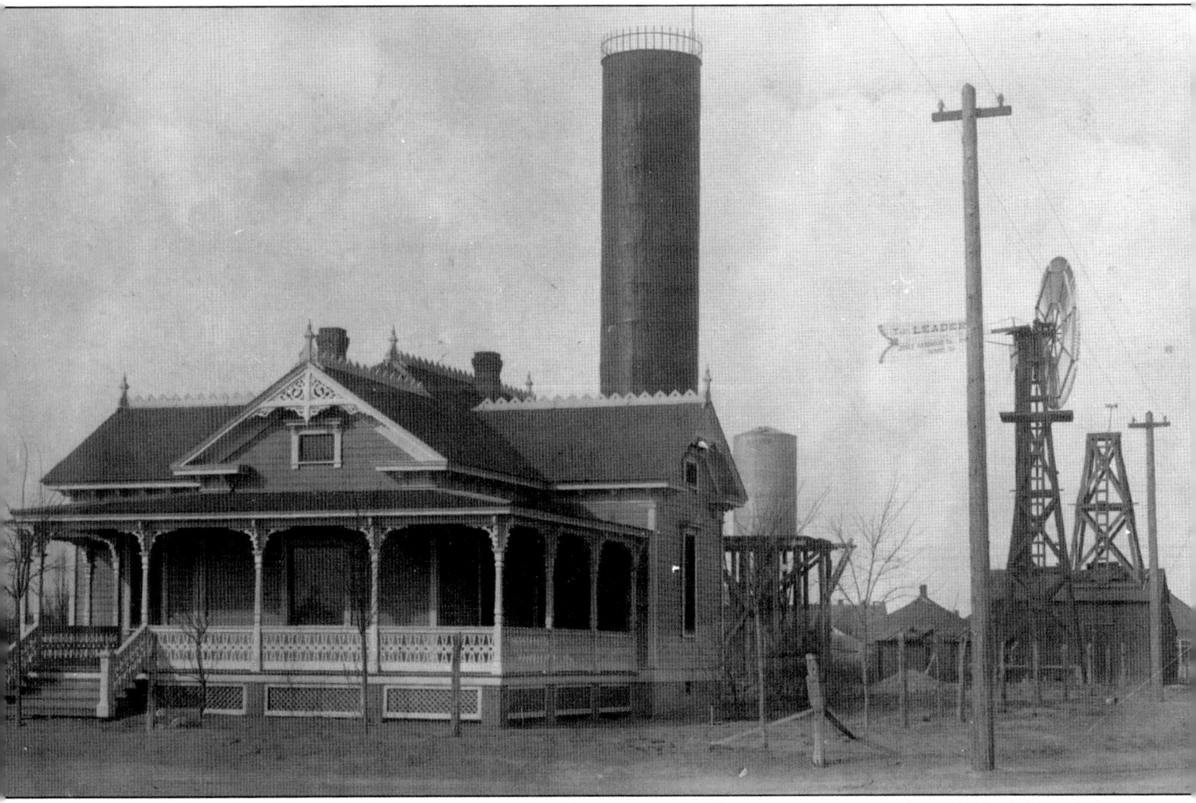

The first waterworks in Dalhart was drilled by C.E. Williams in 1901 and included 3,000 feet of pipe and a 500-gallon tank. Williams also set up a free watering trough for dogs and horses. Williams also put in the first livery stable in Dalhart. He arrived in Dalhart for a town lot sale on May 14, 1901, and purchased 10 lots. He and his wife bought lumber from Dalhart's lumberyard to build their first home, located on Denver Avenue next to the waterworks. In 1918, their young daughter, Mary Emily, was chosen to turn on Dalhart's first streetlights. People gathered for the lighting ceremony. A platform had been built just large enough for Mayor Dave A. Robinson, who was a Rock Island engineer, and little Mary Emily Williams to stand on. Dr. Garner lifted Mary Emily, the mayor pointed to the switch, and she flipped it on as the crowed cheered and the band played.

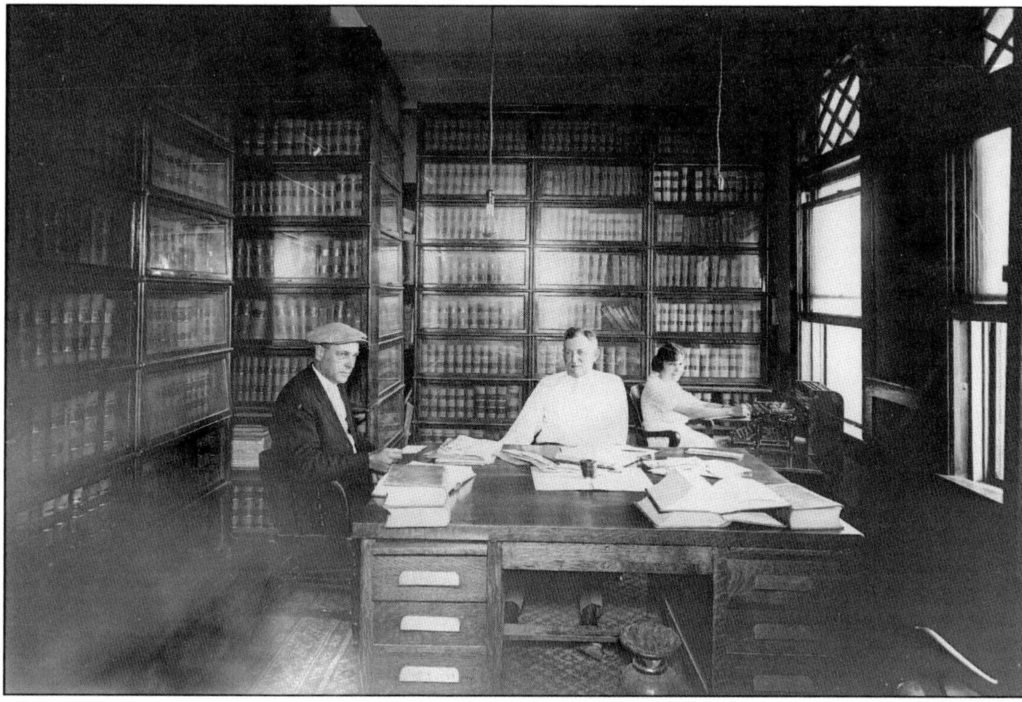

This 1910 photograph shows Frank Tatum in his law office on Denrock Avenue. In a time before everyone had telephones, and nearly a century before email or texting, visiting neighboring businesses was the way to find out what was going on in town. Tatum was known for making the rounds through Dalhart each morning, catching up on the latest gossip. Tatum was a bit of a historian, and he kept many papers that are now part of the permanent collection at the XIT Museum.

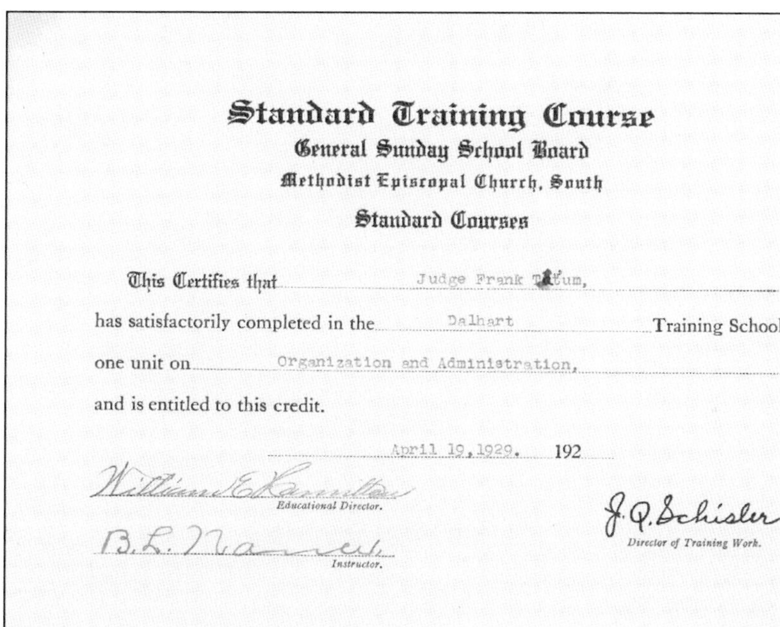

Standard Training Course

General Sunday School Board

Methodist Episcopal Church, South

Standard Courses

This Certifies that Judge Frank Tatum,

has satisfactorily completed in the Dalhart Training School

one unit on Organization and Administration,

and is entitled to this credit.

April 19, 1929. 192

Educational Director.

Instructor.

Director of Training Work.

In April 1929, Judge Frank Tatum completed a course in organization and administration from the Methodist Episcopal Church in Dalhart. Tatum was affectionately known as the "irrepressible lawyer." Close friends with Dr. Dawson, he is said to have teased him relentlessly about how the doctor became so renowned.

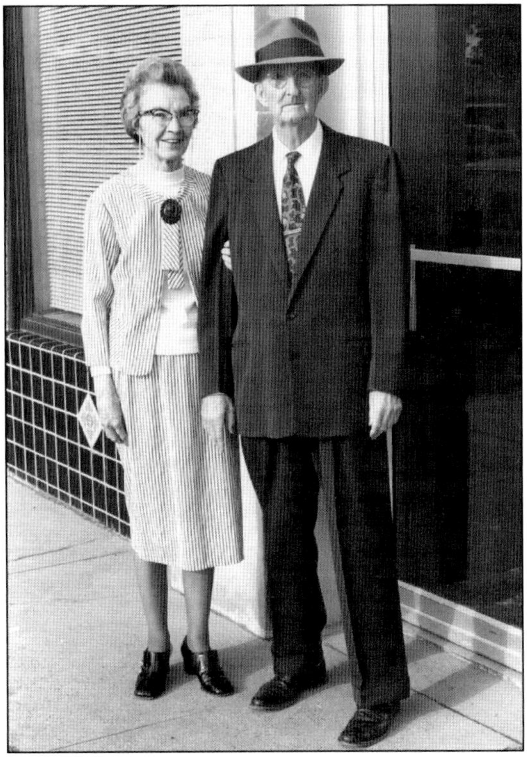

Newspaperman Albert Law wrote in the *Dalhart Texan* about the XIT Ranch and noted that it was the largest range in the world under fence, sprawling from the Yellow House headquarters near Lubbock north to the Oklahoma Panhandle in an irregular strip that was roughly 30 miles wide. Law was editor of the *Dalhart Texan* from 1936 until his retirement in 1982, and a reporter for the paper from 1929 until taking over the editor's position. The Laws stand in front of the *Dalhart Texan* offices in 1982.

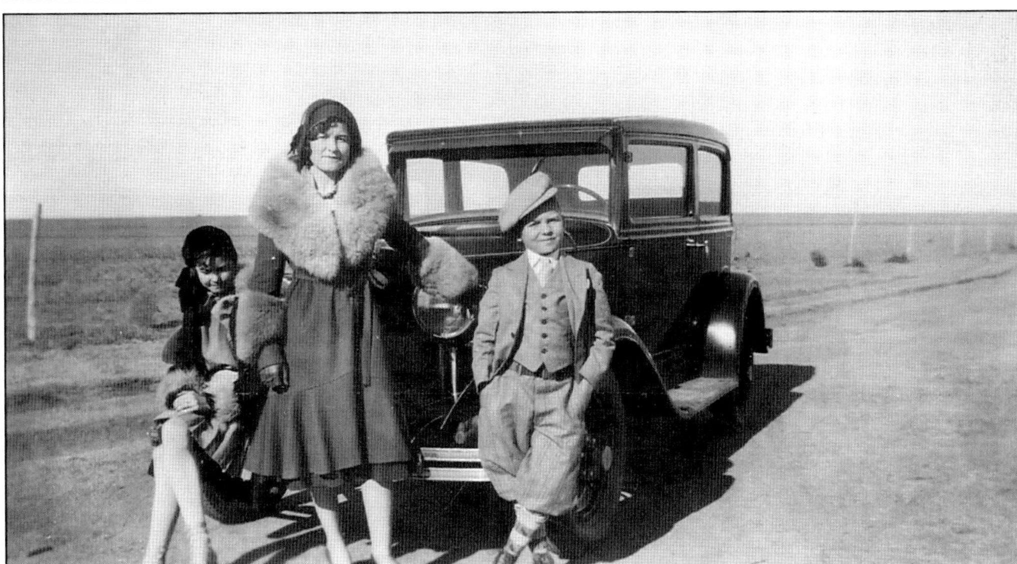

Rubydell "Dell" Steel was born in April 1919 to Charles McClure Steel and Bertie Whaley Steel. She was raised in Dalhart and was a member of the graduating class of 1936. After graduating from high school, Dell became a legal secretary and worked in Midland, Texas; LaJolla, California; Washington, D.C.; and Paris, TX. After retiring, she returned to Dalhart and served as the librarian for the Dallam-Hartley County Library, a columnist for the *Dalhart Texan*, and a volunteer at the XIT Museum. Her brother, Charles, continues to sit on the XIT Museum Board of Directors. Dell passed away in 2008.

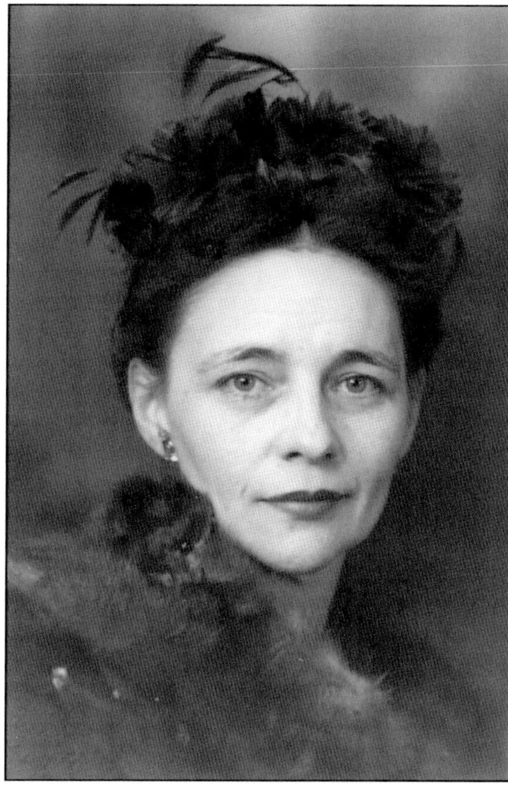

R.S. Coon was referred to as "Uncle Dick" Coon. He came to Dalhart in 1901 on his way to Houston. Dalhart was supposed to be a train stop, but Uncle Dick was intrigued and stayed. He ranched from 1902 until he died in 1941. He was married to Katherine Panky, known as "Aunt Kate." She died in the couple's permanent home at the Rice Hotel in Houston in 1951. Uncle Dick set up a trust, the Coon Memorial Trust, which has greatly benefited Dalhart, including buying the land on which the Loretta Hospital was located. The hospital was operating at a loss, but when Aunt Kate died, the hospital was modernized and enlarged with funds from the trust. The Coon Memorial Home was added, serving 100 elderly residents. The Coons had no children of their own, thus becoming "Uncle" and "Aunt" to everyone in the Dalhart community. (Courtesy of the XIT Museum and Mrs. Anne Davis.)

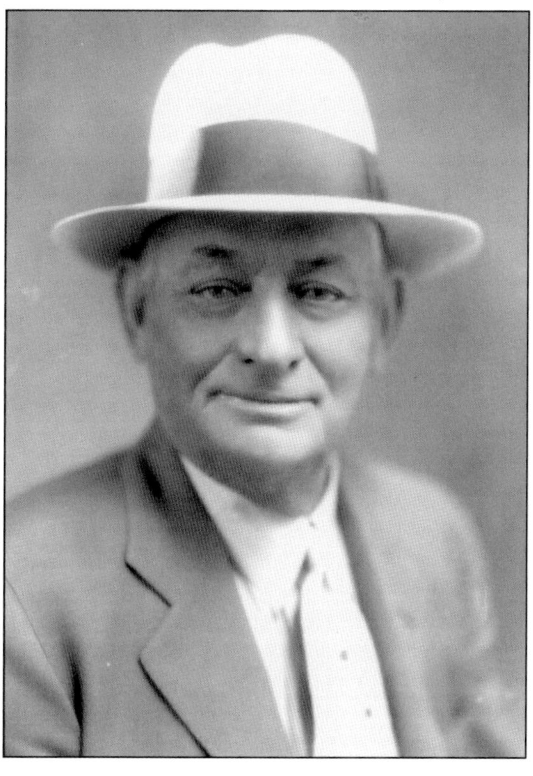

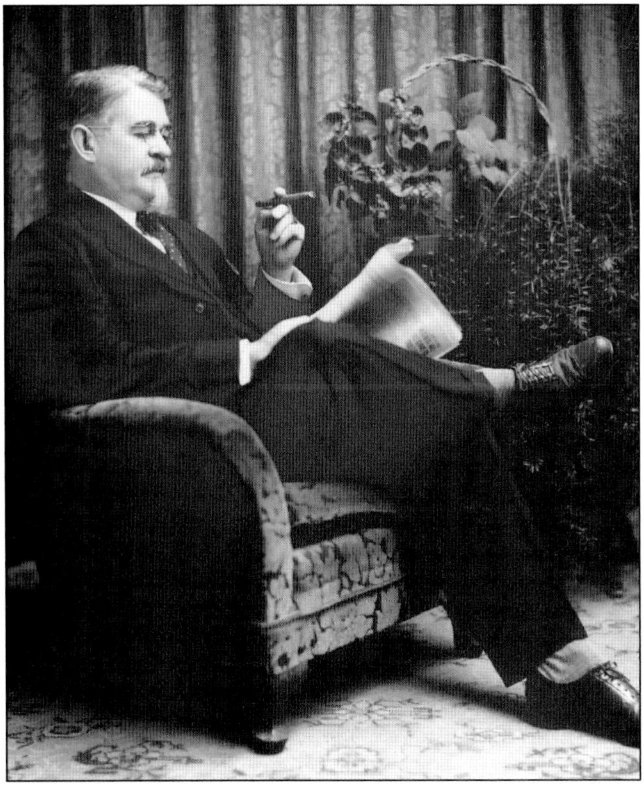

When Dr. G.W. Dawson came to Dalhart from Kentucky in 1907, he became Dalhart's 13th doctor, but managed to make his own mark. In 1912, he and his wife opened the Trans-Canadian Clinic. Mrs. Dawson, Willie Catherine, was the anesthetist and matron. The clinic, located in the 100 block of Denrock Avenue, was very successful, and Dr. Dawson was reported to have performed 2,000 operations from 1912 until the Loretta Hospital opened in 1929. In this photograph, Dr. Dawson sits in a chair reading the newspaper.

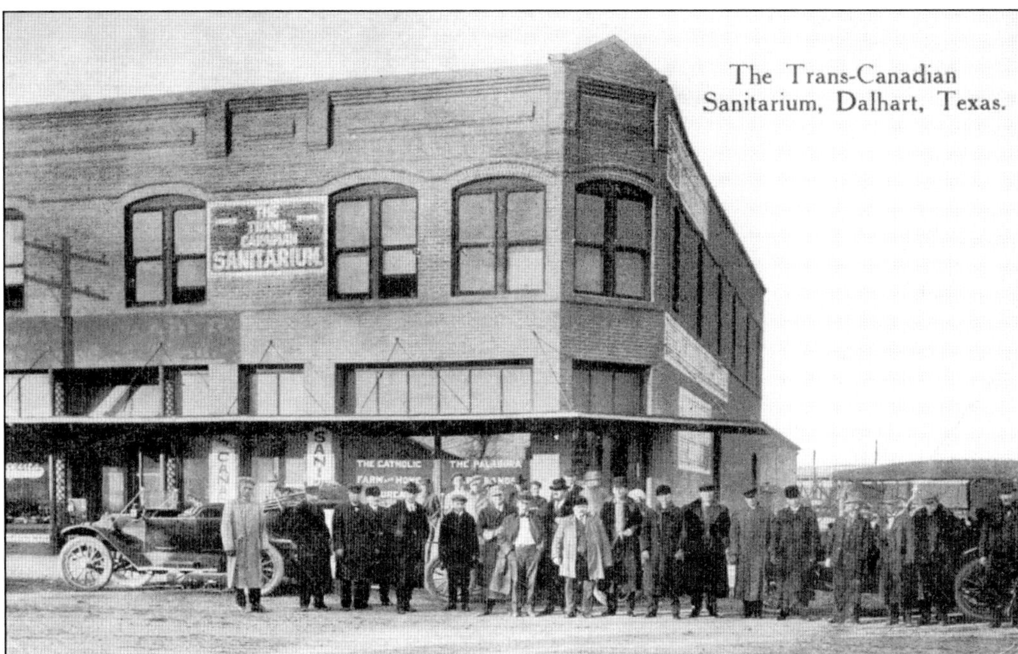

The Trans-Canadian Sanitarium was "very well-equipped for a pioneer sanitarium," and included an x-ray machine brought from Kentucky. Patients came from as far away as Colorado for treatment from Dr. Dawson, who also served as the railroad's surgeon for more than 40 years.

Four

Places in Dalhart

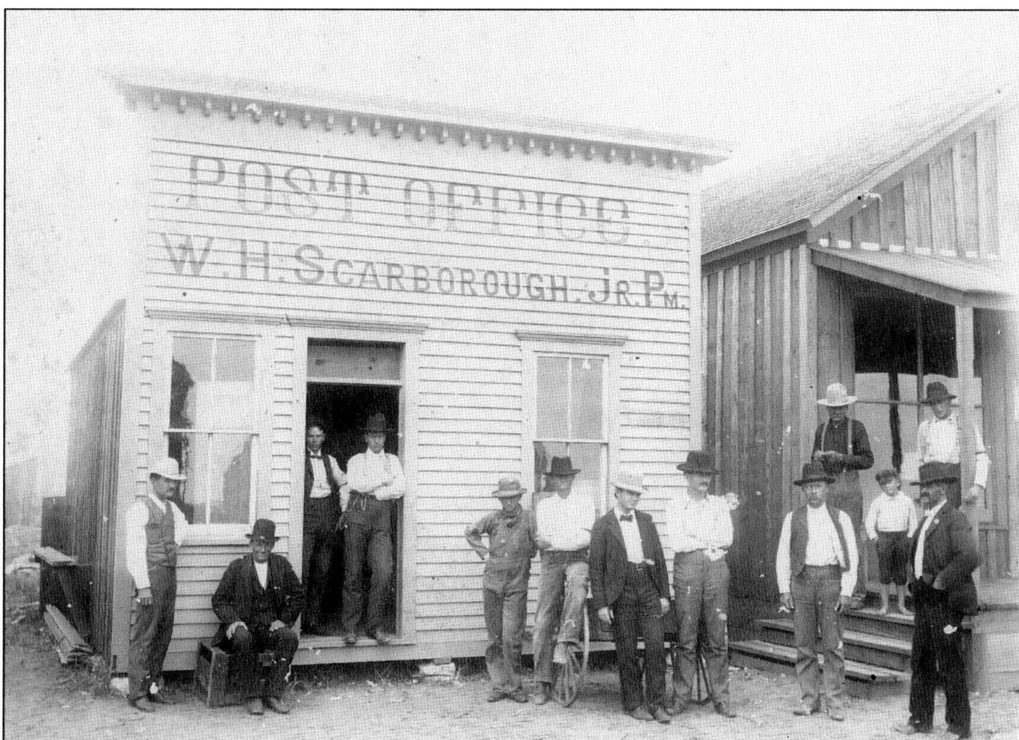

Dalhart's first post office was built in 1901, and W.H. Scarbrough was named its first postmaster. (His brother, Edgar, was the first postmaster in Hartley, 12 miles southeast of Dalhart.) The first post office was located on the corner of First Street and Denver Avenue and was later the site of the Scott Motor Company. W.H. Scarbrough is credited with bringing Dalhart's first building to town, having it moved from Hartley. The building was used for many years as a multipurpose center.

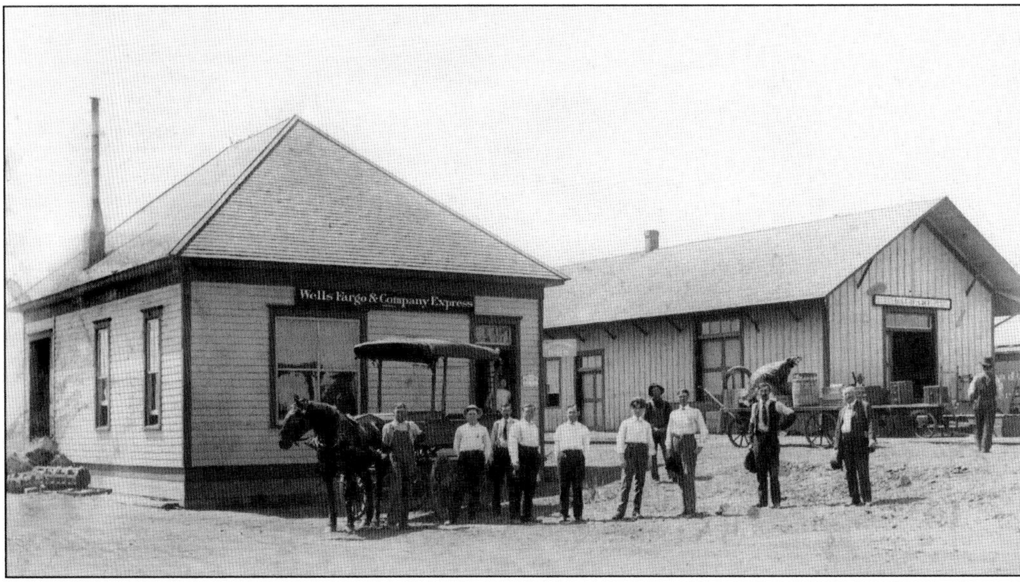

In 1901, Wells Fargo & Company occupied the first business building erected in Dalhart, located at the intersection of what are now US Highways 87 and 54, and part of this building remains standing today. In addition to providing banking services, Wells, Fargo & Company bought gold, sold paper bank drafts, and provided express services—the rapid delivery of gold and other valuables. The prominent business helped secure Dalhart's position as a town. In this 1909 image, men stand in front of the company's offices. The original safe from the business is now on permanent display at the XIT Museum in Dalhart, along with one of the Wells Fargo wagons used to haul items to and from the railroad. Dalhart's first businesses, including Wells Fargo, were located adjacent to the tracks for ease in loading and unloading. (Courtesy of the XIT Museum and Elizabeth Knight.)

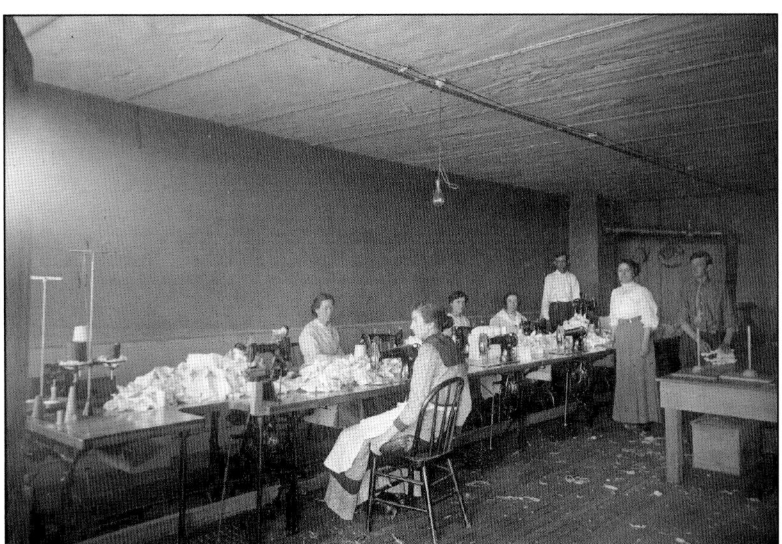

Employees are seen here busily working at a Dalhart glove factory in 1913. Daisy Kirby Tubman is seated in the foreground, and Cecil Ainsworth stands on the far right. Dalhart was also home to a factory that made mattresses, which were hand-stuffed by female employees. (Courtesy of the XIT Museum and Earl McIlroy.)

Seen here in 1910 is the office of Dalhart Ice and Electric, located in the Felton Building at the corner of Denrock Avenue and Third Street. The man on the left is unidentified; the woman is Lucile Sigafoos Lovell; Ben Ethridge is on the right.

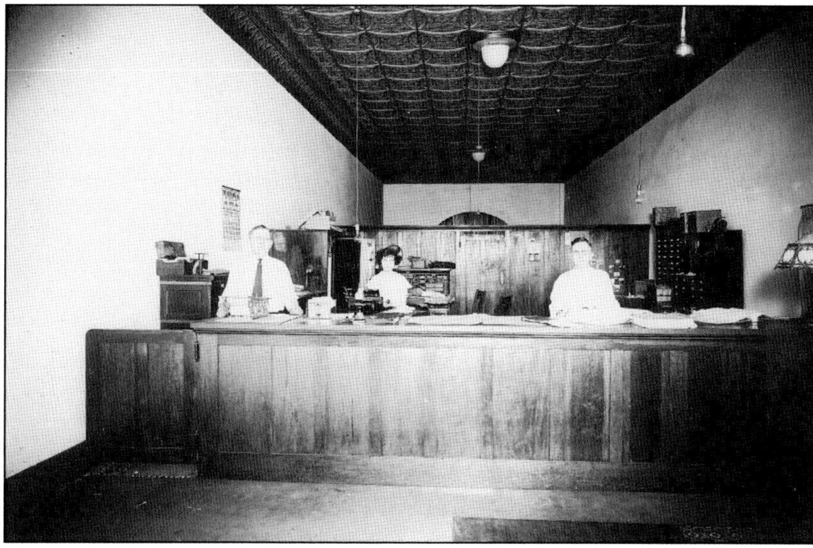

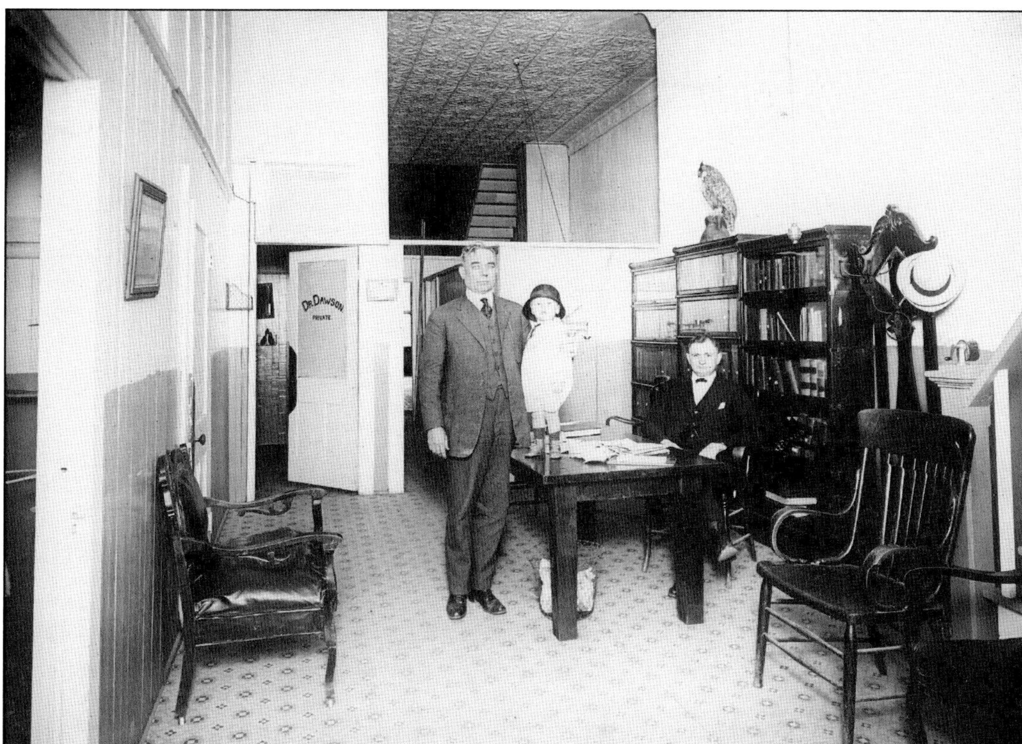

Dr. Dawson's name is seen on the door in the background of this view inside the Trans-Canadian Sanitarium. A Dr. Campbell is seen seated here; Dr. A.J. Lovell stands with Jack. Note the steep staircase with no railing in the back—a common way to reach the second floor. During the Great Depression, people who suffered from mental illness related to the stress of the Dust Bowl are said to have stayed at the sanitarium.

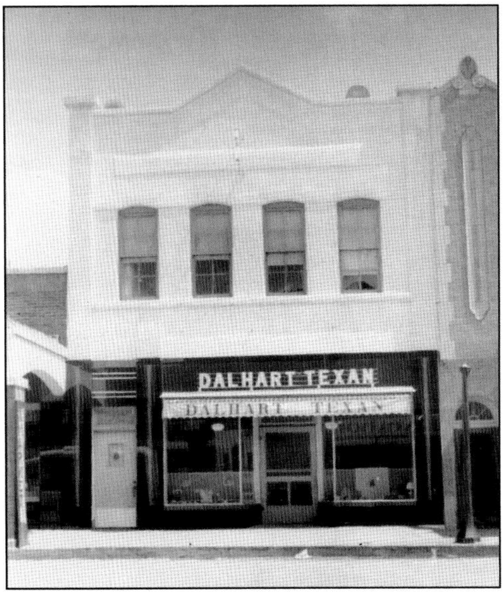

The first edition of the *Denrock Sun* was printed on May 1, 1901. In 1902, the name changed to the *Dalhart Sun*, and the newspaper continues today as the *Dalhart Texan*. The paper still operates from its offices at 410 Denrock Avenue, seen here in 1930. In 1903, the editor of the *Dalhart Sun*, Fred Kornegay, offended a lawyer named W.T. Keith in an editorial. After the newspaper came out, Kornegay passed by Keith's office, and a gunfight ensued, leaving Keith dead. Kornegay was arrested and charged with murder. He pled not guilty, and his trial ended in acquittal. Nearly every Dalhart lawyer was involved in the trial in some fashion, and the newspaper reported on all aspects of the trial.

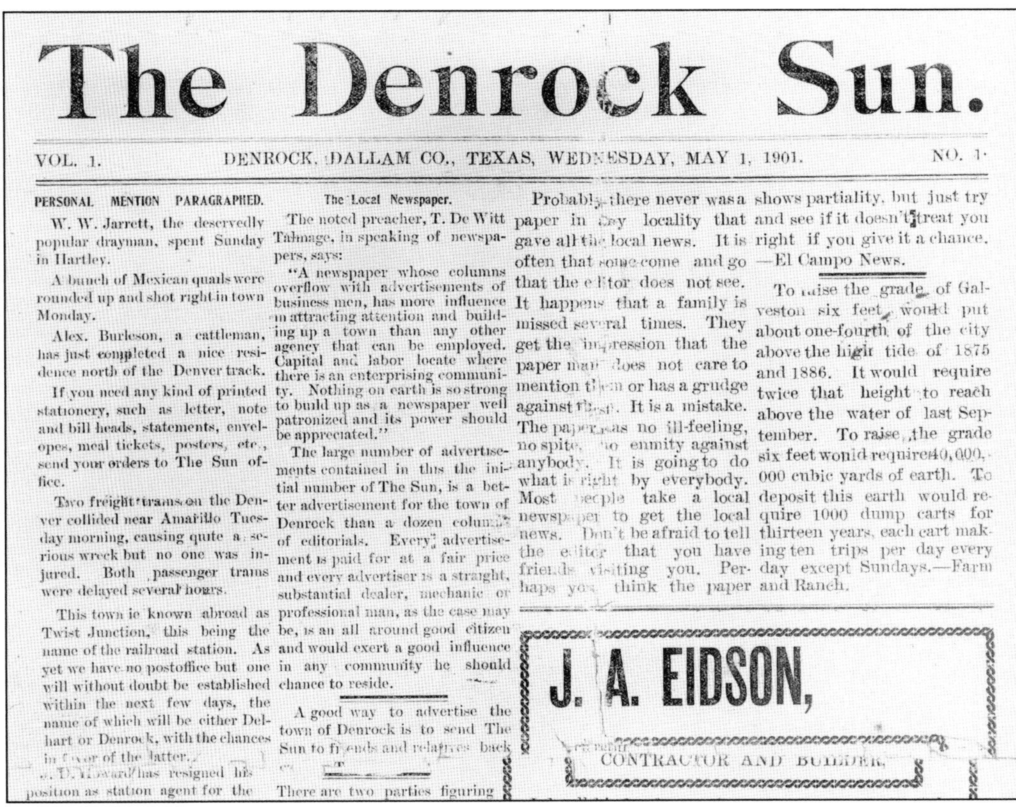

The Denrock Sun.

VOL. 1. DENROCK, DALLAM CO., TEXAS, WEDNESDAY, MAY 1, 1901. NO. 1

PERSONAL MENTION PARAGRAPHED.

W. W. Jarrett, the deservedly popular drayman, spent Sunday in Hartley.

A bunch of Mexican quails were rounded up and shot right in town Monday.

Alex. Burleson, a cattleman, has just completed a nice residence north of the Denver track.

If you need any kind of printed stationery, such as letter, note and bill heads, statements, envelopes, meal tickets, posters, etc., send your orders to The Sun office.

Two freight trains on the Denver collided near Amarillo Tuesday morning, causing quite a serious wreck but no one was injured. Both passenger trains were delayed several hours.

This town is known abroad as Twist Junction, this being the name of the railroad station. As yet we have no postoffice but one will without doubt be established within the next few days, the name of which will be either Delhart or Denrock, with the chances in favor of the latter.

J. T. Howard has resigned his position as station agent for the

The Local Newspaper.

The noted preacher, T. De Witt Talmage, in speaking of newspapers, says:

"A newspaper whose columns overflow with advertisements of business men, has more influence in attracting attention and building up a town than any other agency that can be employed. Capital and labor locate where there is an enterprising community. Nothing on earth is so strong to build up as a newspaper well patronized and its power should be appreciated."

The large number of advertisements contained in this the initial number of The Sun, is a better advertisement for the town of Denrock than a dozen columns of editorials. Every advertisement is paid for at a fair price and every advertiser is a straight, substantial dealer, mechanic or professional man, as the case may be, is an all around good citizen and would exert a good influence in any community he should chance to reside.

A good way to advertise the town of Denrock is to send The Sun to friends and relatives back east.

There are two parties figuring

Probably there never was a paper in any locality that gave all the local news. It is often that some come and go that the editor does not see. It happens that a family is missed several times. They get the impression that the paper man does not care to mention them or has a grudge against them. It is a mistake. The paper has no ill-feeling, no spite, no enmity against anybody. It is going to do what is right by everybody. Most people take a local newspaper to get the local news. Don't be afraid to tell the editor that you have friends visiting you. Perhaps you think the paper shows partiality, but just try and see if it doesn't treat you right if you give it a chance. —El Campo News.

To raise the grade of Galveston six feet would put about one-fourth of the city above the high tide of 1875 and 1886. It would require twice that height to reach above the water of last September. To raise the grade six feet would require 40,000,000 cubic yards of earth. To deposit this earth would require 1000 dump carts for thirteen years, each cart making ten trips per day every day except Sundays.—Farm and Ranch.

J. A. EIDSON,

CONTRACTOR AND BUILDER.

The first edition of the *Denrock Sun* included a report about a train wreck on the Fort Worth and Denver City Line near Amarillo. Following that report was, "This town is known abroad as Twist Junction, this being the name of the railroad station. As yet, we have no post office, but one without doubt be established with the next few days, the name of which will be either Delhart or Denrock, with the chances in favor of the latter." Note that Dalhart was misspelled as "Delhart," in the report.

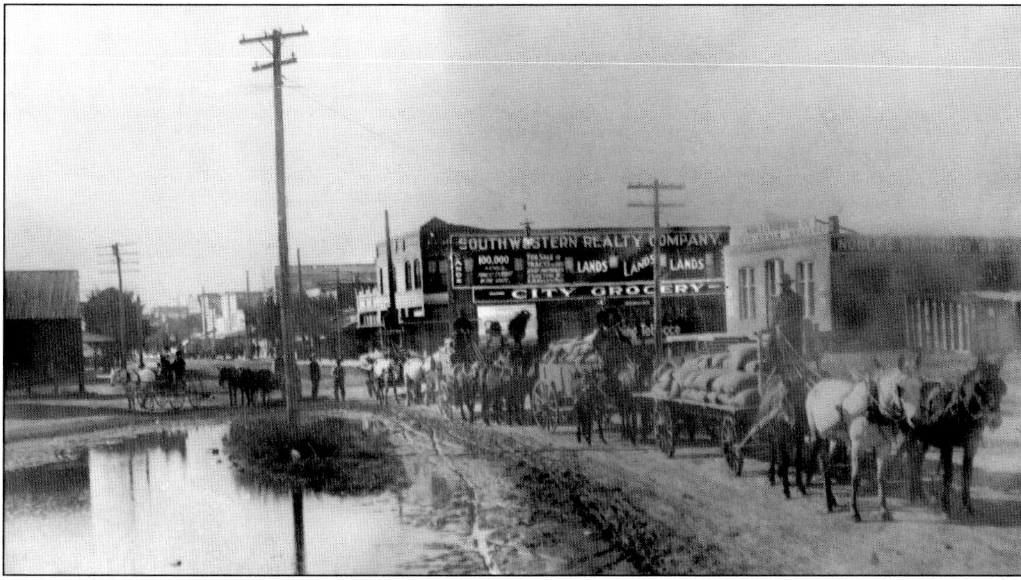

By 1903, Denrock Avenue was Dalhart's main street and home to Dalhart's most notable businesses. Dalhart's first bank, the Bank of Dalhart, was another thriving Denrock Avenue business. This photograph shows the northernmost edge of Denrock Avenue, a street named by combining the names of the Fort Worth and Denver Railroad and the Rock Island Railroad, which were responsible for Dalhart's success as a burgeoning town in the late 1800s.

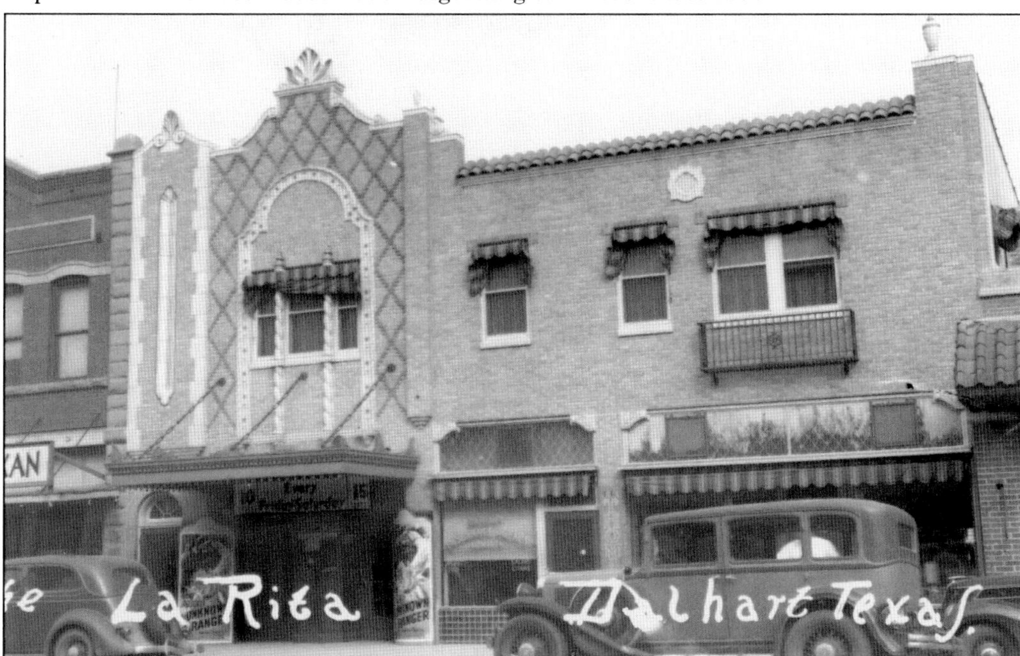

The La Rita Theatre opened in 1921. It was closed for many years and then reopened in the 1980s as a playhouse. Currently, the La Rita holds several performances each year including a melodrama during XIT Rodeo and Reunion weekend in August, a play in October, a play at Christmastime, and a dinner theater for Valentine's Day. The restoration of the building maintains its 1920s flavor.

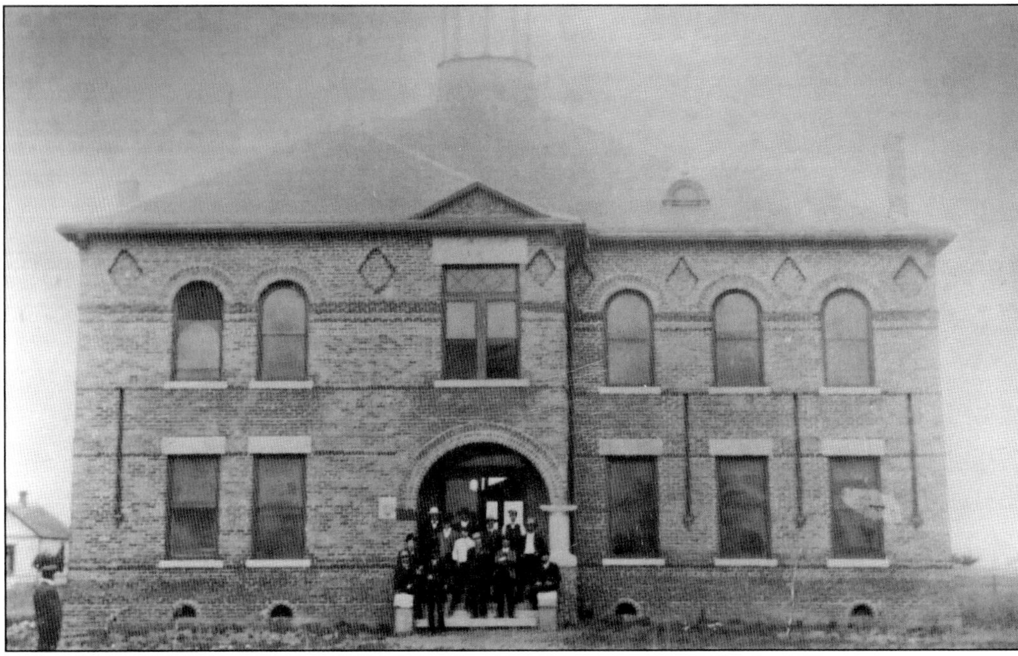

Texline, 38 miles northwest of Dalhart, was the county seat for Dallam County until 1901, when Dalhart assumed this role. As with many other Dalhart endeavors, the unique intersection of the Fort Worth and Denver City Railway and the Chicago and Rock Island Railway gave Dalhart an advantage over other Dallam and Hartley County communities. In 1901, the Dallam County Courthouse was built, but was only in use for a handful of years. It is pictured here in 1912.

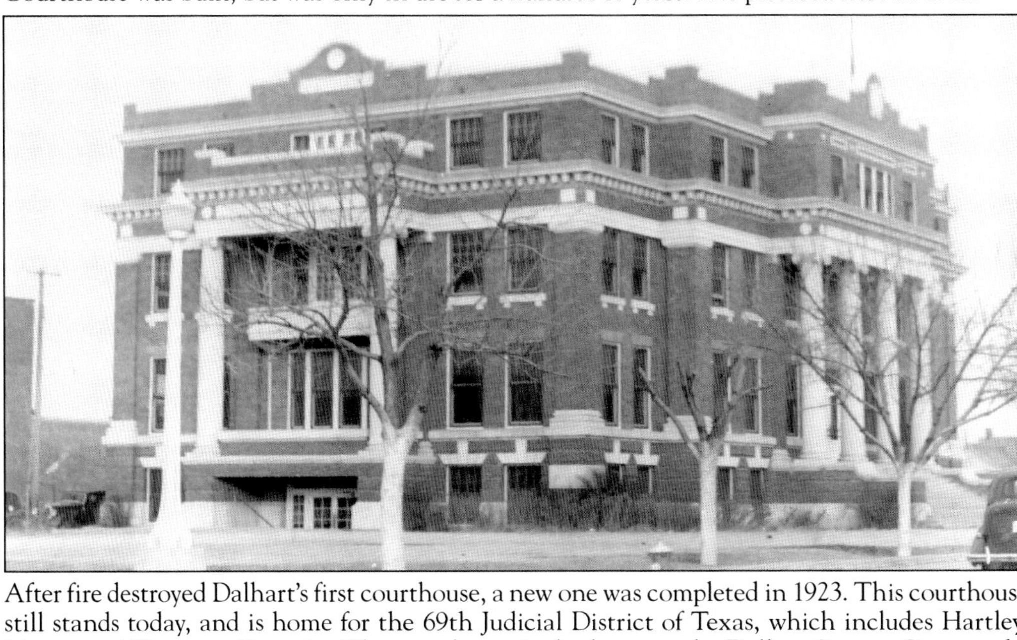

After fire destroyed Dalhart's first courthouse, a new one was completed in 1923. This courthouse still stands today, and is home for the 69th Judicial District of Texas, which includes Hartley, Moore, and Sherman Counties. The courthouse is also home to the Dallam County Court and a presiding county judge. Unlike the courthouses in several nearby communities, the Dallam County Courthouse building is quite large, and at one time included the Dallam County Jail. Today, both Dallam and Hartley Counties share a jail located across the street from the courthouse.

Grocers popped up all along Denrock Avenue beginning in 1901. The stores carried everything from fresh fruits and vegetables to non-perishables. T.L. Swearingen and Company was one of Dalhart's first grocers, along with Noble Brothers. Pictured here is wrapping paper from the T.L. Swearingen & Co. Fancy Groceries, which reads, "Hello, give me no. 6 and 350," likely the telephone numbers for the grocery.

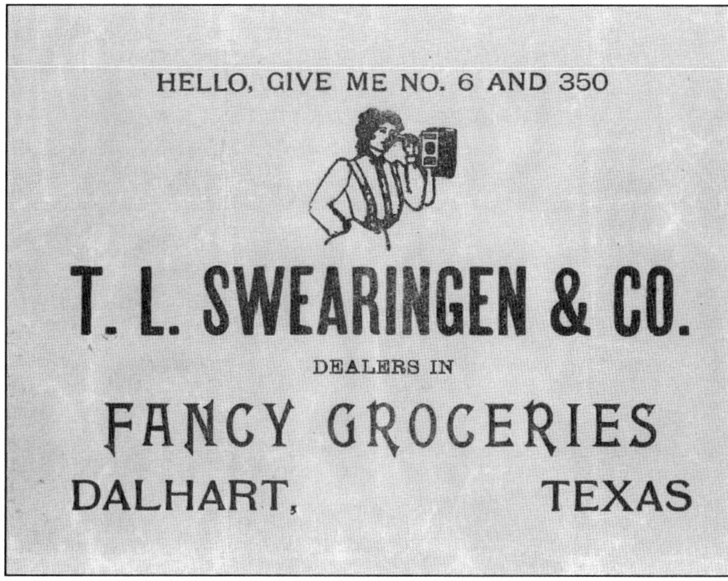

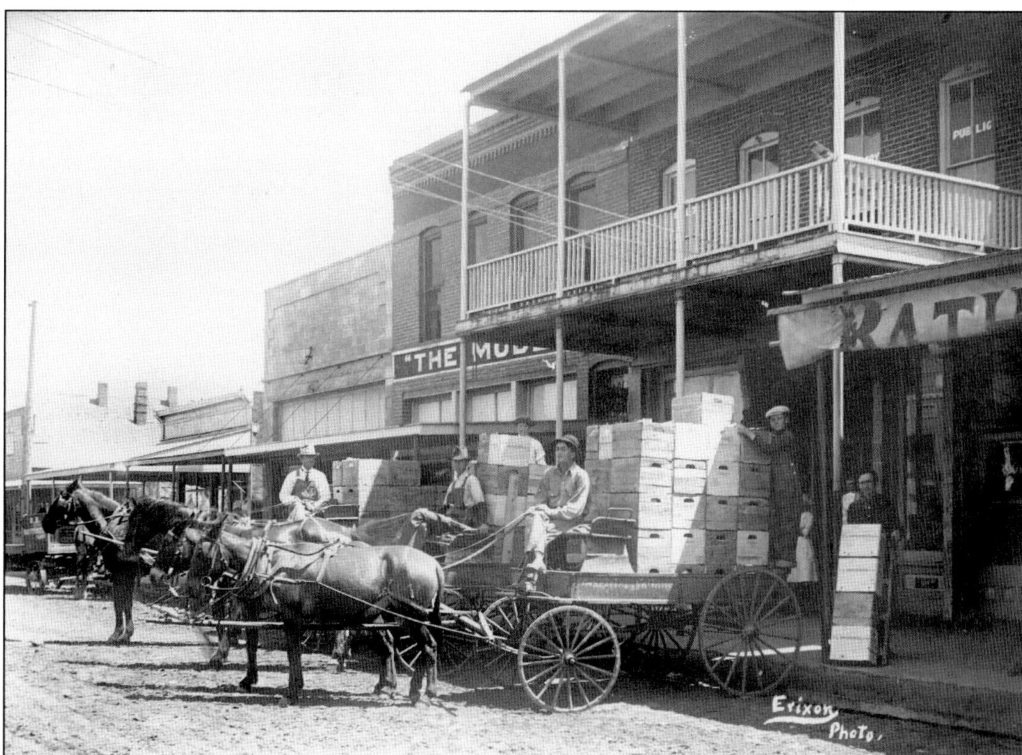

This photograph was taken outside of the Swearingen Grocery Store, showing buggies and supplies in 1905. The store was owned by T.L. Swearingen. Inside the grocery, Ada Mae and Eula Swearingen sat elevated in a cage, and buckets with transactions were hoisted up to them for handling and accounting. The store was operated in the same location for 50 years.

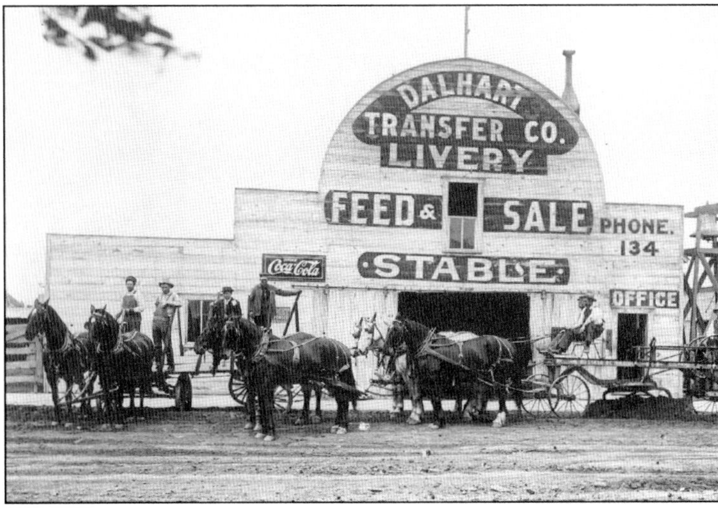

Pictured here is the Dalhart Transfer Company Livery in 1909. Note that Coca-Cola has an advertisement on the outside of the business, and the phone number is 134. Coca-Cola advertising is seen in many old photographs in Dalhart. The company later opened a distribution plant in Dalhart, now closed. (Courtesy of the XIT Museum and Henry and Dora Tandy.)

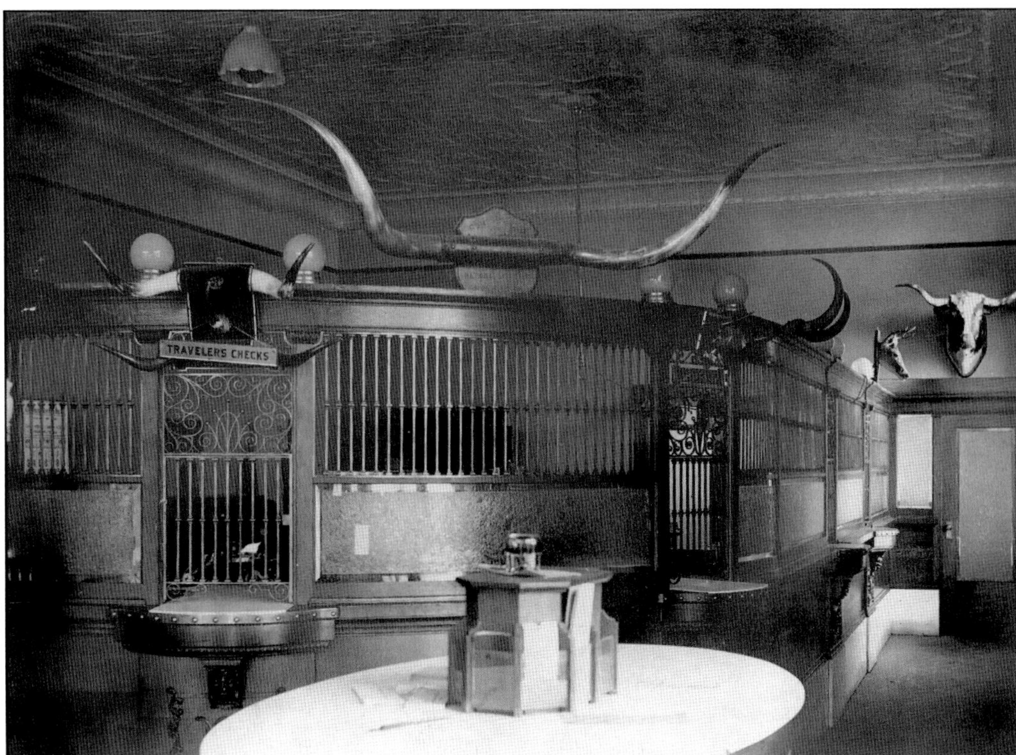

The interior of the Midway Bank and Trust, located at 202 Denrock Avenue, is shown here. In 1920, when this photograph was taken, the bank president was Charles C. Woods, W.E. Farwell was cashier, and R.U. Counts was secretary. One of Dalhart's most prominent early residents, Andy James, once held a principal interest in the bank. In 1919, after James's 17,000 head of cattle died in a great blizzard, he was broke and having a terrible time keeping the bank open, so Charles "Charlie" Woods bought out James's interest in the bank. (Courtesy of the XIT Museum and Bill and Mary Spencer.)

Seen here in 1920, the Edwards and Scott Motor Company was located on the same spot where Dalhart's first post office was originally built. Because of its location, the motor company is seen in many of the photographs of downtown Dalhart during the Dust Bowl years.

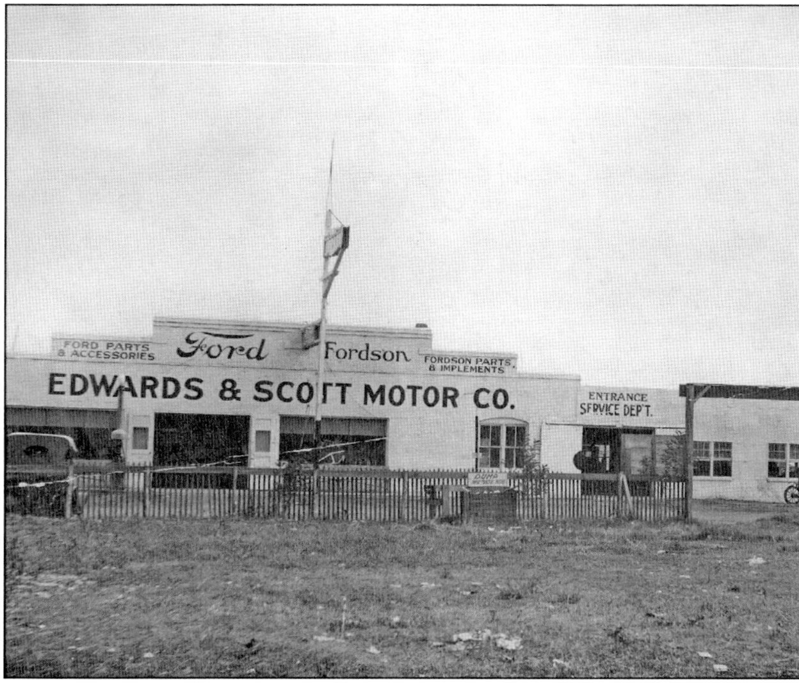

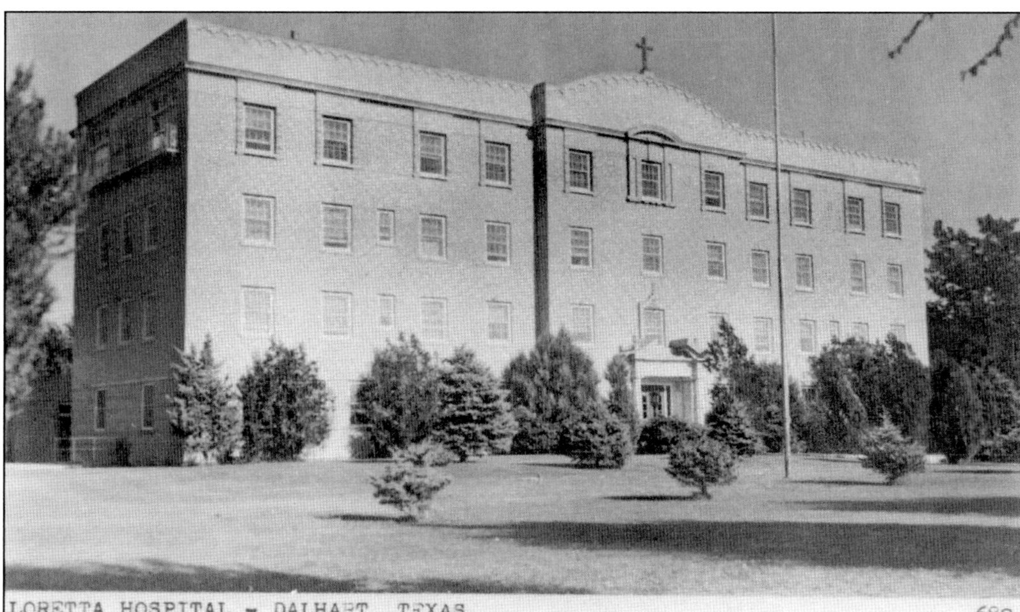

The Loretta Hospital was built in 1929, largely replacing the Trans-Canadian Sanitarium run by Dr. G.W. Dawson. The Loretta Hospital remained until Coon Memorial Hospital was built in the 1950s with funds from the Coon Memorial Trust.

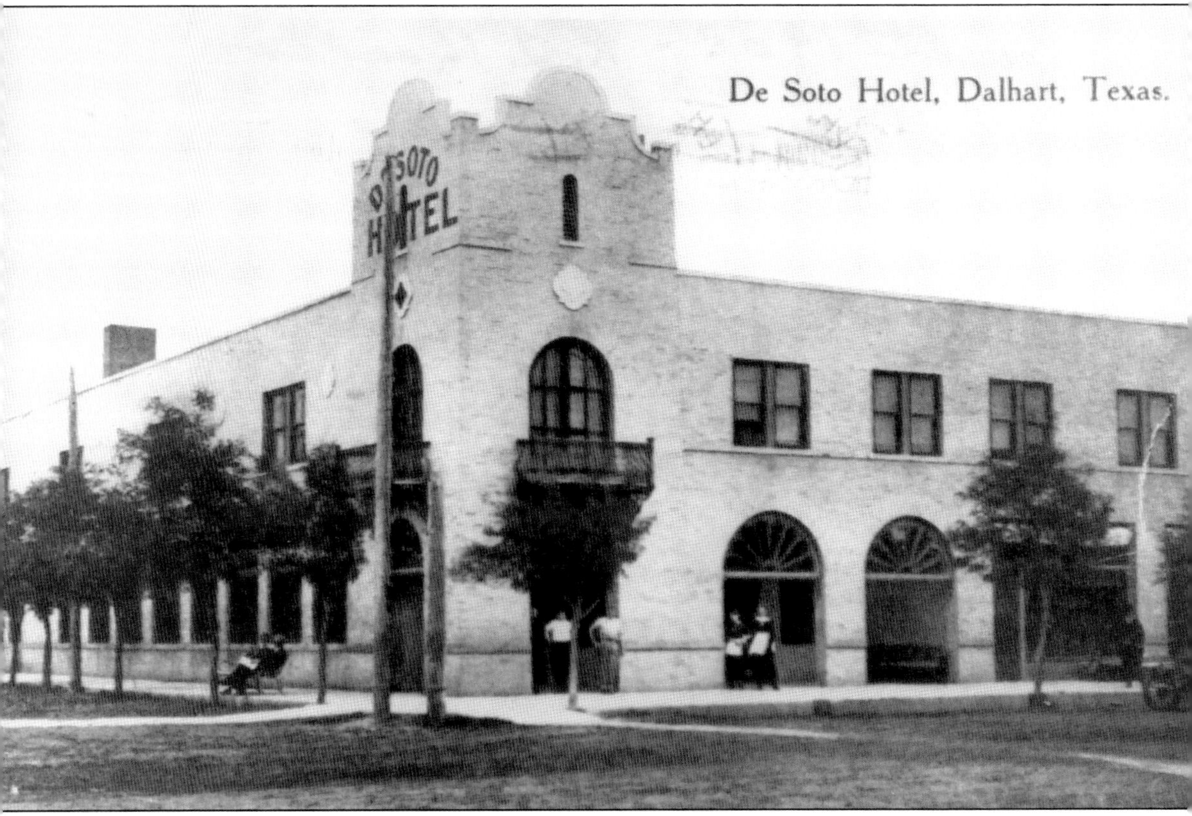

The yellow-brick DeSoto Hotel built between 1908 and 1910 became an iconic spot. Its owner, C.R. Woods, became known for his benevolence in helping out down-on-their-luck families. Woods was determined to build the finest hotel in Texas, including the finest accommodations, food, and service. Every room in the hotel had a bathroom with hot and cold running water and a toilet. Rooms also had telephones. A manned horse-drawn hack met every train to pick up passengers headed for the brick palace, and a bellhop was on call to meet the needs of patrons. Woods named his hotel after the Spanish explorer credited with discovering the Mississippi River, Hernando De Soto.

Five

The Dirty Dust Bowl to the Booming 1950s

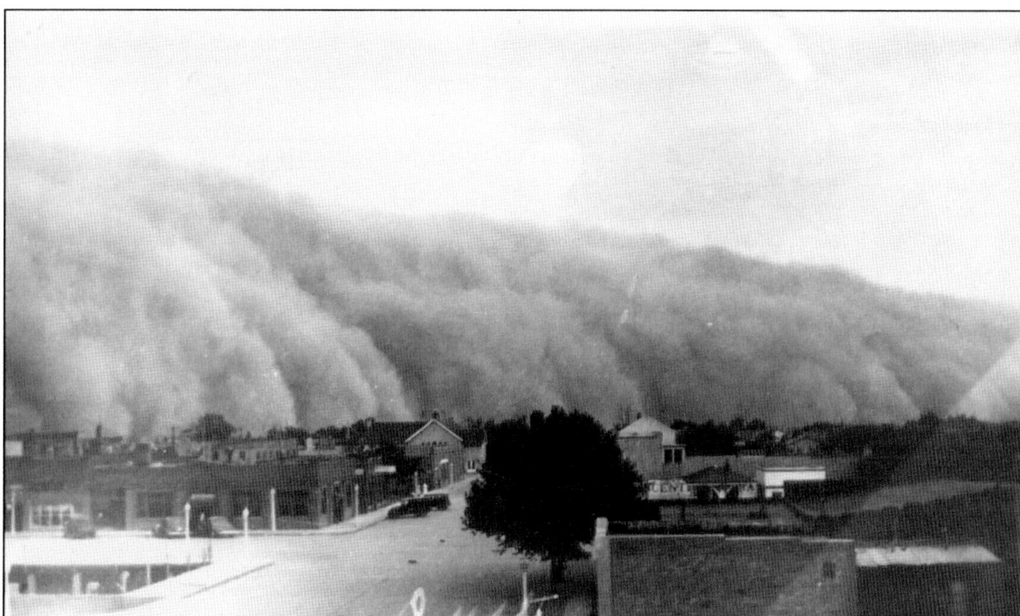

The city of Dalhart was centrally located in the area known as the Dust Bowl. Although the Dust Bowl years are a well-known part of American history, Dalhartans rarely speak of them unless a traveler asks. In Dalhart, the Dust Bowl era is referred to as "The Dirty Years." When the massive dust storms entered the area, visibility dropped to zero, and people were forced to wait out the storm, unable to move even a few feet. Reports of being unable to see one's own hand or of sitting in a convertible and not being able to see the person riding in the passenger seat are numerous. (Courtesy of the XIT Museum and the Clapp family estate.)

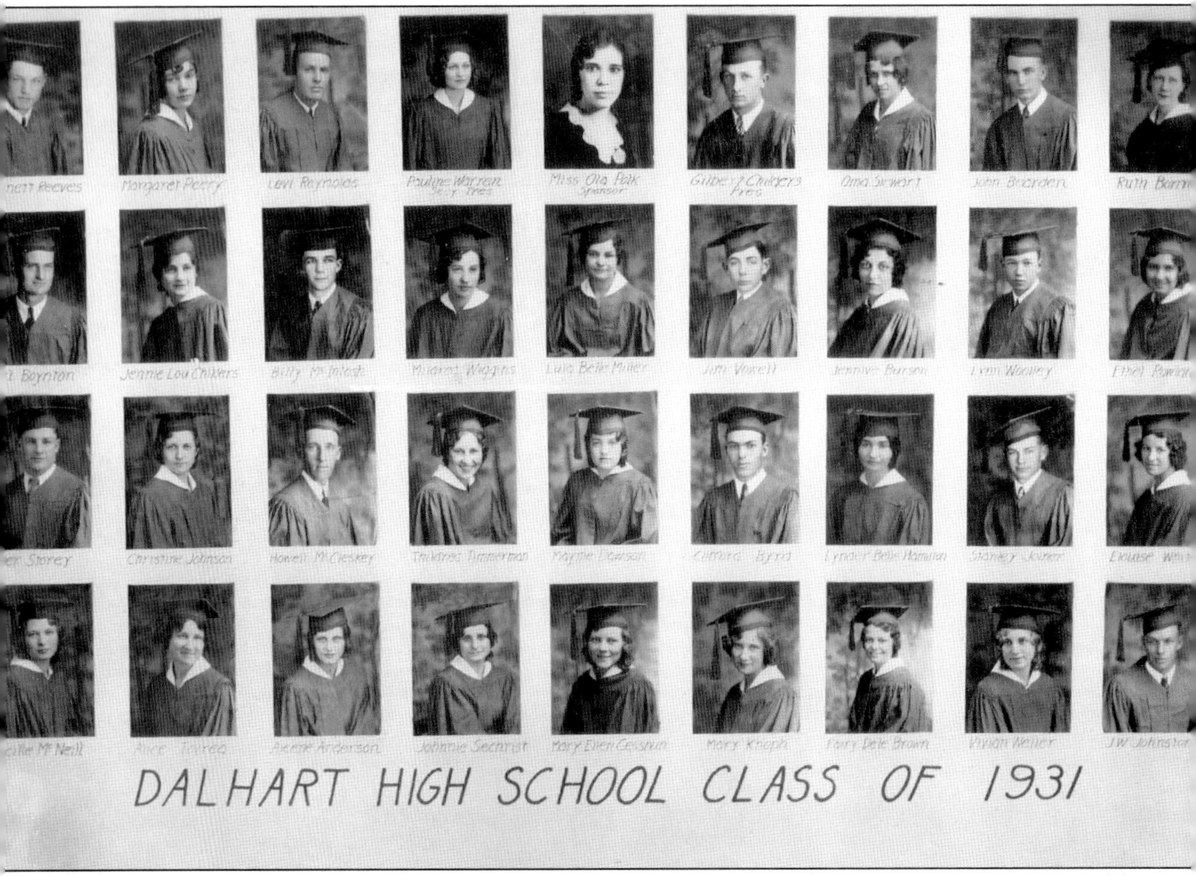

At the onset of the Dust Bowl, students in Dalhart had no idea what the next several years would bring. The graduating class of 1931 held high hopes for their lives. For those who remained in Dalhart, however, the years between graduation and 1937 were unimaginably difficult. Lives were turned upside down and even lost as the dust kept tearing its way through the area. (Courtesy of the XIT Museum and Novelyn Richards.)

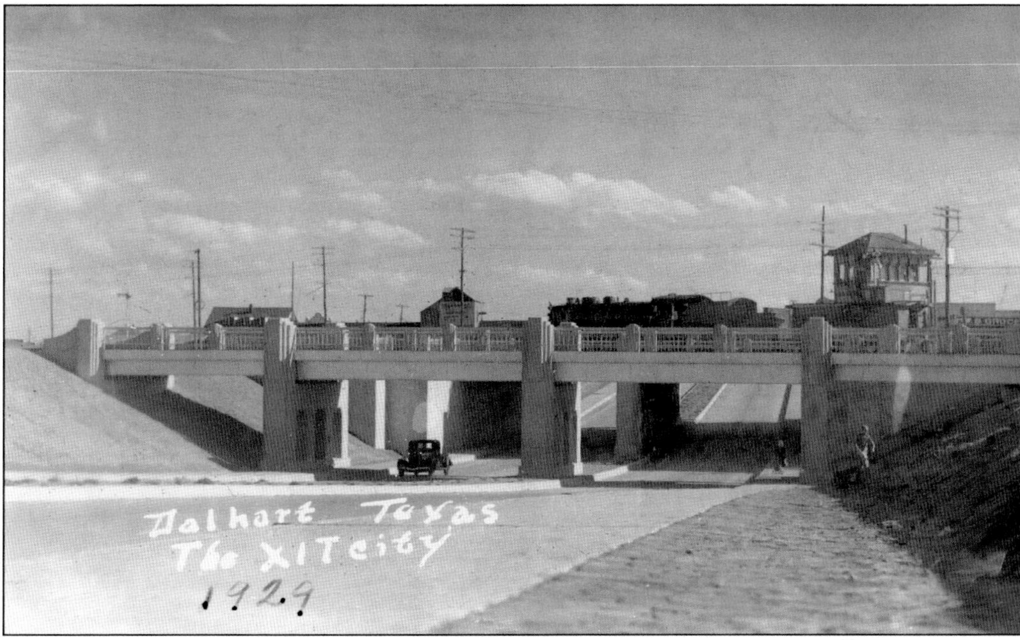

Just before the Dust Bowl began to blow its way through Dalhart, city streets were clean and free from dirt and debris. The underpass on Highway 87, shown in 1929, reveals life before the destructive storms began. In the background on the right is the depot, a two-story structure. The underpass looks much the same today, but it has been slated for renovations: the big-rig semi trucks that were nonexistent in the 1920s and 1930s now frequently get stuck underneath the bridge, and during inclement weather, vehicles cannot make it up the steep slope.

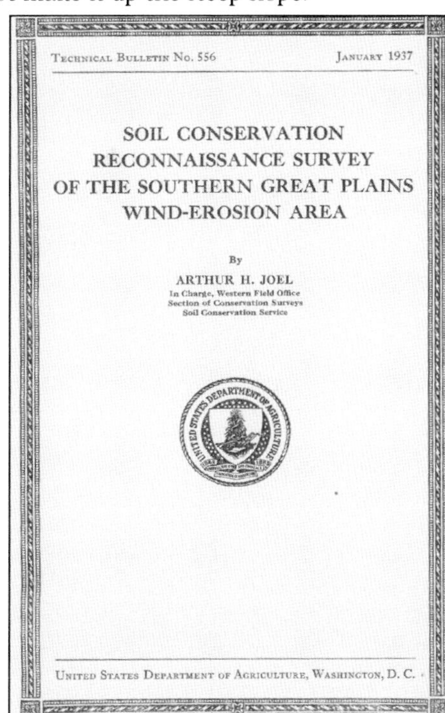
Technical Bulletin No. 556 — January 1937

SOIL CONSERVATION
RECONNAISSANCE SURVEY
OF THE SOUTHERN GREAT PLAINS
WIND-EROSION AREA

By

ARTHUR H. JOEL
In Charge, Western Field Office
Section of Conservation Surveys
Soil Conservation Service

United States Department of Agriculture, Washington, D. C.

For sale by the Superintendent of Documents, Washington, D. C. - - - - - - Price 25 cents

The Dust Bowl was largely created by farmers overworking land, which caused soil erosion. The devastation caused during the Dust Bowl led to many improvements aimed at soil conservation, including better farming techniques and irrigation. Even with the marked improvement in the factors that led to the Dust Bowl, however, the city of Dalhart and surrounding areas still carry visible signs that the Dust Bowl was once alive and lingering behind every weather front. (Courtesy of the XIT Museum and Gary Nall.)

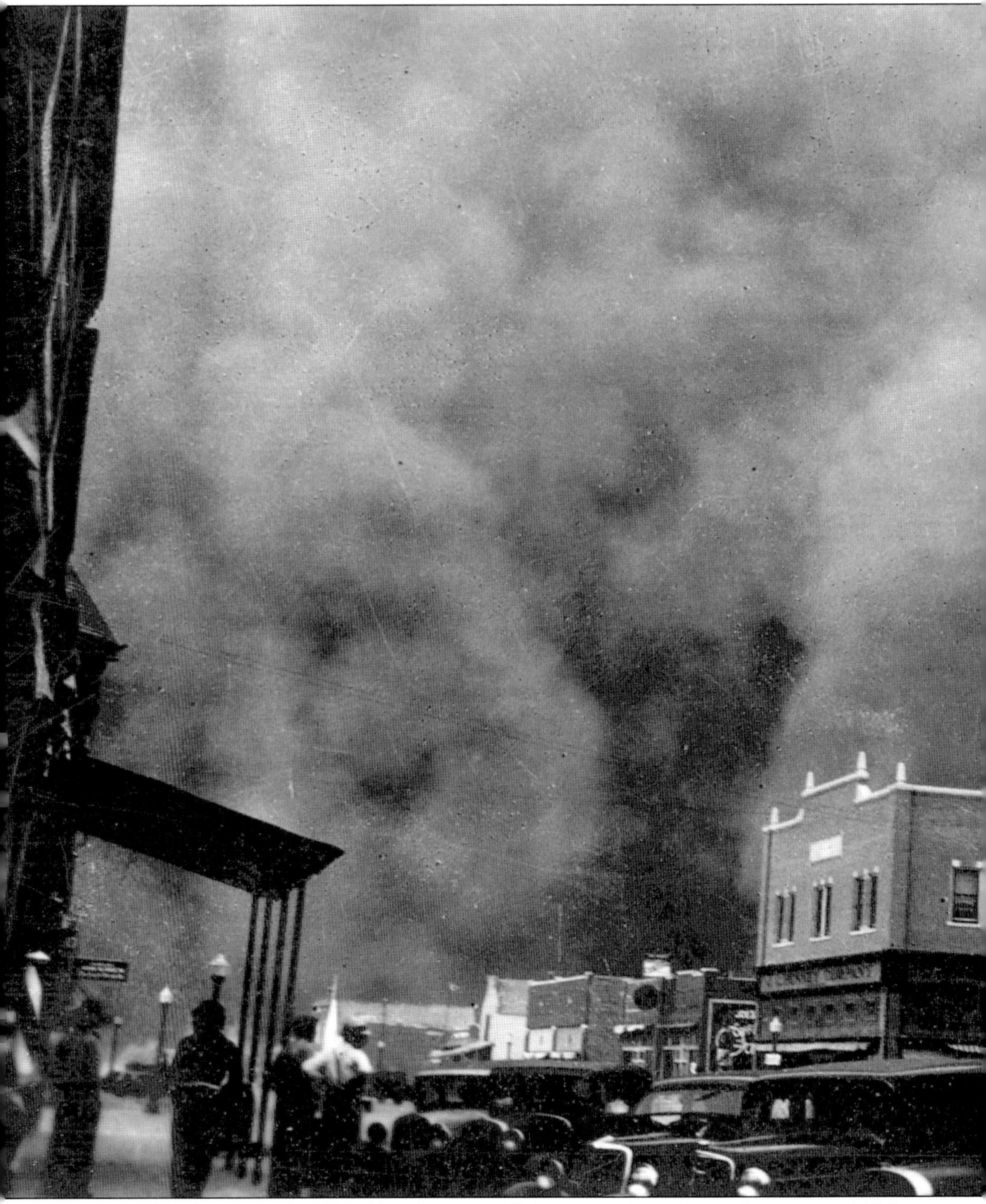

Storms like this, seen nearly engulfing downtown Dalhart near Scott Motor Company and Midway Bank and Trust, were a common sight in the 1930s. Here, people stand outside watching what would become a regular event for nearly a decade. People quickly adopted techniques to help them

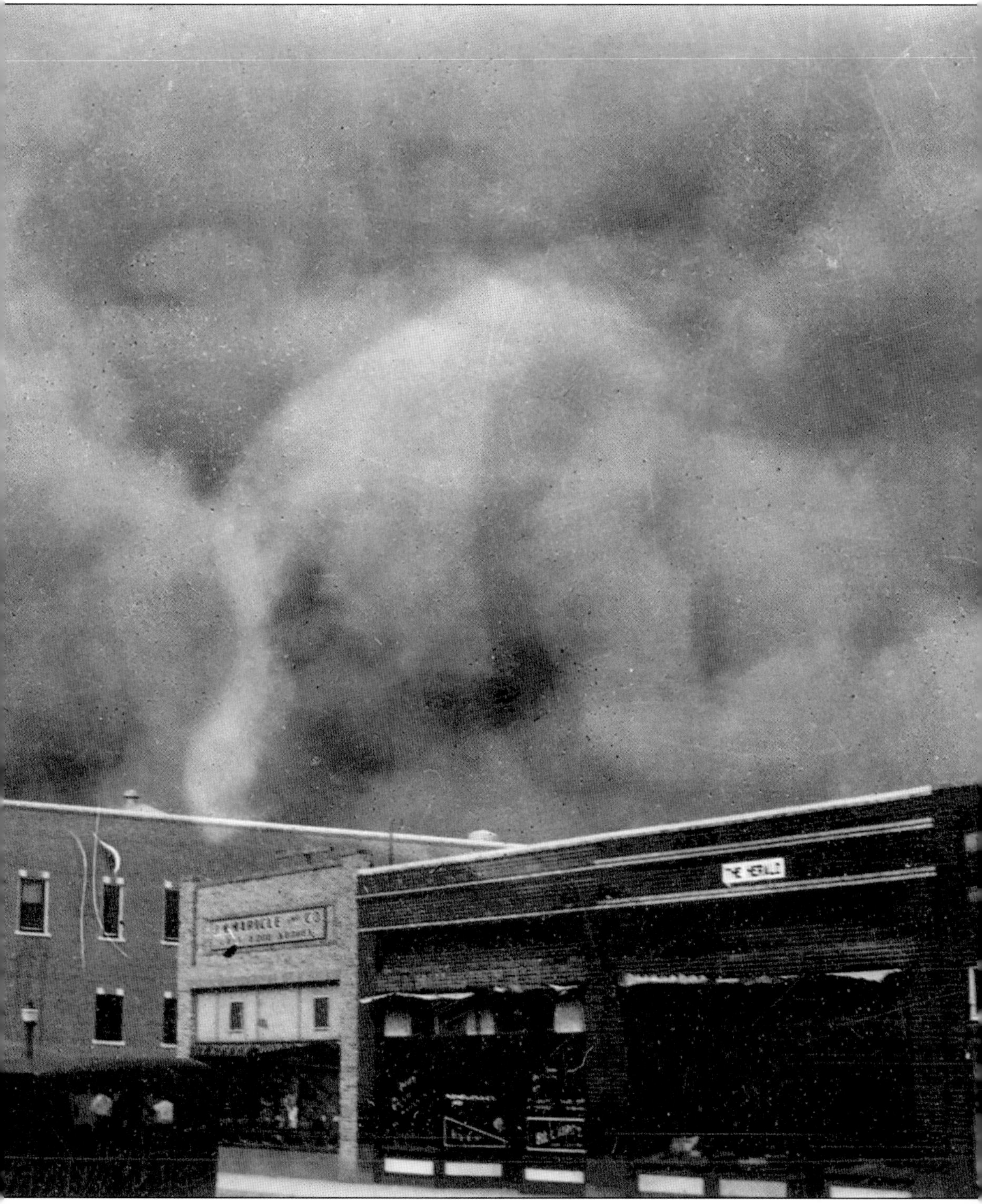

endure the dust storms; survivors from those years state that they would put wet sheets over the dinner table to keep the sand from covering food, but that everything was still gritty. (Courtesy of the XIT Museum and Bill and Mary Spencer.)

Stop Wind Erosion On Cropland

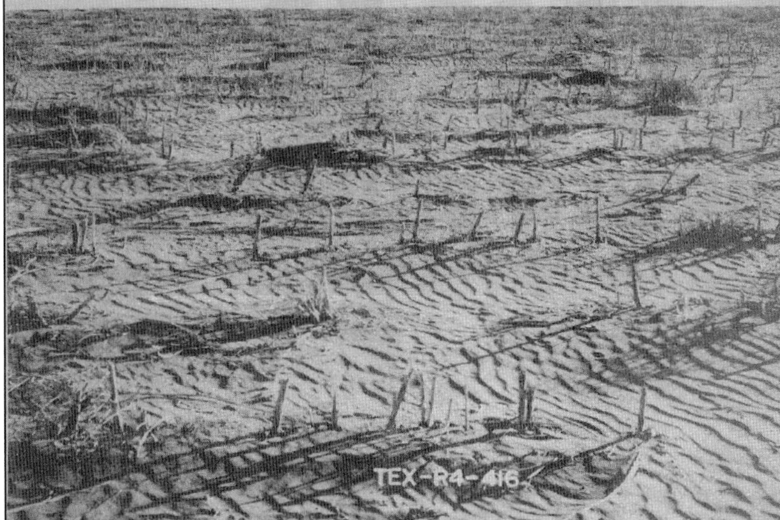

TYPICAL RESULT OF WIND EROSION if cropland is not protected by a dense cover of stubble. This picture was taken in Dallam County in April of 1939 by the Dalhart SCS Research Station, of sorghum stubble planted in 36-inch rows, as a study of soil movement.

Cropland is best protected from wind erosion by keeping a good, dense cover of a growing crop, or crop residue on the surface of the soil at all times, says Cecil Seitz, range conservationist for the Dallam County Soil Conservation Service. The way farmers handle the residue from grain sorghum and corn after harvest this fall can determine if that land will have a wind erosion hazard on it next spring and during the windy erosion, he pointed out.

Some things that can be done to help keep cropland covered and give protection against wind erosion, include planting small grain early, so a good ground cover can be made before it gets too cold for these crops to make growth; do not graze cropland to the point of creating a wind-erosion hazard; leave grain sorghum and corn stalks standing undisturbed in the field as long as possible before commencing seedbed preparation for the next crop.

Do not burn crop residues; eliminate as many tillage operations as possible, as each tillage operation reduces the amount of residue left; perform tillage operations with implements that are adapted to leaving residue on the top of the soil. Planting no-til in undisturbed crop residue; narrowing the row spacing down on corn and grain sorghum, with 20 or 30 inch spacing giving better protection than the 40-inch rows, Seitz pointed out. Also manure applied to small areas that have started to blow, will keep them from spreading. Anything that can be done to help control erosion is important and in the absence of a good cover, emergency tillage can be used to help control wind erosion, he said.

Don't be afraid of your shadow — it's only one of the cloak-and-giggle boys practicing.

One day after the worst dust storm to occur during the Dust Bowl years, the *Dalhart Texan* ran an article titled "Black Gale Sweeps Panhandle Territory Sunday Night." This storm began on Sunday, April 14, 1935, at approximately 6:30 p.m. The article stated that dust-laden winds turned the day into a nightmare. Later, the newspaper reported on methods of stopping wind erosion. (Courtesy of the XIT Museum and Lillian Maynard Maples.)

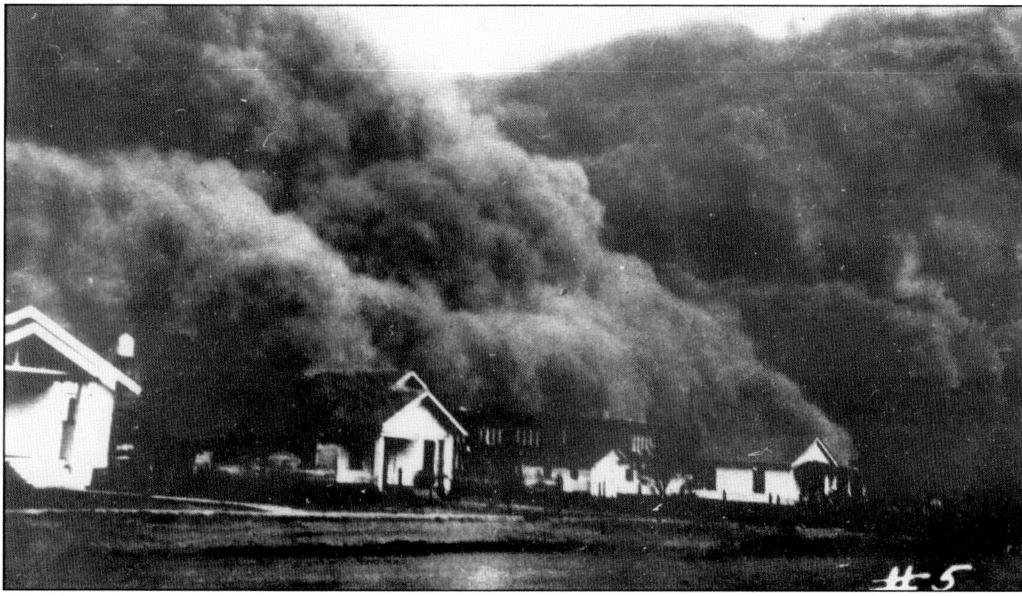

The storm in Dalhart that fateful night engulfed the area at 6:20 p.m. Traffic was paralyzed, and the darkness was like midnight though there had been brilliant sun a moment before. Former storms had rolled up slowly, but the storm on what became known as "Black Sunday" moved with awe-inspiring speed. On April 16, 1935, H.T. Collman, meteorologist for the US Weather Bureau, predicted "A southwest duster today" after noting a low-pressure area to the northeast. March had 20 dust storms; the first 15 days of April had 10.

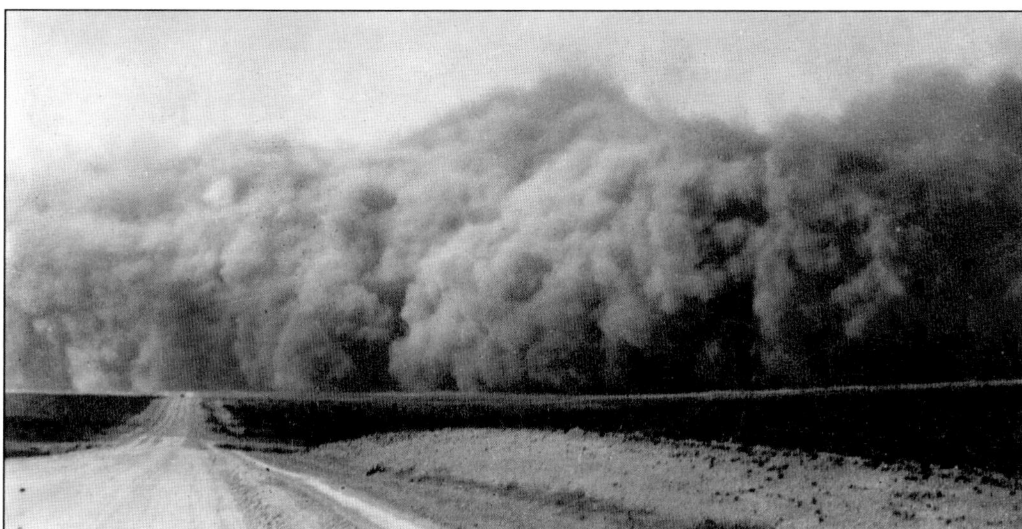

On Black Sunday, the weather was reported in the *Dalhart Texan* as a beautiful, warm, balmy spring day, and remained so until the storm struck with sudden fury. Not only were cars unable to move in the storm, but all train traffic was halted as well. The passengers due in Dalhart at 7:30 p.m. Sunday on the southbound from Denver did not arrive until after midnight. Cars and trucks were parked all over the streets and roads. In this photograph, in the distance, a car tries to stay ahead of the 70-mile-per-hour storm. (Courtesy of the XIT Museum and Sue Nelson.)

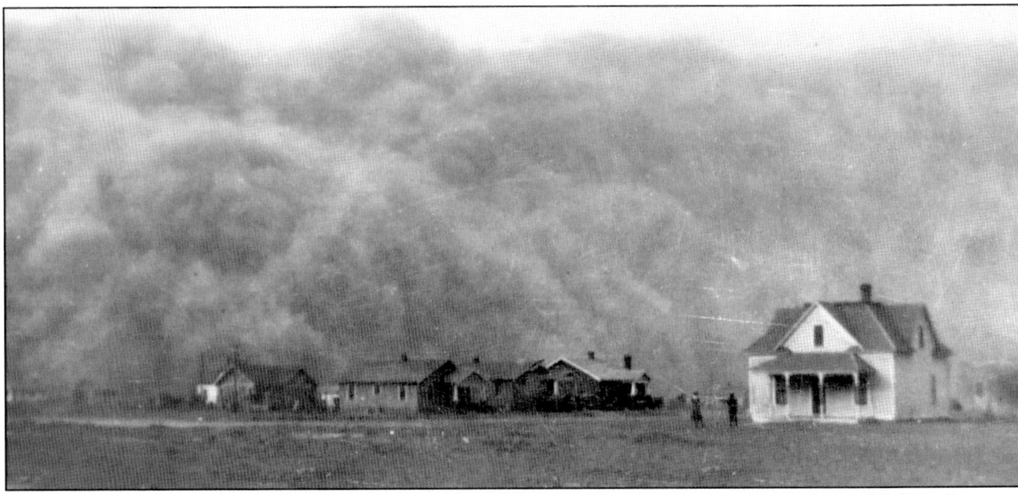

W.T. Farr, who lived about seven miles southwest of Dalhart, stated, "I was about 75 feet from my barn. I was more than an hour finding it. I tried to keep close to my saddle horse, but the horse was so charged with static electricity that I was nearly knocked down every time I touched the animal." (Courtesy of the XIT Museum and the Clapp family estate.)

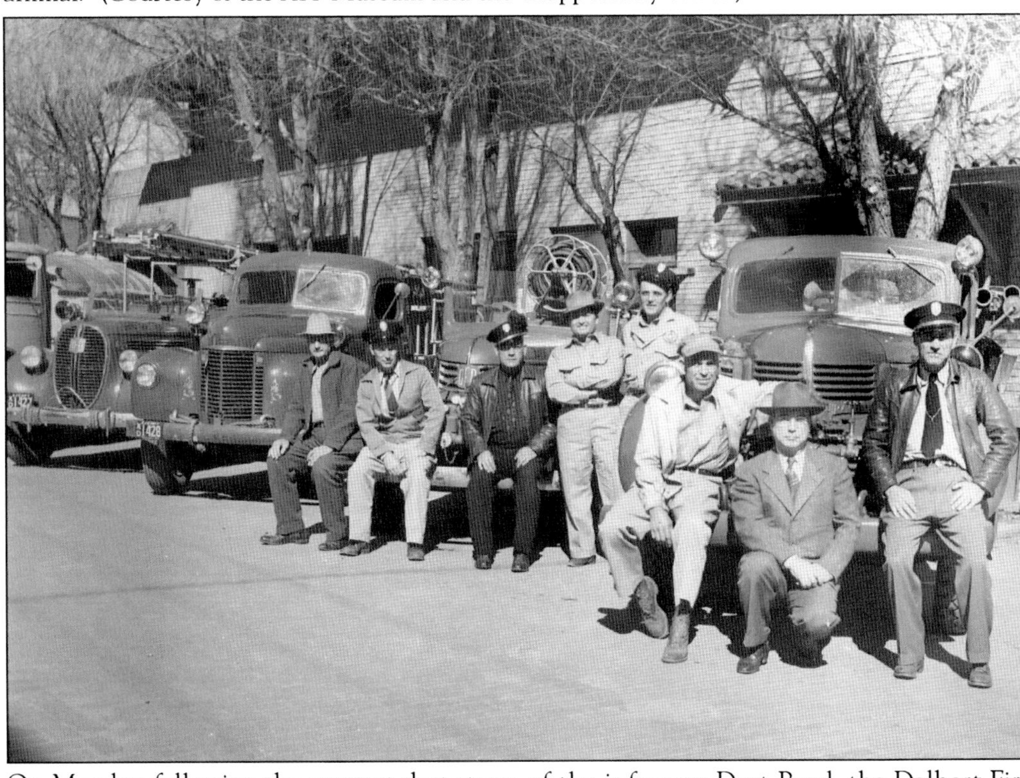

On Monday, following the greatest dust storm of the infamous Dust Bowl, the Dalhart Fire Department and the West Texas Utilities Company began clearing the streets of the sand and dirt left behind. The *Dalhart Texan* reported a "fine bath in the streets of the downtown section this morning. The fire boys donated their services and the West Texas Utilities donated the water. A noticeable improvement in the atmosphere was evident after the streets and sidewalks were washed."

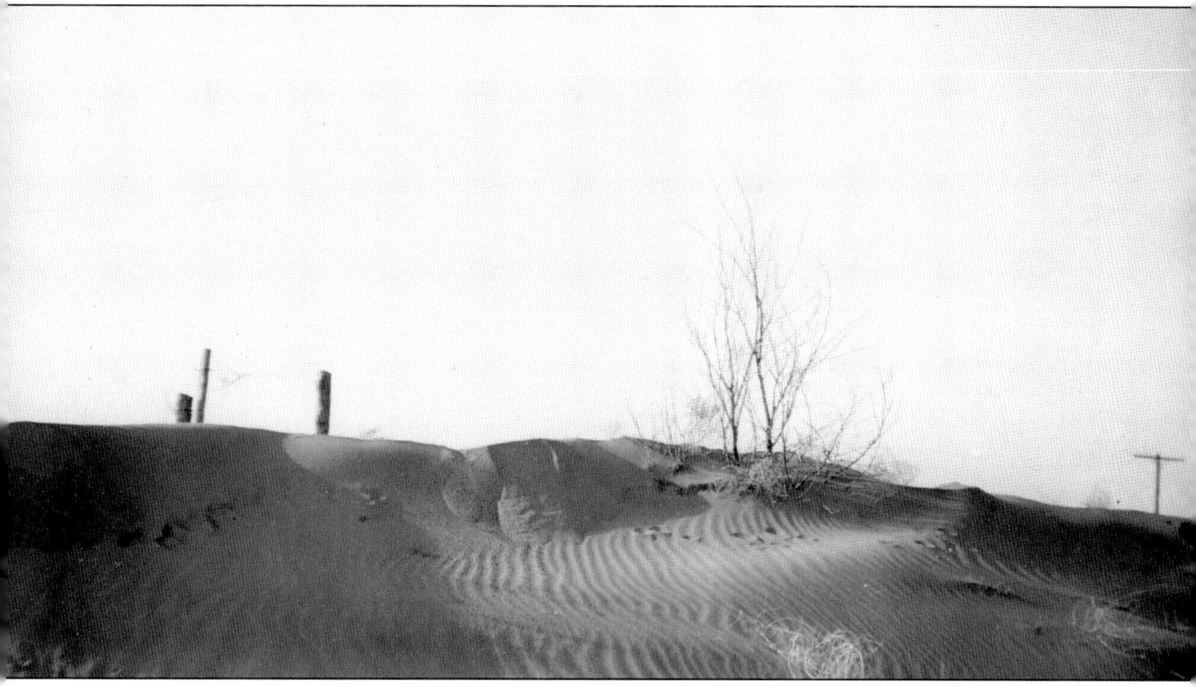

During the week after the storm, the headlines in the *Dalhart Texan* included: "Dalhart has since its inception been the headquarters for the US Soil Erosion Service in this section," "Approved Wind Erosion Work on 200,000 acres in County," "Moisture statistics no cause for wild alarm," "Trace of rain here clears atmosphere," and "Agriculture Assistant In Inspection of Drought Area." The only photograph that appeared of the Dust Bowl in the *Dalhart Texan* was followed by one phrase: "Black Plague." (Courtesy of the XIT Museum and Sue Nelson.)

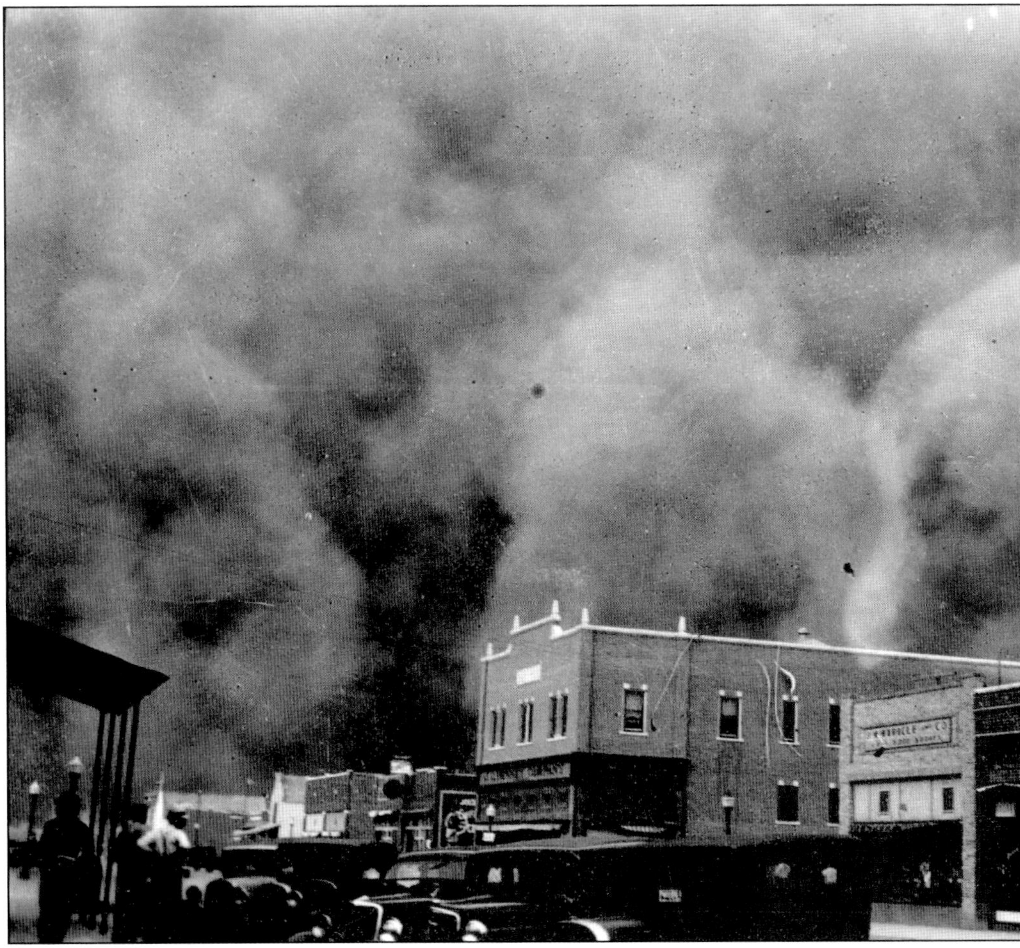

Harry H. Lawrence, a columnist for the *Dalhart Texan*, noted, "The black dust storm which swept out of the north Sunday night and buried the Panhandle under a choking pall has been adequately described as far as words can tell of its immensity and terrifying aspect. Such a storm is impossible to describe, and it is equally impossible to convey to people who have not seen one, its scope and power; they cannot believe it, and it defies credulity." The Dust Bowl is synonymous with the Great Depression, and Dalhart was not immune from the fury of both. Many area residents fled to California, and some reports show that the population dipped to 500. (Courtesy of the XIT Museum and the Clapp family estate.)

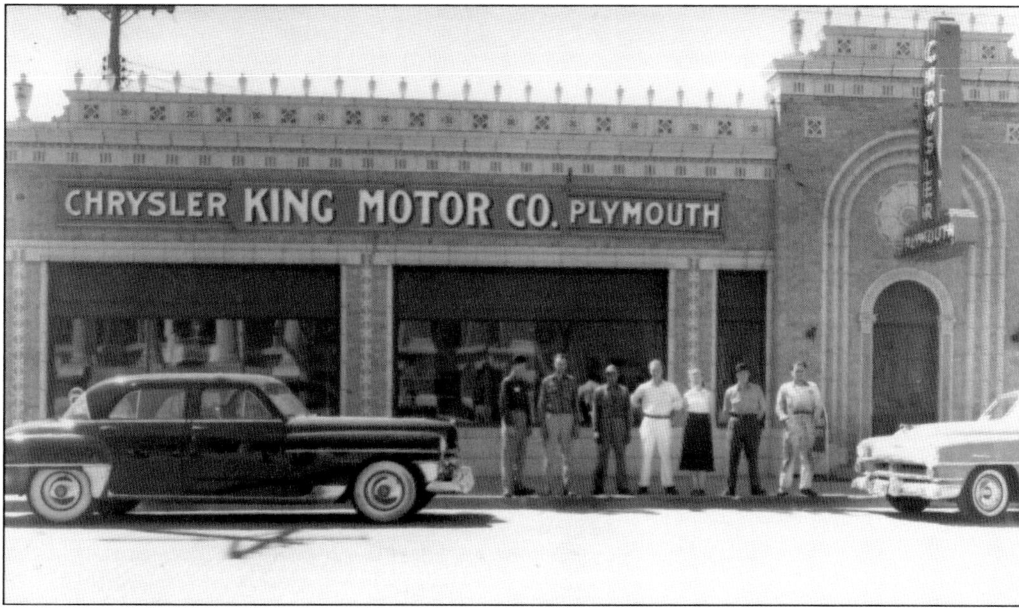

The World War II years saw some regrowth in Dalhart. Land was cheap, and the economy was rebounding. By the end of the war, growth had become nearly exponential, and people resettled into the once barren and sand-filled landscape. By the 1950s, the population of Dalhart flourished and steadily increased. Pictured is the King Motor Company, located in the same building where the XIT Museum sits today.

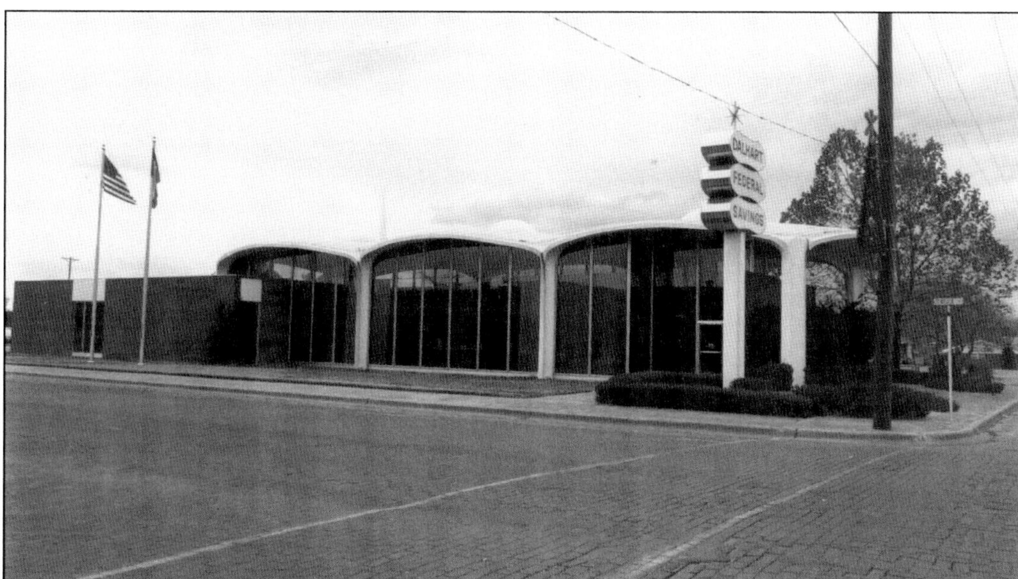

Dalhart Federal Savings and Loan had the nerve to open its doors in 1934 as the Dust Bowl was gaining steam, and the business has steadily grown. Located at the corner of Denrock Avenue and Fifth Street, the bank provides service to customers all over the Dallam and Hartley County area, as well as from the Tri-State area. The bank moved to its current location in 1965 and renovated in 1994, and again in 2010. Several employees in 2010 had been with the business for nearly 30 years.

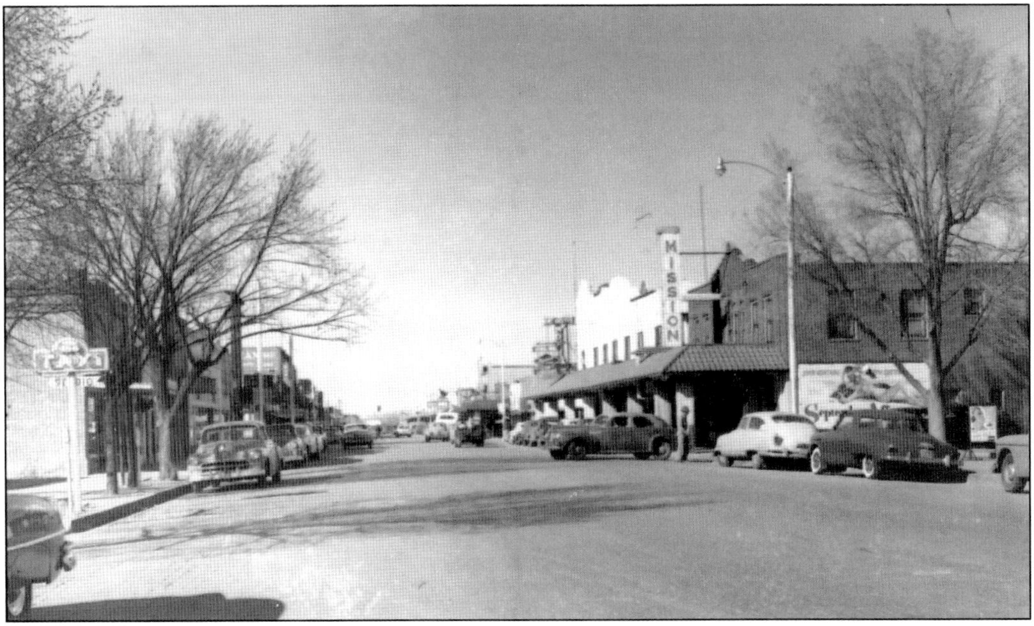

The Mission Theatre stands on the right of this image. Note the sign that reads "Taxi" on the left. Taxis haven't been seen in Dalhart for many years, but after World War II, not everyone had a car. The Mission Theatre is called the Mission Twins today, and when both projectors are working, area residents have their choice of movies. The theater is located across the street from the *Dalhart Texan* office.

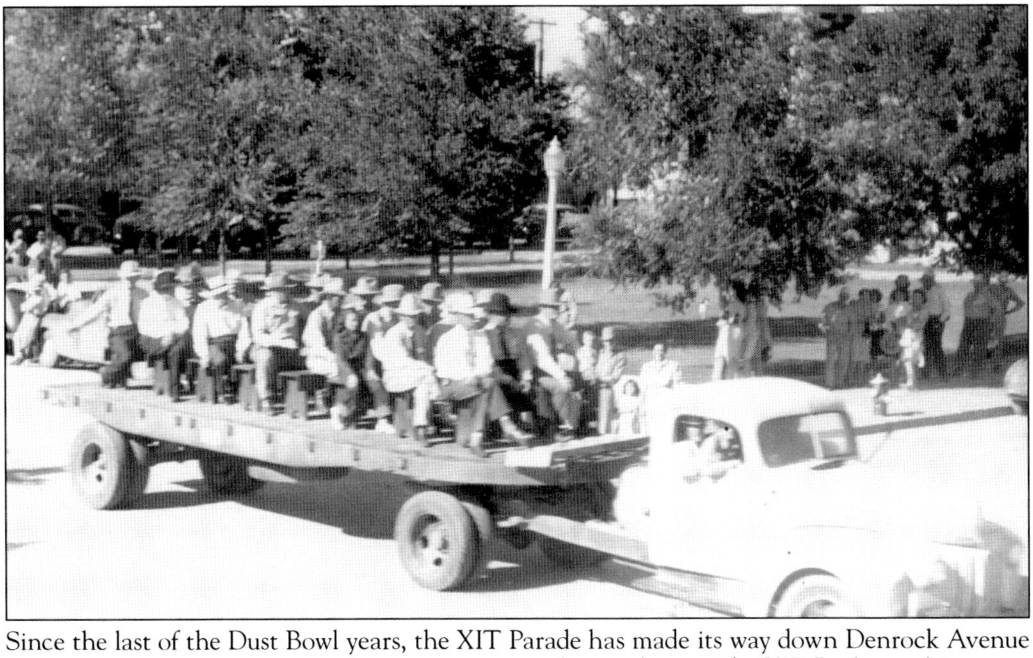

Since the last of the Dust Bowl years, the XIT Parade has made its way down Denrock Avenue in Dalhart, almost as if to say, "You can't keep a good town down." The XIT Rodeo and Reunion was founded in 1936 and celebrated its 75th Anniversary in 2011. The parade takes place each year during the weeklong event, with area businesses, clubs, and organizations getting in on the fun by riding on cars, tractors, motorcycles, or bicycles, or simply walking.

One of Dalhart's leading industries is agriculture, and not just cattle. Growing grains to use as feed was well established by 1950 and continues today. Gooch's Best Feeds was located next to the railroad on Highway 87. All of the buildings remain today; however, the small single-room building on top of the grain elevators is quite run down. (Courtesy of the XIT Museum and Don and Lynn Gilbert.)

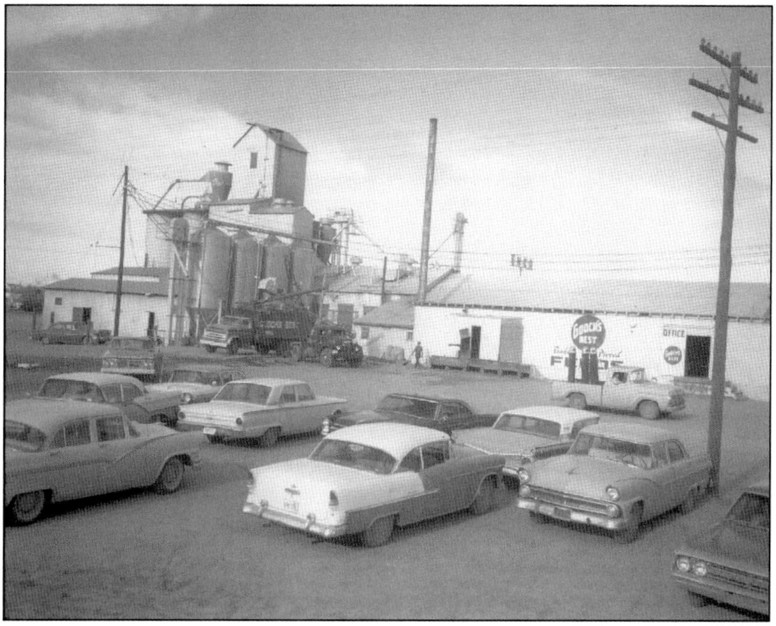

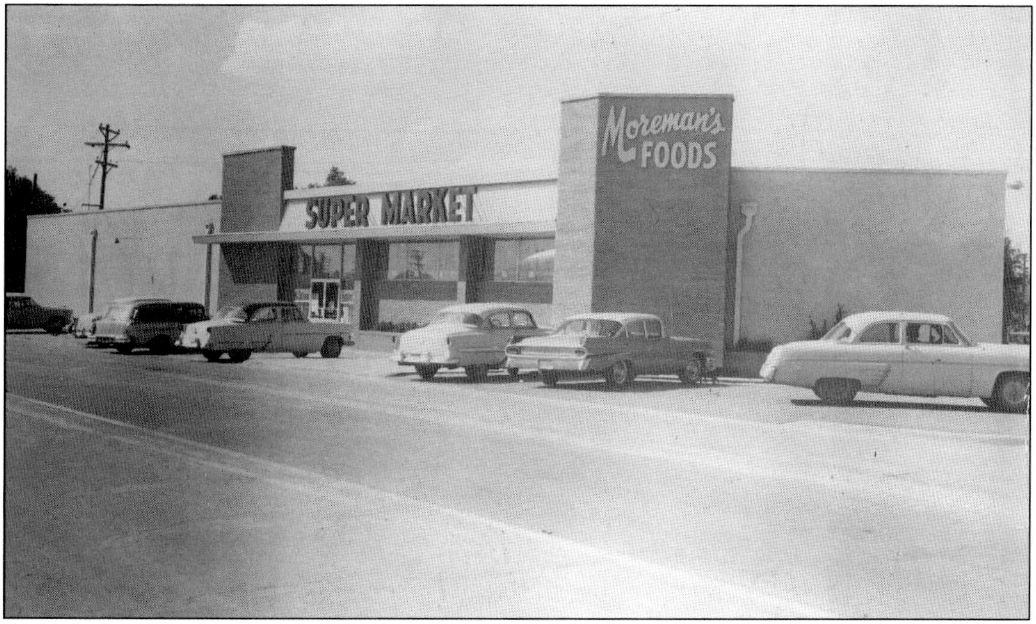

One of Dalhart's supermarkets, Moreman's Foods, was located on Highway 87 next door to where McDonald's is today. The building has been the home of many different businesses, including a sporting goods store and a barbershop, but stands empty today. One reason that businesses may have had a difficult time staying open at this location was the lack of available parking. (Courtesy of the XIT Museum and Don and Lynn Gilbert.)

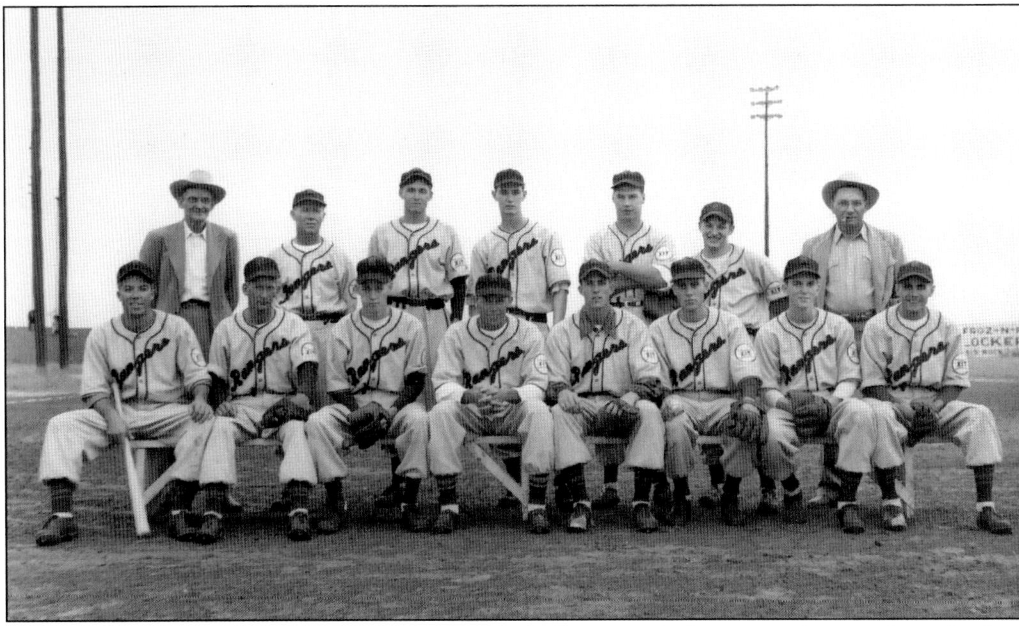

Seen here in August 1950, the XIT Rangers, who are regularly seen riding on horseback in Dalhart parades, had a bit of fun playing baseball in the 1950s. The XIT Rangers coordinate a parade during the XIT Rodeo and Reunion each year as well as the Veterans Day Parade held on November 11 each year. The XIT Rangers have "play days" for area residents, with a focus on children. They maintain a headquarters and horse stalls and rodeo arena off of Highway 281 near the Rita Blanca Coliseum.

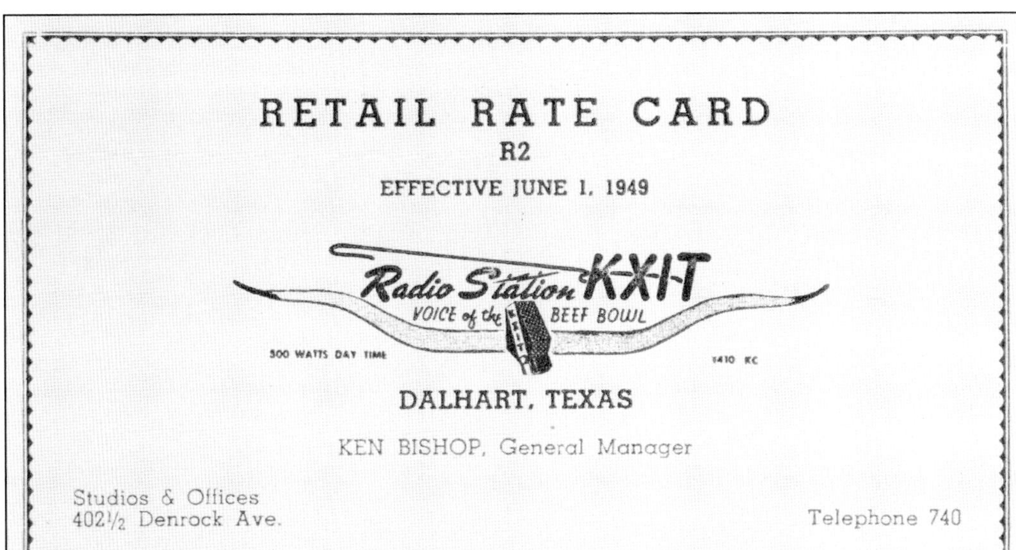

RETAIL RATE CARD

R2

EFFECTIVE JUNE 1, 1949

Radio Station KXIT

VOICE of the BEEF BOWL

500 WATTS DAY TIME

1410 KC

DALHART, TEXAS

KEN BISHOP, General Manager

Studios & Offices
402½ Denrock Ave.

Telephone 740

KXIT Radio has been in Dalhart for many years and is still on the airwaves today. The rate for advertising in June 1949 was $2.40 for an announcement of up to 100 words, but if the same announcement was broadcast 1,095 times or more, the rate dropped to $1.25.

Six

DALHART SCHOOLS

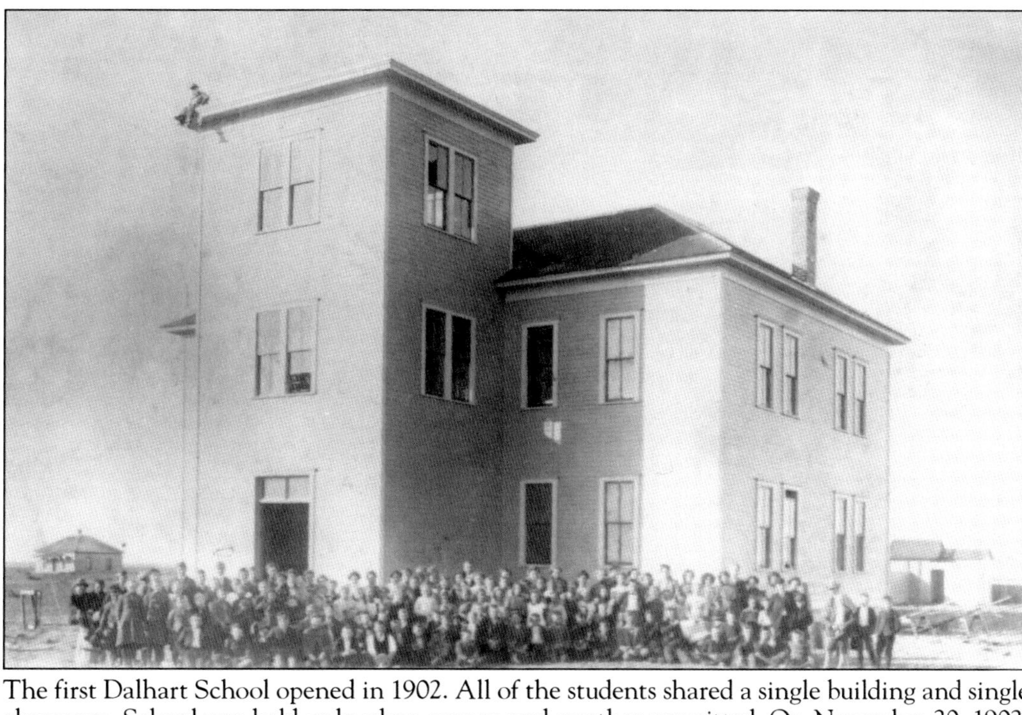

The first Dalhart School opened in 1902. All of the students shared a single building and single classroom. School was held only when money and weather permitted. On November 20, 1902, the *Dalhart Texan* reported on students who made the Honor Roll, "It requires perfect lessons, good behaviors, and excellent deportment each week to entitle pupils to have names entered on the Honor Roll. The teachers' great object in view is the success of the first public free school in Dalhart. Parents should see that the children study on lessons each night and encourage the child to prepare as many of their daily lessons at home each night, by doing so you will greatly relieve the teachers of extra work by detaining pupils for poor lessons and requiring them to bring up the work before leaving school."

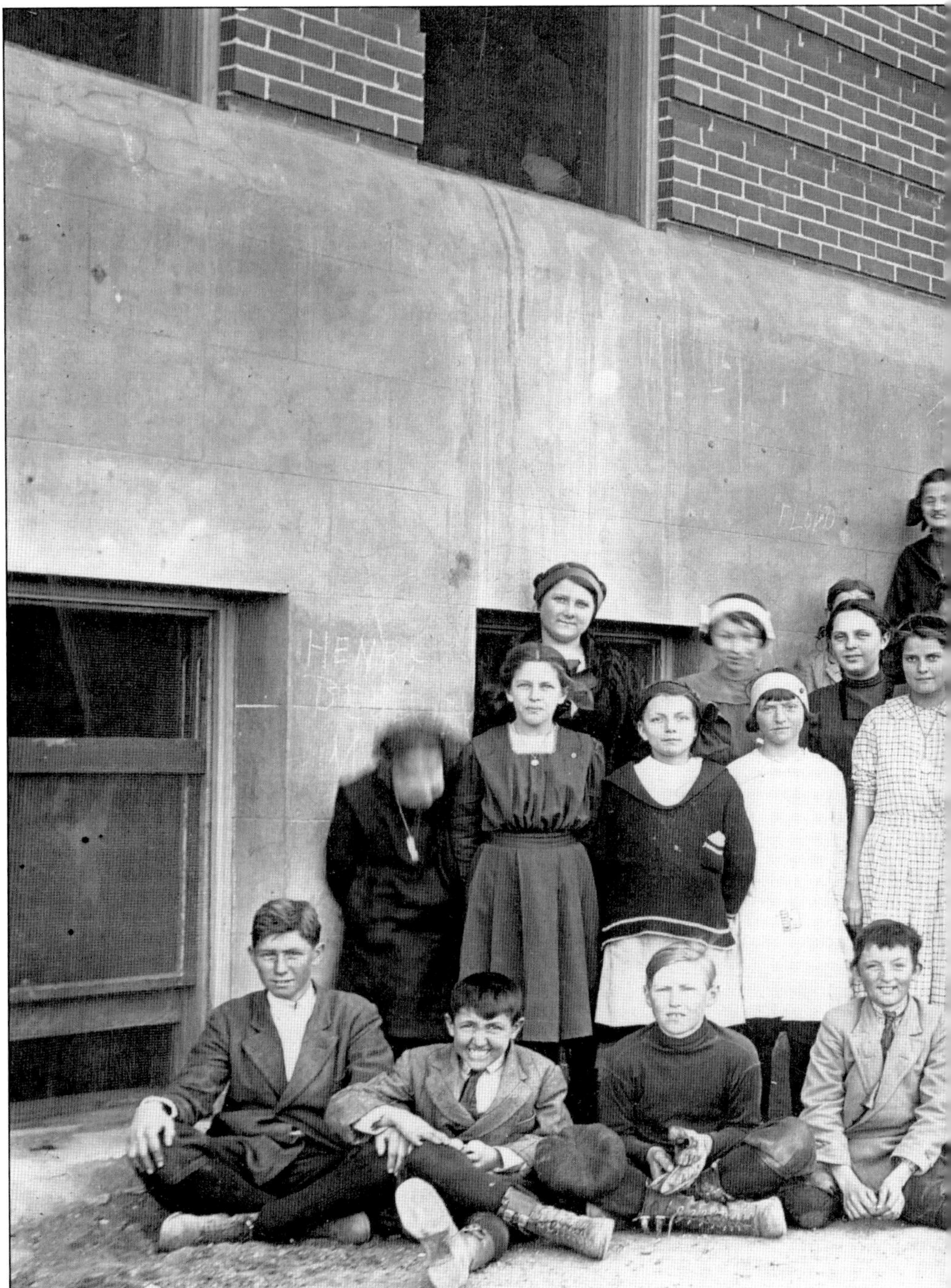

The sixth-grade class attending the Dalhart School poses for a photograph in 1910. In the photograph are Rena Barrett Boston and Ada Mae Swearingen. Note that most of the children are not smiling. The school was built in 1902 and burned down in 1922. In 1905, the *Dalhart Daily Texan* proudly reported, "Public Schools are now in full blast with an increased attendance

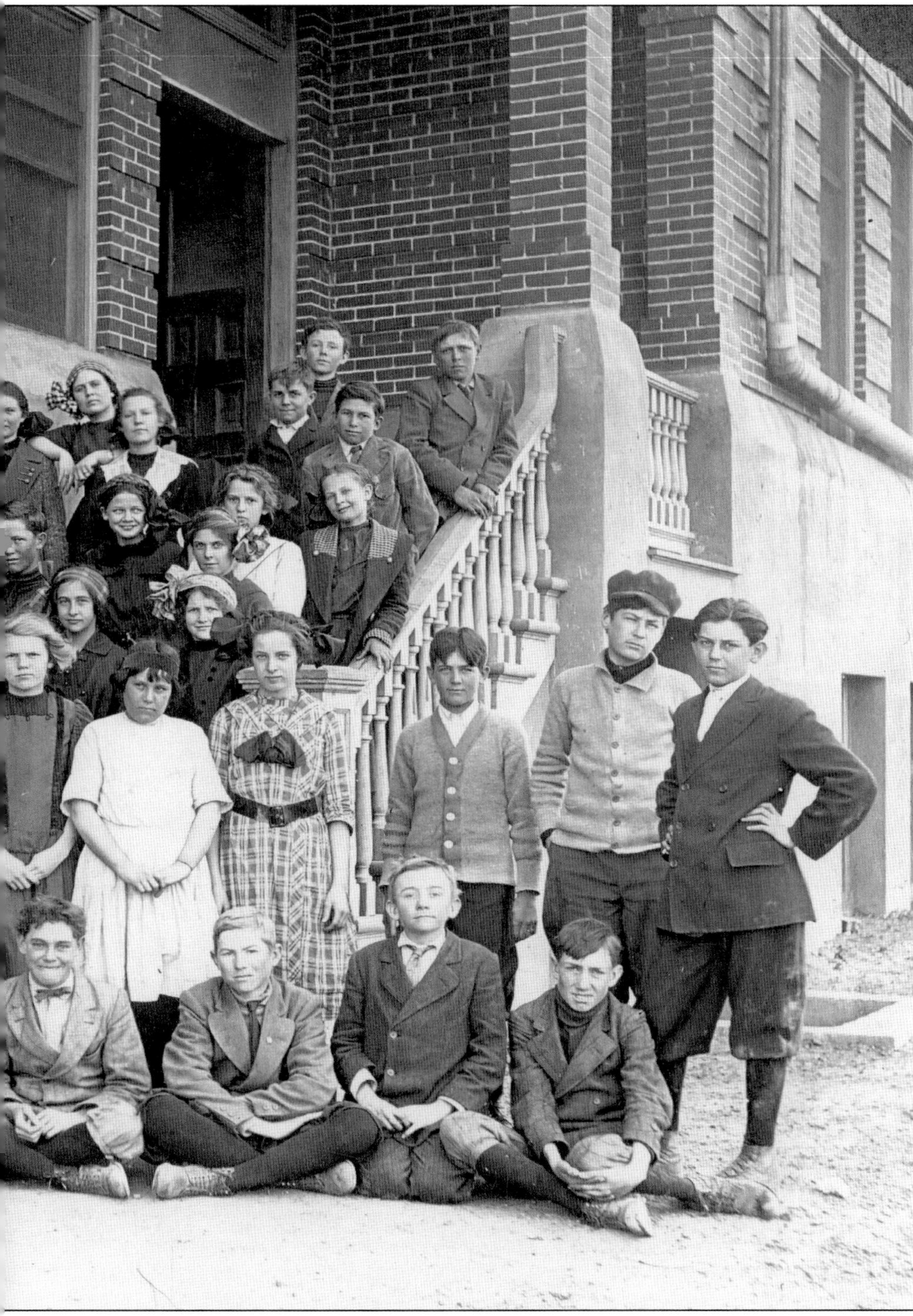

over former opening week. Dalhart is building up the best public schools in this section of the Panhandle." In March 1906, the report was profound, stating, "We never go this way but once. Neglected duty and opportunity for cultivating the child's mind and developing moral character is soon passed, never to return." (Courtesy of the XIT Museum in Dalhart and J.T. Mann.)

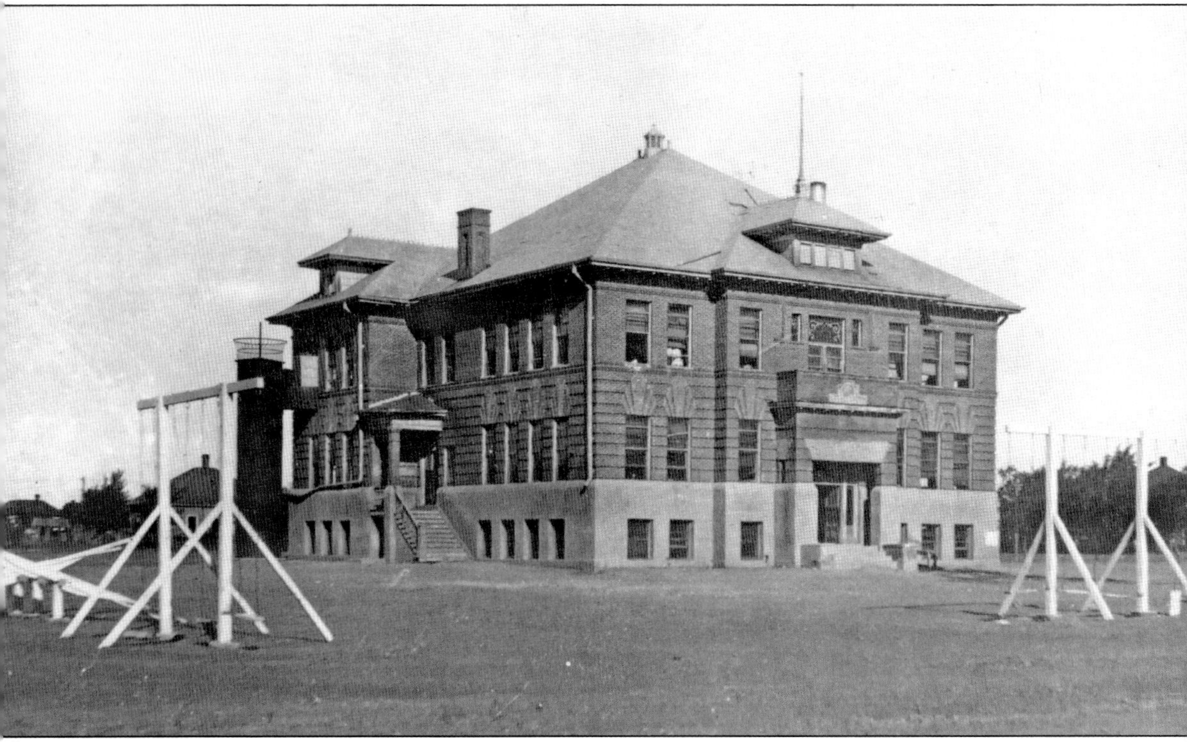

Seen here is the South Ward School, opened in September 1903. That same month, the *Dalhart Daily Texan* reported, "The public school opened Monday morning September 21. Prospects are bright for a long and successful school term. The school board has provided a fund large enough to cover the need of this rapidly growing town. The school building will be equipped with up-to-date maps, charts, globes, new desks, etc. Each teacher is qualified by education and experience to do efficient work."

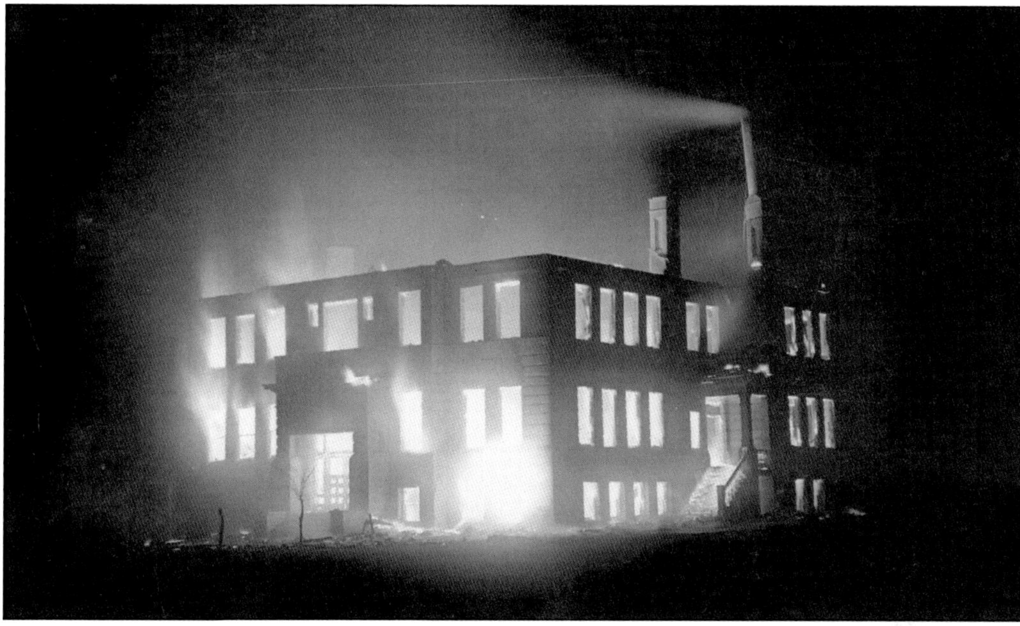

The South Ward School was located at 514 Conlen and burned to the ground in the middle of the night in November 1922 as the entire town watched helplessly. The photograph is from a postcard created after the fire, which seems an odd thing to make by today's standards. However, the school's burning was one of the most notable events of its day in Dalhart.

The North Ward School in Dalhart was located at 1001 Dallam Street. The school was built in 1924. In December 1996, Jake and Robbie Britz purchased the abandoned building. All of the windows were broken out, but they managed to renovate enough to move into the school in June 1997. The gym of the old school was sunken and is now the couple's TV room. (Photograph courtesy of The XIT Museum and Ruth Shewbert.)

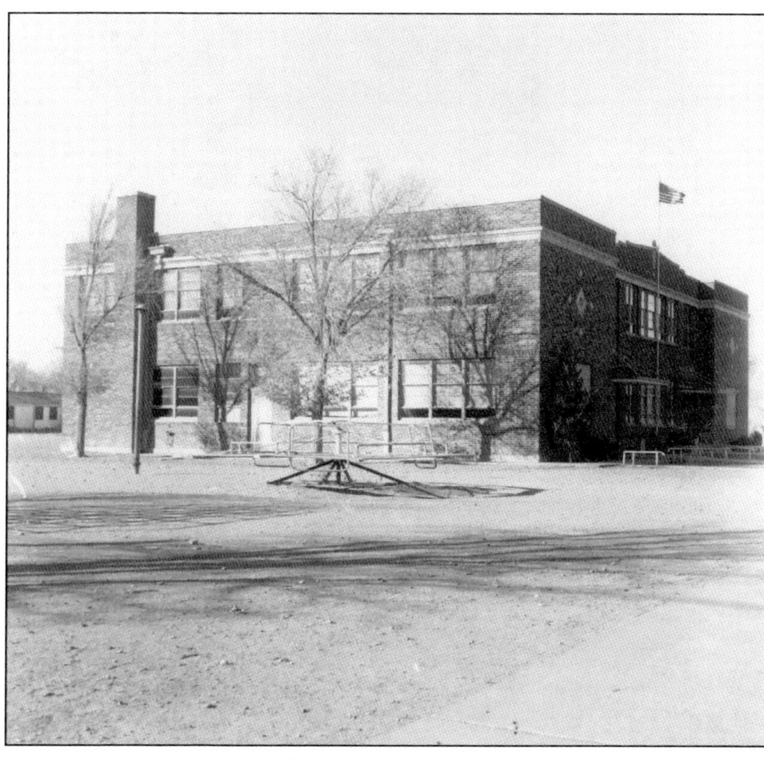

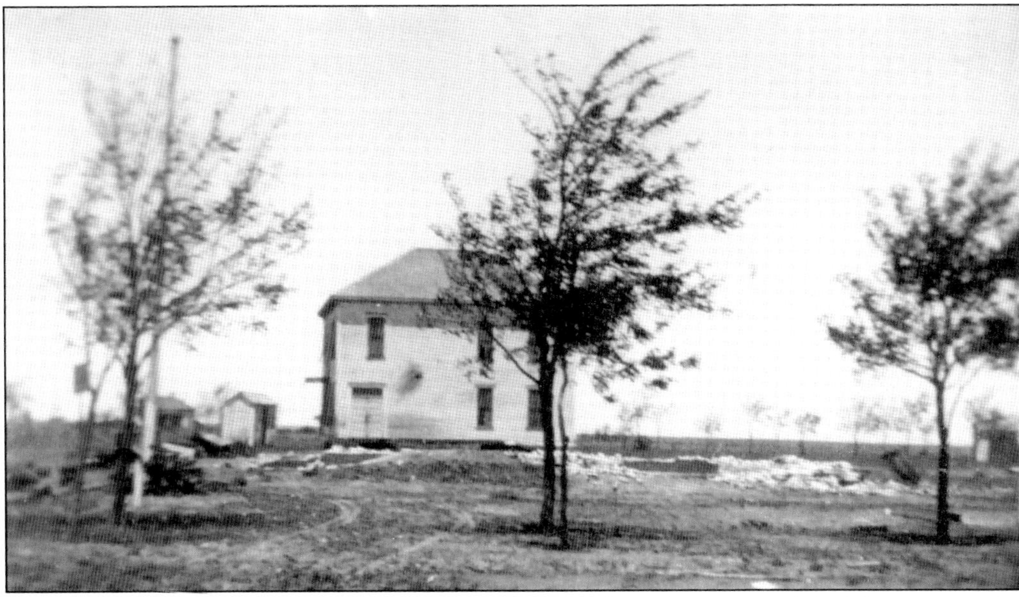

The North Ward School was moved in 1902. When Dalhart first emerged, buildings were often moved from one location to another, and some buildings were even moved from other cities to Dalhart. A lumberyard was established immediately, with lumber being transported into Dalhart by wagon and rail.

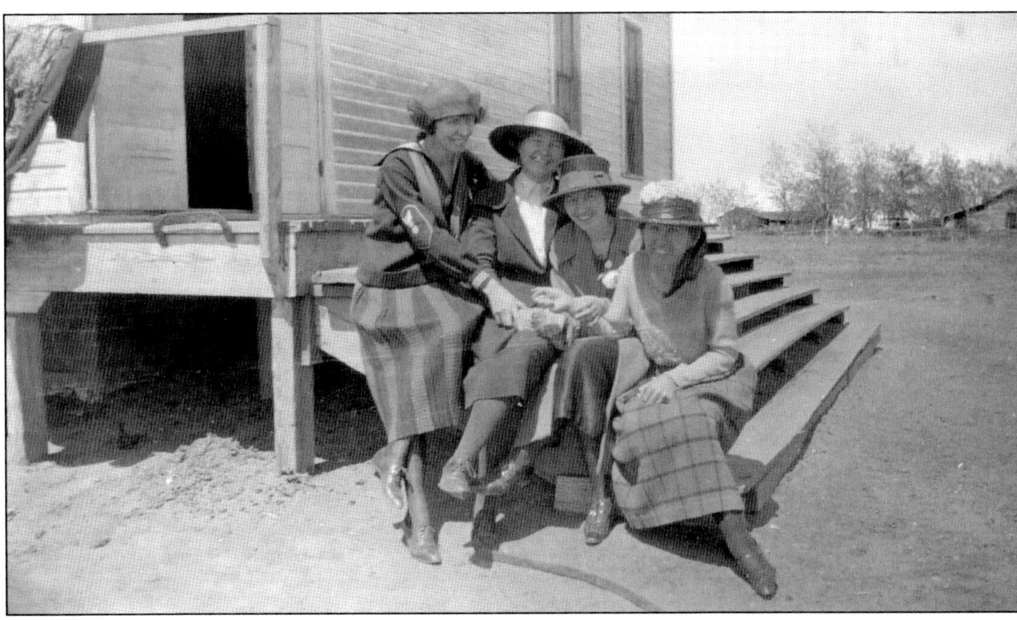

Four teachers in hats sit on the steps of Dalhart's North Ward School in 1921. One of the teachers, Janey Stidham Fitzimmons, came to Dalhart to teach in 1913. She married W.H. Fitzsimmons, and the couple lived in Dalhart. Janey earned her AB degree from Panhandle A&M (now Panhandle State College) at Goodwell, Oklahoma, in 1935. During the Depression, her salary was reduced from $120 per month to $60, paid in warrants. She taught English at Dalhart High School until her retirement.

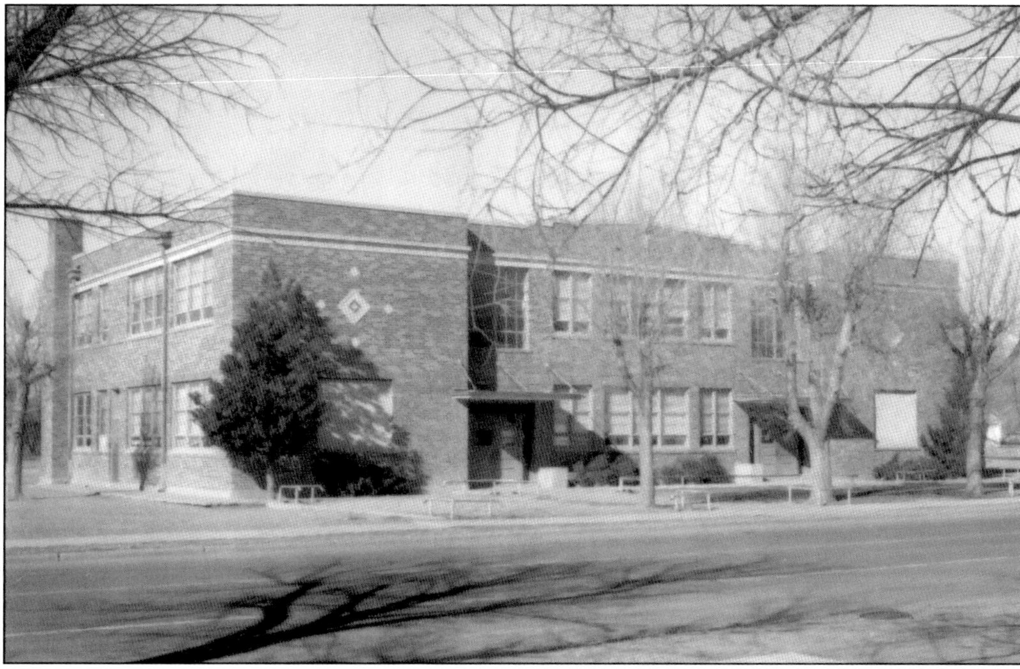

The South Ward School was rebuilt in 1924 at 514 Conlen. A report from the school superintendent stated, "The principal wishes to correct an error that the primary department is overcrowded and people are keeping their children home. All children seven years old the 1st of September are entitled to free education. We teachers are a unit in our purpose to give Dalhart a thorough and up-to-date school, and we are doing so. But we do not undertake to control any long-tongued gossip. We ask you to sit on them and sit hard."

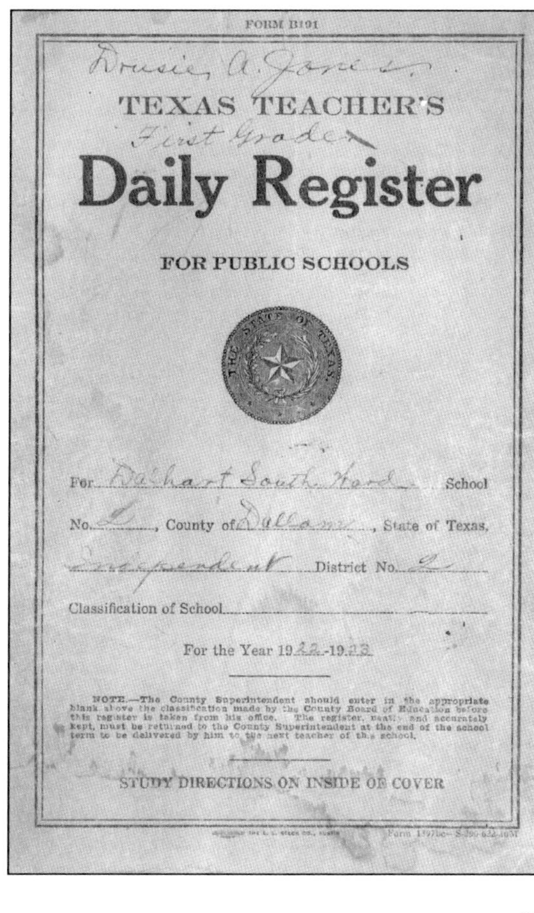

FORM B191

Dousie A. Jones

TEXAS TEACHER'S

First Grade

Daily Register

FOR PUBLIC SCHOOLS

For Dalhart South Ward School

No. 2, County of Dallam, State of Texas.

Independent District No. 2

Classification of School

For the Year 1922-1923

NOTE.—The County Superintendent should enter in the appropriate blank above the classification made by the County Board of Education before this register is taken from his office. The register, neatly and accurately kept, must be returned to the County Superintendent at the end of the school term to be delivered by him to the next teacher of the school.

STUDY DIRECTIONS ON INSIDE OF COVER

The grade book of Miss Dousie A. Jones's first-grade class from the 1922–1923 school year listed each child, the child's father, the father's occupation, and the child's grades in agriculture, arithmetic, deportment, drawing, geography, Texas history, language, music, physiology, reading, spelling, and writing. The booklet also contained general direction to teachers; rules and directions for requisitioning, caring for, and distributing free textbooks; excerpts from school law; and instructions for display of the flag.

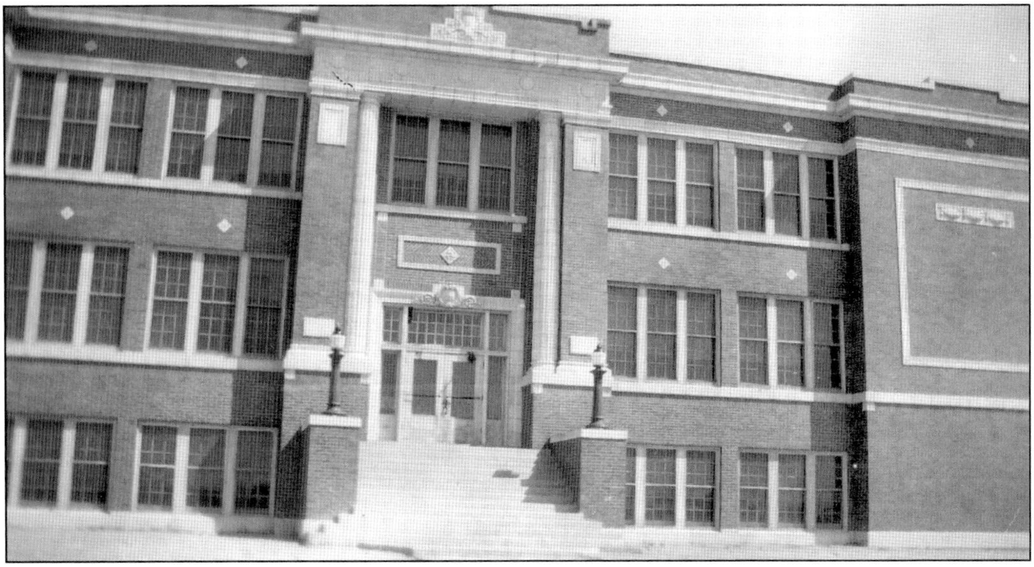

Dalhart's first high school was built in 1922 at 800 Oak Street. It also became the second Dalhart school to burn down, on July 20, 1949. When it was rebuilt, it went from a three-story structure to a two-story structure, which may have been due to the difficulty in putting out the fire. Unlike Dalhart's first school, which burnt in the middle of the night, Dalhart High School burned in the afternoon. Students relocated to tents while the school was rebuilt.

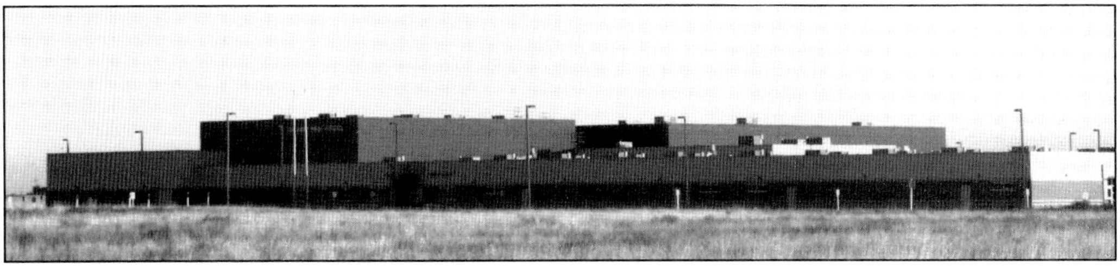

Dalhart's newest high school opened for its first classes in the fall of 2009. The school continued to use Memorial Stadium for football games through 2010, with a new stadium built for the 2011 school year. The new stadium is located next to the high school, while the old stadium is located next to the administration building and Dalhart Intermediate School, which once housed high school students.

Mary Emily Williams, daughter of C.E. Williams, was chosen as a young girl in 1918 to turn on Dalhart's first electric lights. Here she is seen with her cousin, Laura Blanch Atkinson, in their Dalhart Pep Squad uniforms in 1925.

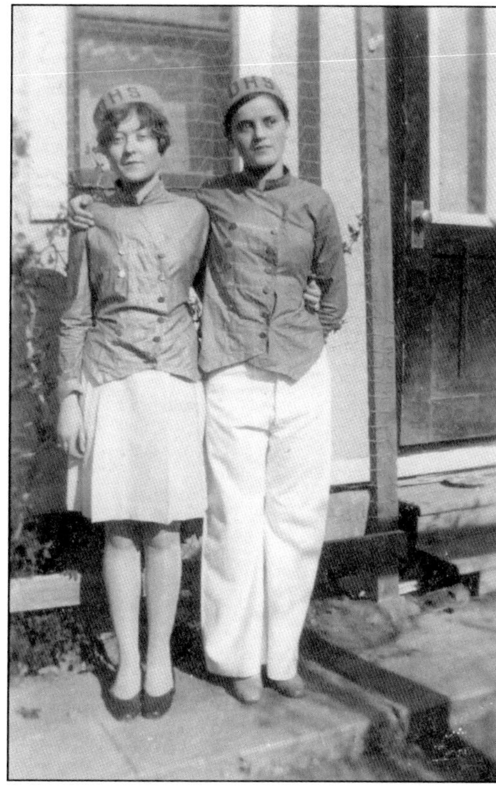

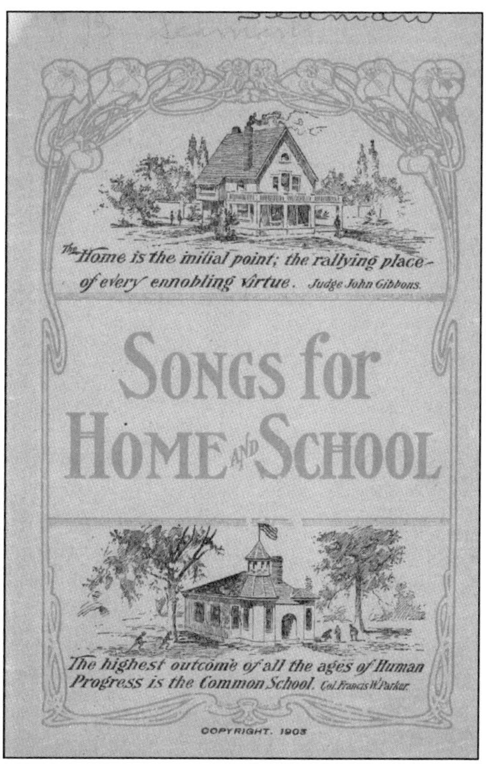

Dalhart schoolchildren enjoyed lessons in music. The 1903 "Songs for Home and School" booklet included advertising throughout and songs such as "Battle Hymn of the Republic," "Home Sweet Home," and "The Star Spangled Banner."

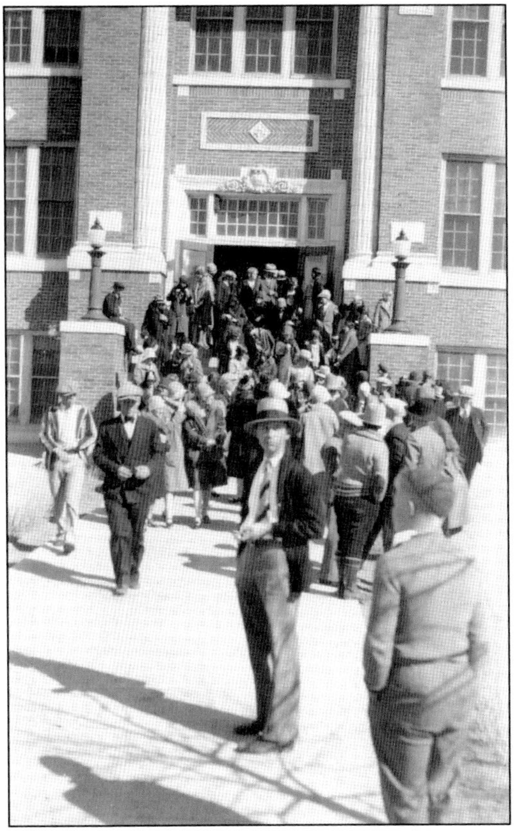

The impressive three-story Dalhart High School, located at 800 Oak Street, stood from 1922 until it burned in 1949. Rebuilt as a two-story structure, the school was later repurposed as a junior high school, and then as an intermediate school, as new buildings were built for the higher classes. In this photograph, students pour out of school. The boys all wear hats, coats, and ties, and the girls wear dresses and hats.

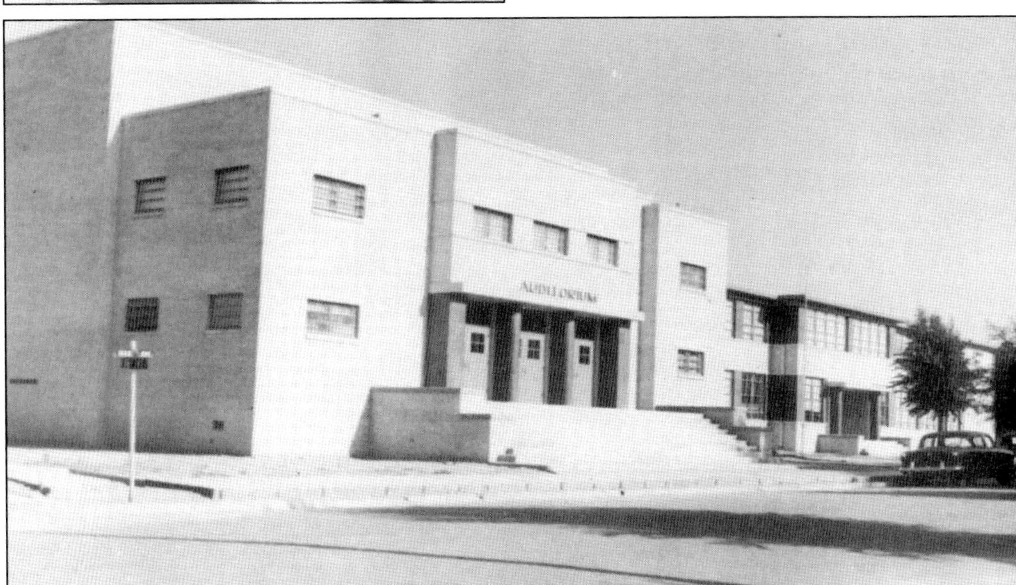

When a new high school was built on Sixteenth Street, the junior high school students moved to the building at 800 Oak Street. This postcard depicts the building that replaced the high school after it burned down in 1949. Junior high students occupied the location until they moved to the building on Sixteenth Street in 2009. (Courtesy of the XIT Museum and Zelda Beth Lang.)

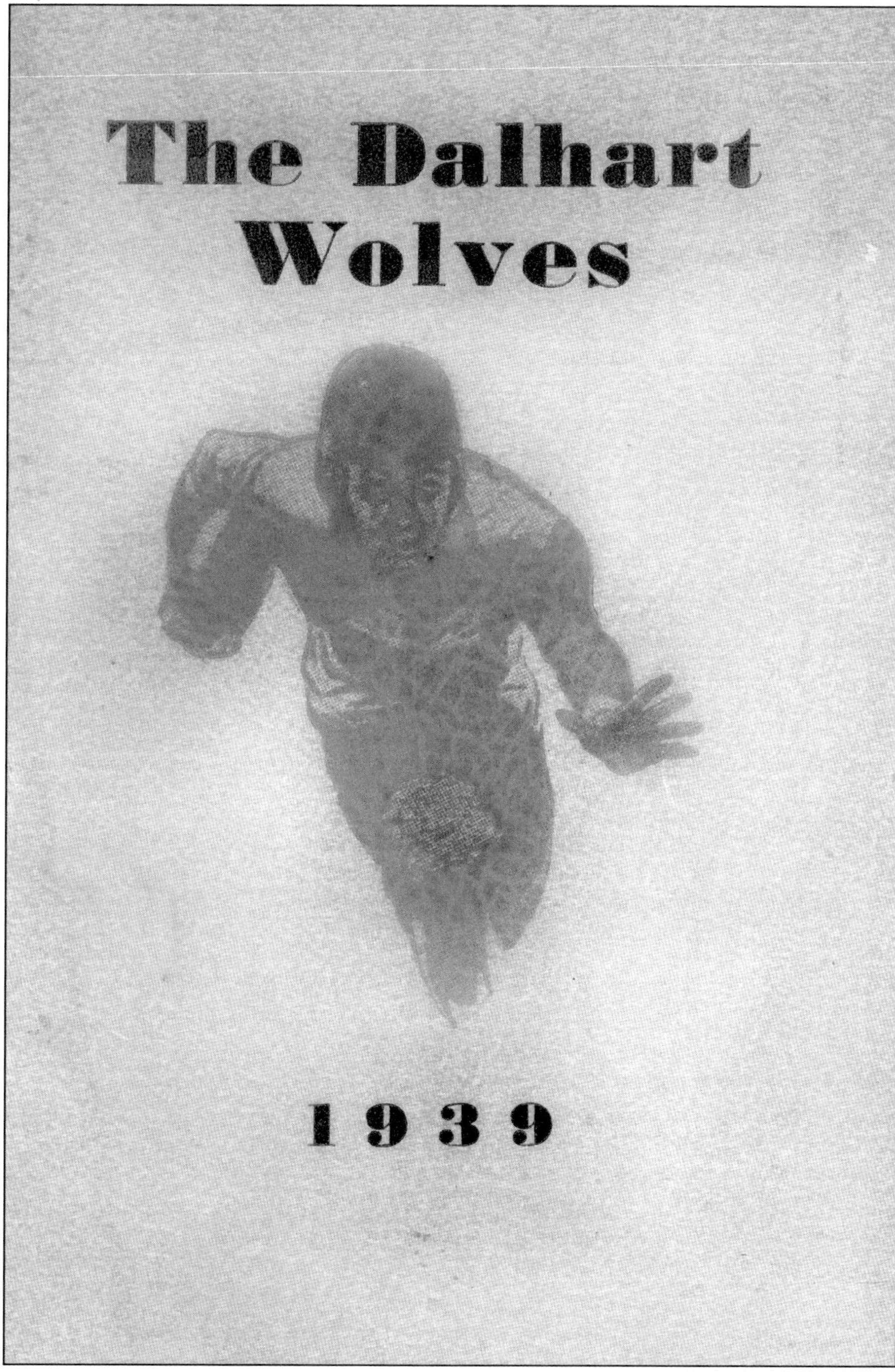

Football is one of the great Friday night activities in any Texas town, and Dalhart is no exception. In 1939, booklets were given out at the games with photographs and mini biographies about each player. In that same year, R.M. Thompson Jr. was the Wolf coach. He came to Dalhart in 1926 and began coaching in 1938. The back of the booklet contains the school song, with the lyric, "Far out on the western prairie, standing plain to view, is our dear old Dalhart High School, tow'ring toward the blue."

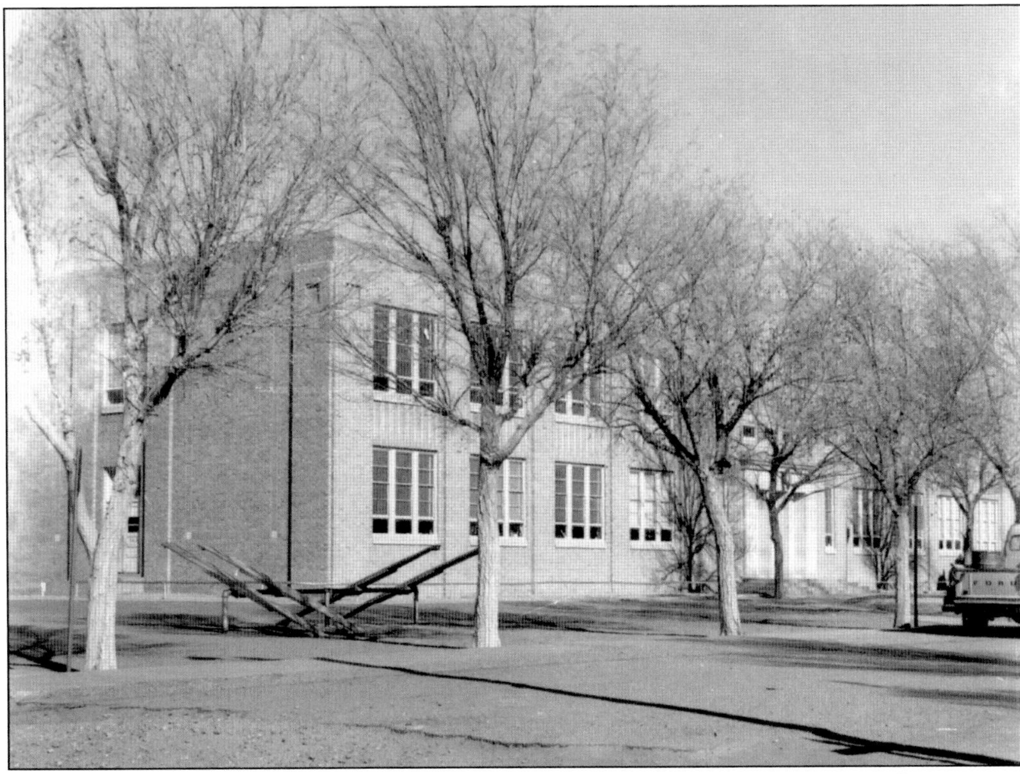

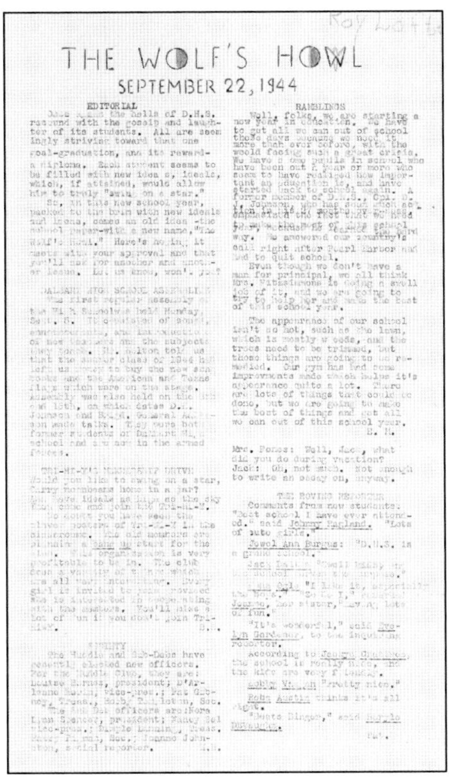

THE WOLF'S HOWL

SEPTEMBER 22, 1944

EDITORIAL

Once again the halls of D.H.S. resound with the gossip and laughter of its students. All are seemingly striving toward that one goal-graduation, and its reward-a diploma. Each student seems to be filled with new ideas, ideals, which, if attained, would allow him to truly "swing on a star."

So, in this new school year, packed to the brim with new ideals and ideas, comes an old idea -the school paper-with a new name, "The Wolf's Howl." Here's hoping it meets with your approval and that you'll ask for another and another issue. Let us know, won't you?

[illegible]

RAMBLINGS

Well, folks, we are starting a new year in education. We have to get all we can out of school these days because we need it more than ever before, with the world facing such a great crisis. We have [illegible] pupils in school who have been out a year or more who seem to have realized how important an education is, and have started back to school again. A former member of D.H.S., Cpl. D. J. Johnson, [illegible] the fact that we need to make the most of this school year, [illegible] way. He answered our country's call right after Pearl Harbor and had to quit school.

Even though we don't have a man for principal, we all think Mrs. Fitzsimmons is doing a swell job of it, and we are going to try to help her and make the best of this school year.

The appearance of our school isn't so hot, such as the lawn, which is mostly weeds, and the trees need to be trimmed, but those things are going to be remedied. Our gym has had some improvements made which helps it's appearance quite a lot. There are lots of things that could be done, but we are going to make the best of things and get all we can out of this school year.

E. H.

Mrs. Fones: Well, Jack, what did you do during vacation?
Jack: Oh, not much. Not enough to write an essay on, anyway.

THE ROVING REPORTER

Comments from new students: "Best school I have ever attended." said Johnny Ragland. "Lots of cute girls."

Jewel Ann Burgus: "D.H.S. is a grand school."

[illegible]

Kella Hill School was built in 1930 and was located at the corner of Kendrick and Heights Streets in Dalhart. (Photograph courtesy of the XIT Museum in Dalhart and Ruth Shewbert.)

The September 22, 1944, edition of the *Wolf's Howl*, Dalhart High School's typed newsletter, included an editorial section, ramblings, a society page, sports section, favorite nursery rhyme of the seniors ("rings on their fingers, bells on their toes, they shall have music wherever they go"), and notes on clubs including the pep squad and sub debs. The three-page newsletter also reported comments from new students, including Johnny Ragland, who said, "Best school I have ever attended. Lots of cute girls."

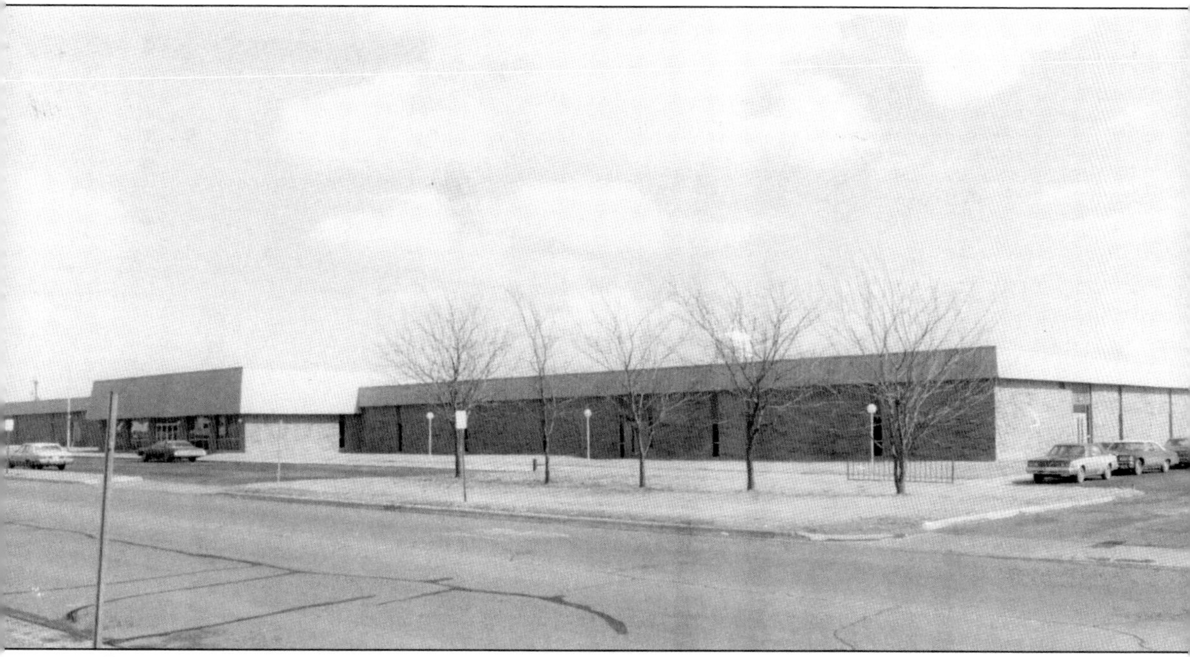

Dalhart Elementary School was built in 1971 and remains in use today. The school is located at 1401 Tennessee Avenue and is home to students in pre-kindergarten through the third grade. The elementary school children enjoy the benefit of having a building designed just for their use. In 2008, the school was expanded to add an entire new wing, now home to pre-kindergarten classes.

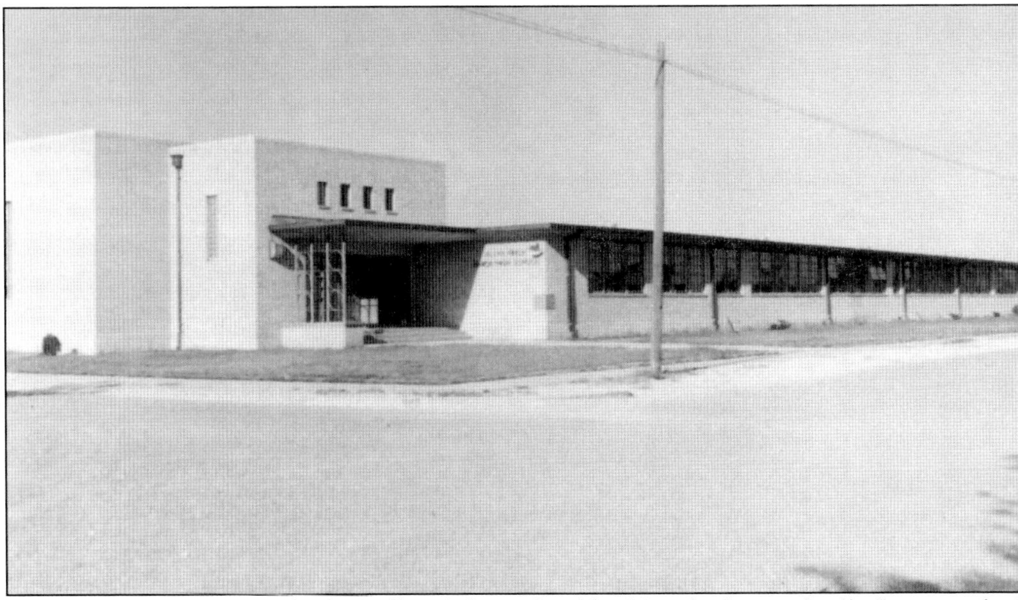

Allyn Finch is the namesake for Dalhart's first school building built specifically for junior high school students. Finch was one of the first directors for the XIT Rodeo and Reunion. Dalhart ISD now houses its administrative offices and XIT Secondary School in this building.

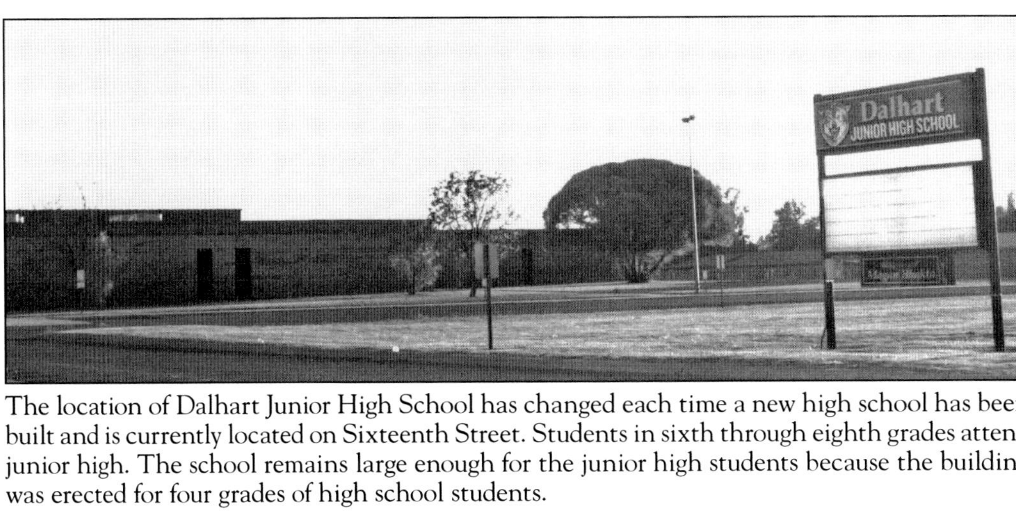

The location of Dalhart Junior High School has changed each time a new high school has been built and is currently located on Sixteenth Street. Students in sixth through eighth grades attend junior high. The school remains large enough for the junior high students because the building was erected for four grades of high school students.

Seven

The Outlying Communities

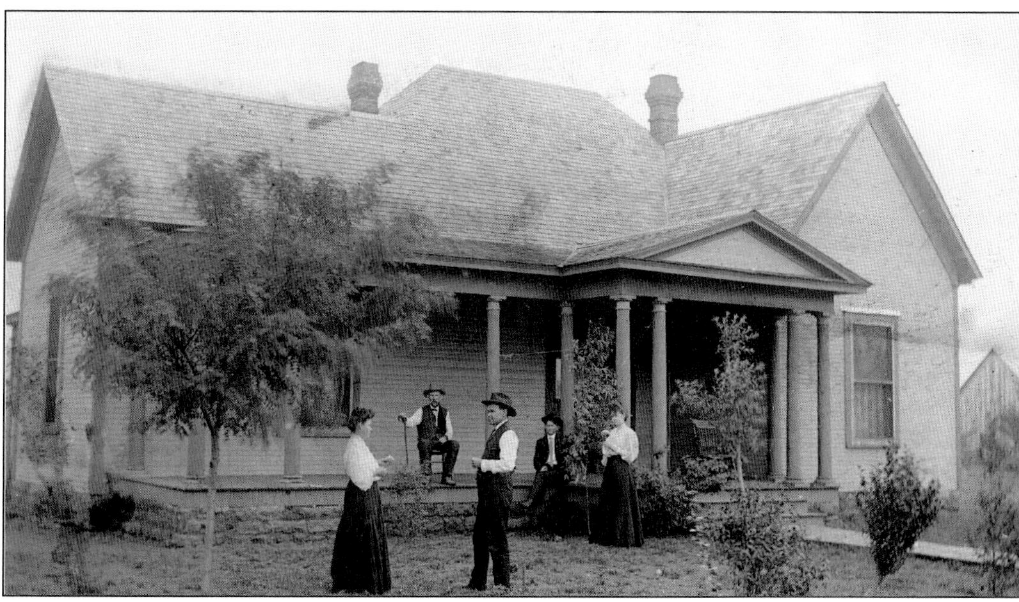

Several communities also sprouted up in Dallam and Hartley Counties due to the railroad. The earliest, Texline, was briefly the county seat for Dallam County. Conlen, a large farming community, is home to one of Dallam County's most prominent farming and ranching families. Perico is known for bringing the Catholic Church to Dallam County, and Wilco nearly disappeared after the railroad passed on plans to go through the small community. Other communities included Buffalo Springs, Bunker Hill, Middlewater, and Kerrick. Each community helped to establish Dallam and Hartley Counties as agriculturally significant, and farming and ranching remain their mainstay. Seen in the foreground of this 1901 photograph are Mr. and Mrs. Tobe Pitts at a home in Texline.

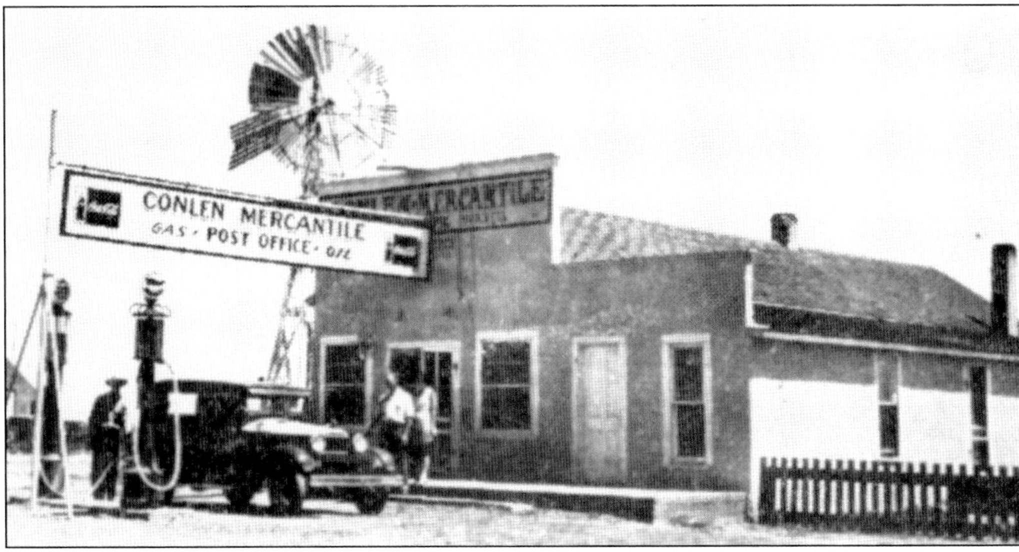

The community of Conlen is located 19 miles northeast of Dalhart. Conlen was founded in 1903 and named after Captain J.H. "Jim" Conlen, the engineer responsible for building the tracks that brought the Rock Island Line from Kansas to New Mexico, passing through Dalhart. Conlen's early survival was due to agricultural endeavors. The community's 1940 pre-war population of 150 declined to less than half that number by 1948. The 1990 census showed 61 people living in the area, which increased in the 2000 census to 69. The town is shown on the official state map today with an estimated population of 18 people. A prominent family in the Conlen and Colony School area is the Summerours, who continue to farm and ranch today. Pictured here is the Conlen Mercantile, post office, and service station. (Courtesy of the XIT Museum and Kathrine Crabtree.)

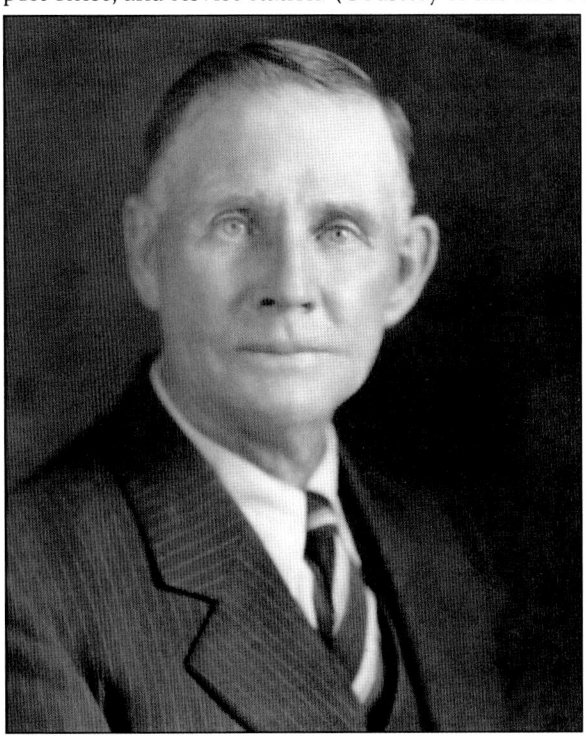

The Summerour family settled in Dallam County in the Colony School area and Conlen in 1916. The family patriarch, James Elmer Summerour Sr., was known as "Elmer," and was a World War I veteran. He married Dorothy "Polly" Pronger in 1929, and they began the Summerour Ranch. Elmer and Polly lived most of their married life on the ranch in the Conlen community. (Courtesy of the Edward Berry Summerour family.)

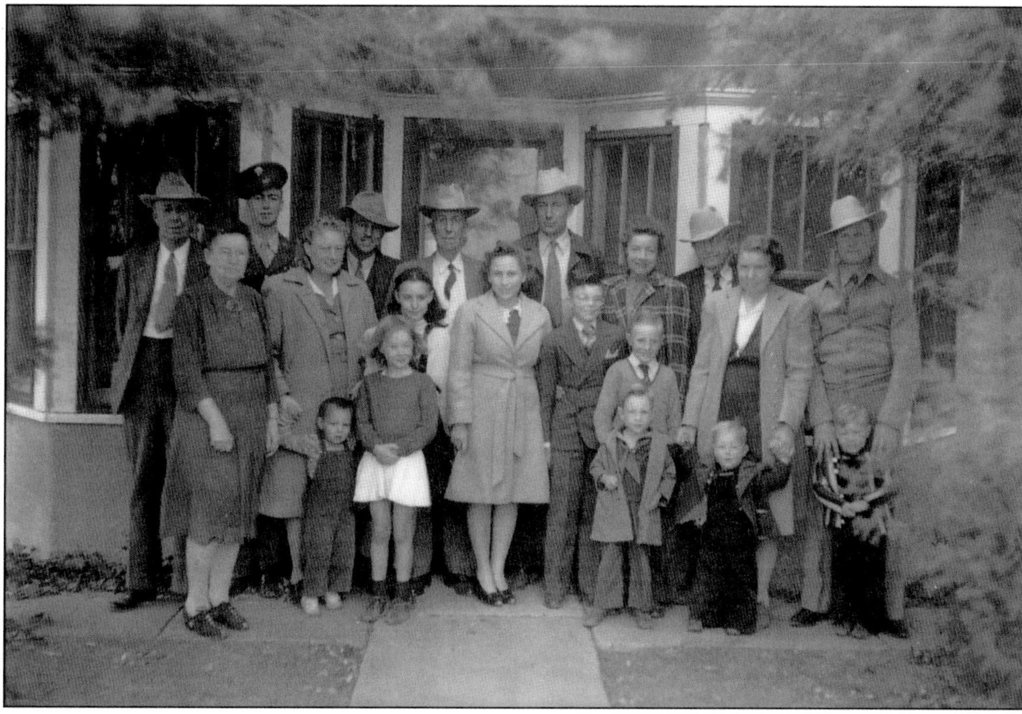

The Summerours parented four children, and the three oldest, all boys, continue to reside at the ranch. Elmer died in 1969, and Polly passed away in 1995. James Elmer "Jimmy" Summerour (born on October 27, 1930), Johnny Summerour (born on December 9, 1934), and Edward Berry "Buzz" Summerour (born on June 13, 1939), continue to reside at the ranch. The youngest sibling, Donna Summerour, was born on her parents' 18th anniversary, October 17, 1947. (Courtesy of the Edward Berry Summerour family.)

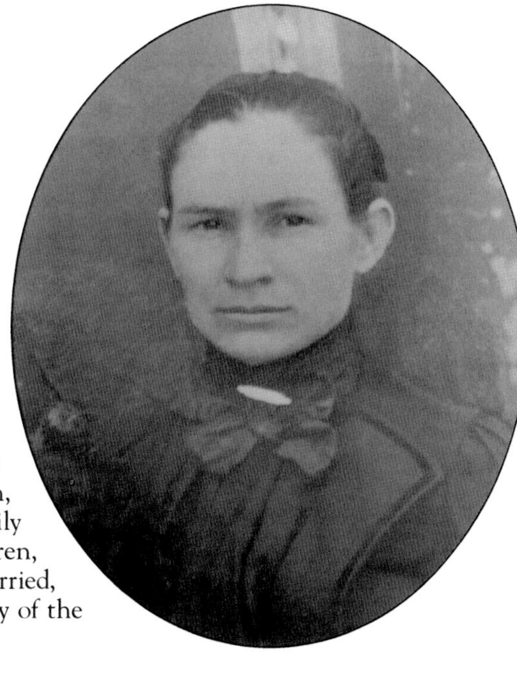

Elmer's father, James Berry Summerour, was born on September 2, 1864, and died on July 22, 1948. Elmer's mother, who had her father's first name, was Henry Melvina Dawson Summerour, born on January 25, 1871. She died on August 25, 1907, at the age of 36. Melvina was part Cherokee Indian and came from Indian Territory. After Melvina's death, her sister moved in with the Summerour family to care for James and Melvina's young children, including Elmer. James and the sister later married, and had one daughter of their own. (Courtesy of the Edward Berry Summerour family.)

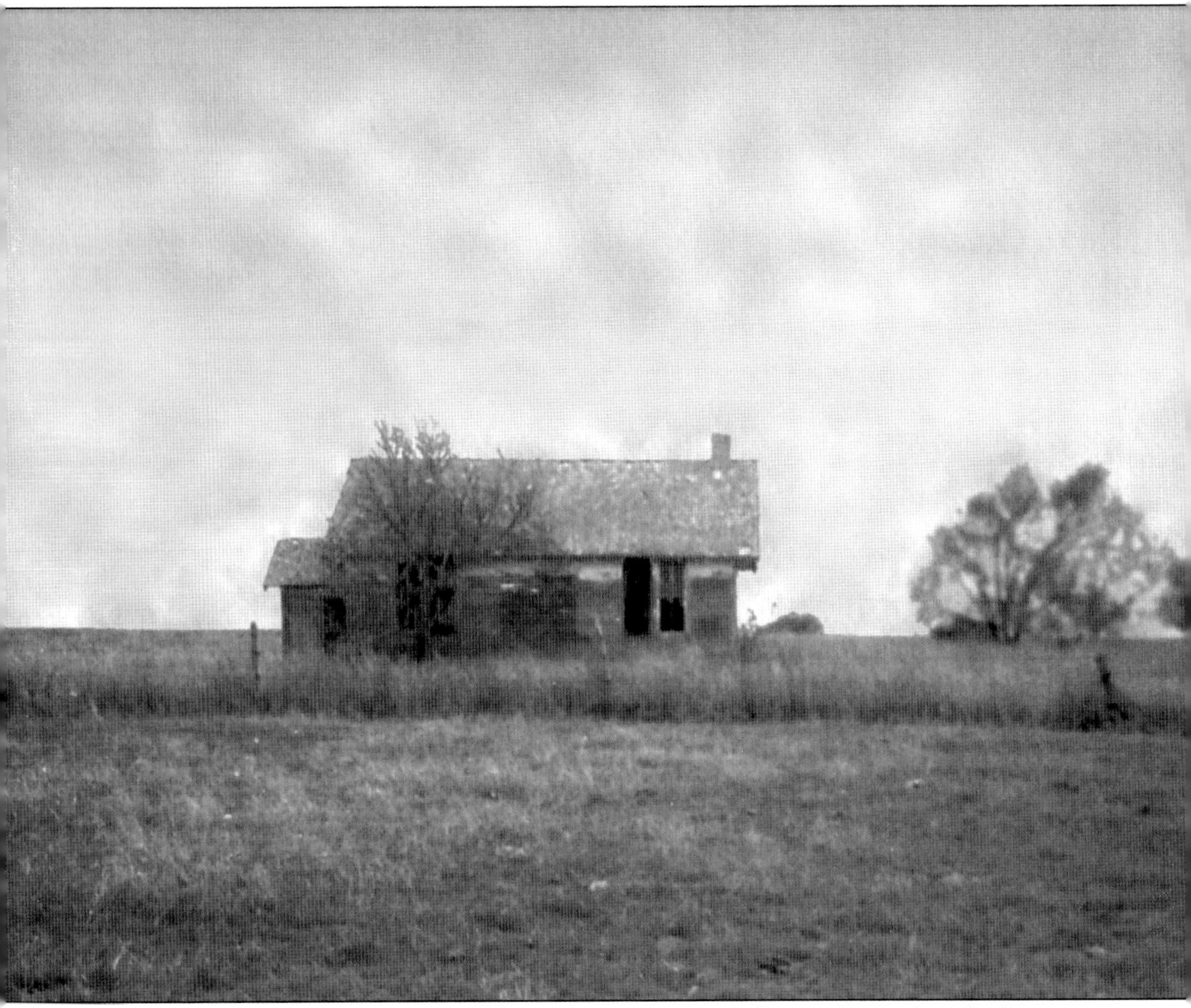

The Summerour boys attended the Colony School, which was three miles south of the Summerour Ranch. The one-room school was used for Sunday services each week as well as community events. Several teachers taught at the Colony Schoolhouse during the eight years that each of the Summerour children attended; often, these teachers were very young. Buzz was the ring-bearer for his 18-year-old teacher, Mavis Rose, when she married. Later, Buzz was able to retrieve the old piano from the schoolhouse. The school still stands today on Summerour Lane, just east of Moore Road. (Courtesy of the Edward Berry Summerour family.)

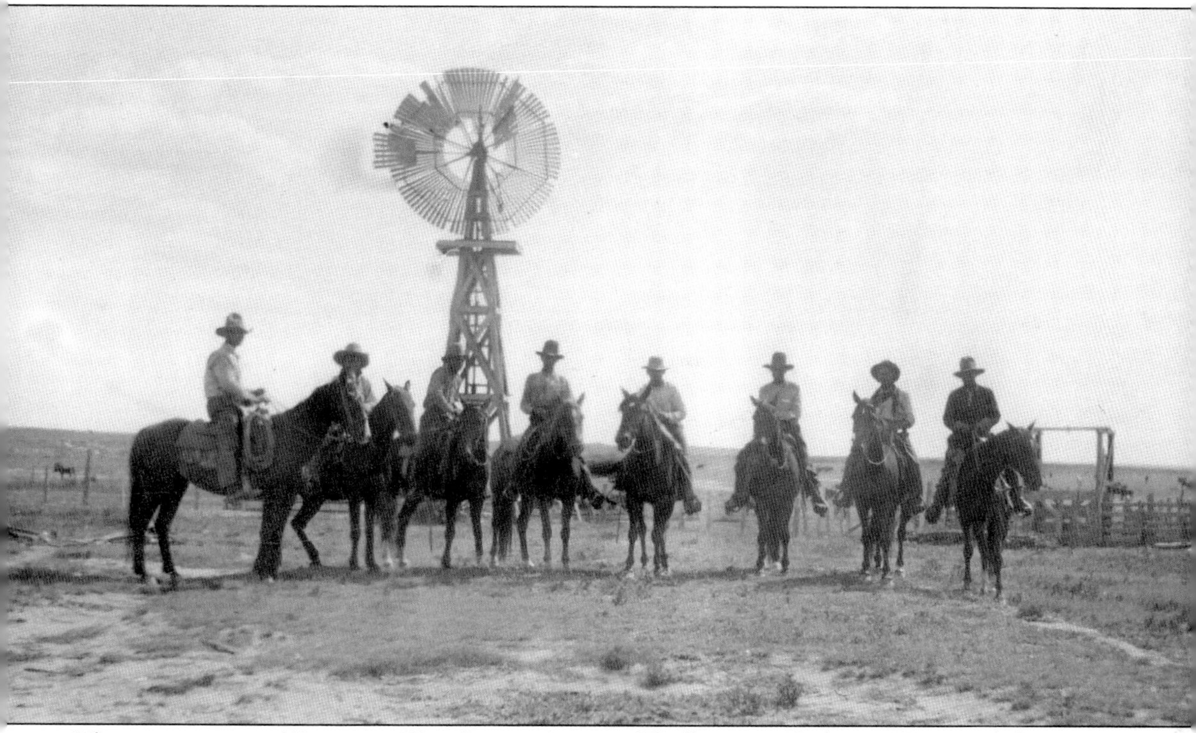

The community of Perico is 25 miles northwest of Dalhart on Highway 87 toward the New Mexico border and is largely a ghost town today. Perico was a siding on the railroad and was originally named Farwell after Charles and John Farwell, who were instrumental in establishing the XIT Ranch. In 1905, the railroad changed the town name to Perico. The community had a depot made from boxcars placed next to one another, a water tower, and a bunkhouse for railroad workers. Perico was promoted by W.P. Soash, and received its own post office in 1907. (It closed in 1970.) Thirty German farming families from Illinois were the first residents in Perico in the late 1880s. The Henry Schniers and the George Reilman families were first to the Perico area. Other original families included the Barths, Lambergers, Bolks, Theismans, and Kohrmans. This photograph shows Bob Duke of Perico on horseback near Perico.

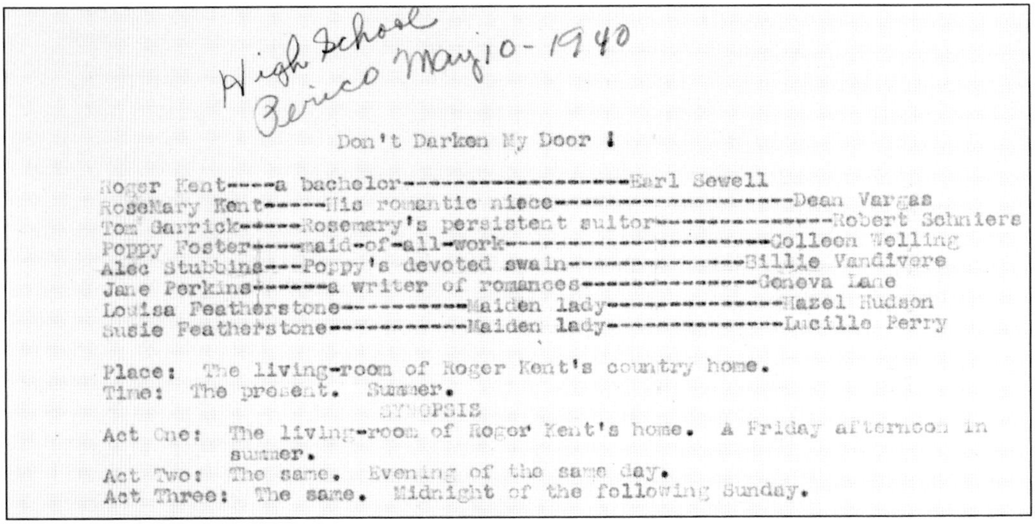

High School
Perico May 10-1940

Don't Darken My Door !

Roger Kent----a bachelor------------------Earl Sewell
RoseMary Kent-----His romantic niece-------------------Dean Vargas
Tom Garrick-----Rosemary's persistent suitor---------------Robert Schniers
Poppy Foster----maid-of-all-work---------------------Colleen Welling
Alec Stubbins---Poppy's devoted swain--------------Billie Vandivere
Jane Perkins------a writer of romances--------------Geneva Lane
Louisa Featherstone----------Maiden lady--------------Hazel Hudson
Susie Featherstone-----------Maiden lady--------------Lucille Perry

Place: The living-room of Roger Kent's country home.
Time: The present. Summer.

SYNOPSIS

Act One: The living-room of Roger Kent's home. A Friday afternoon in summer.
Act Two: The same. Evening of the same day.
Act Three: The same. Midnight of the following Sunday.

Perico's first school was built in 1907, and in 1924, a larger school was built. It now sits abandoned, just feet away from Highway 87. During the school's years, only about 50 students attended. The school was modern in that it had indoor plumbing, running water, and a heating system. The program for a play, *Don't Darken My Door*, from May 10, 1940, included eight students in three acts.

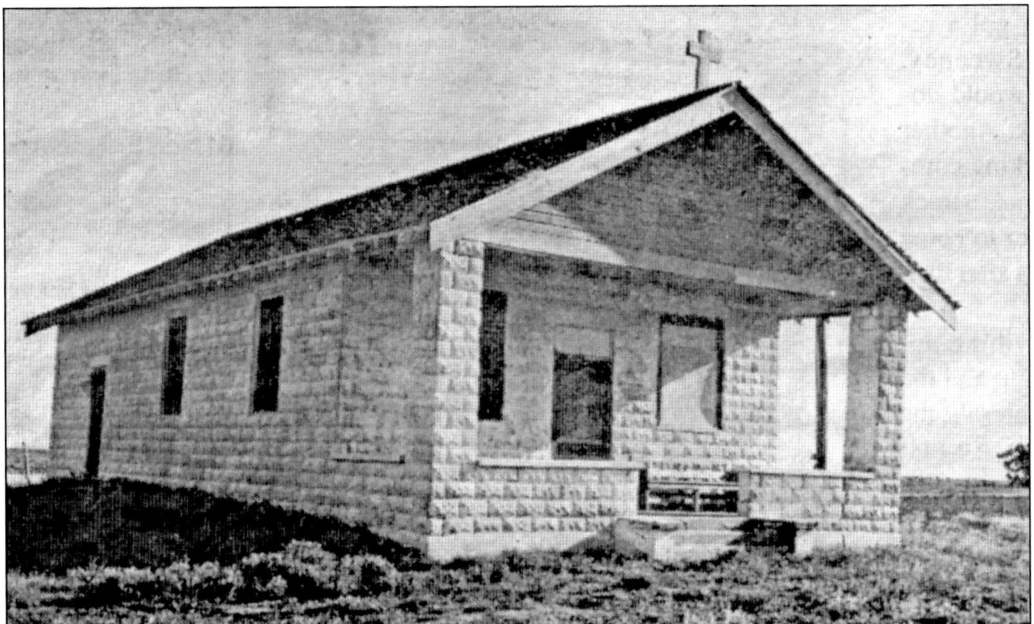

Early Perico businesses included the Theodore W. Timmerman store and the Blotz-Henneman Grain Company elevator. Timmerman was also the postmaster. (The XIT Museum has a straightedge razor engraved with "T.W. Timmerman" within its collections.) Hugh Hamilton Sr. operated a Phillips 66 gas station, and a second gas station was run by Grady Edge. By 1947, the population decreased to just 30. In the 1980s, Perico's recorded population was two, and just one business remained. The St. Mary's Catholic community began in 1910 at Perico. Priests from Clarendon and Amarillo rode the Fort Worth and Denver City Railway, a freight train, to offer Mass in the homes of parishioners.

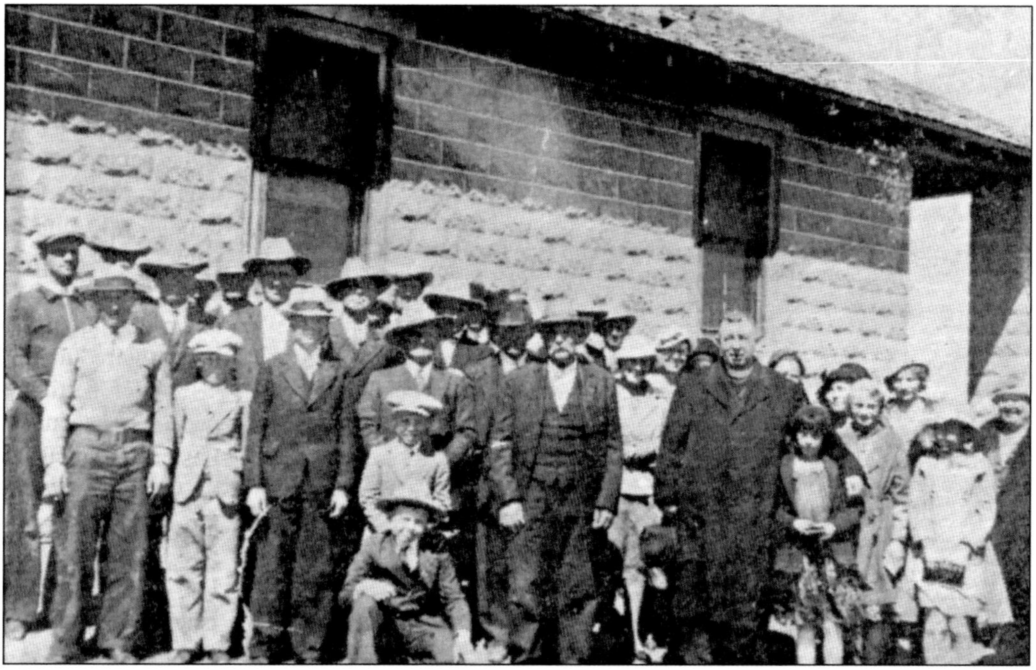

The first Mass in Perico was given on August 18, 1910, and three years later, the "Church on the Prairie" was built with a $750 grant from the Catholic Church Extension Society, along with money raised by families in the community. T.W. Timmerman donated the land where St. Mary's was built. A cemetery was also created west of the church. Built of concrete, the building still stands today, alone and abandoned on the prairie.

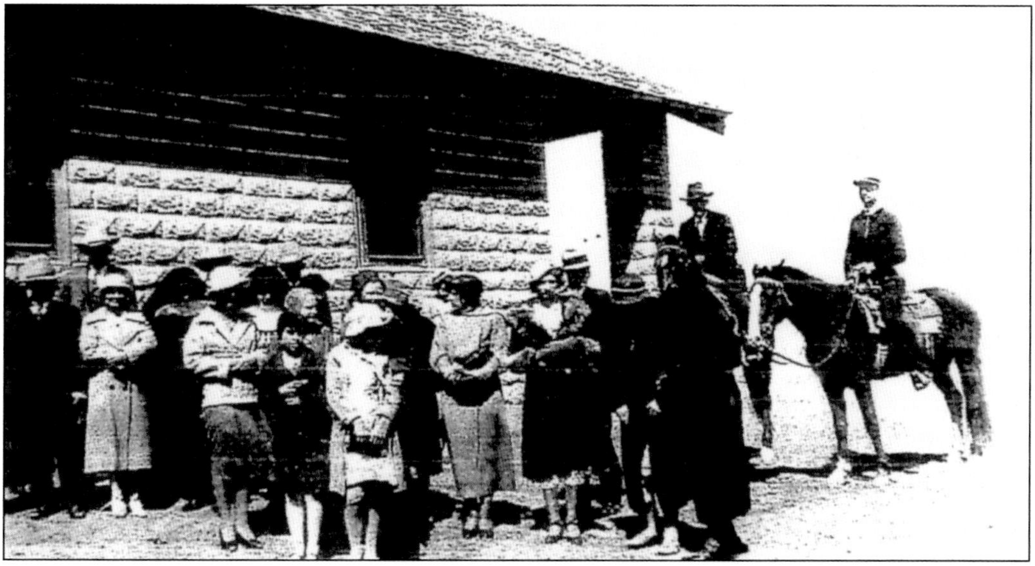

The Catholic community of Perico was served by priests who rode the train up from Clarendon, Amarillo, or Dalhart to say Mass every two or three months in the home of one of the local Catholic families. By 1980, St. Mary's was in such a state of decline that a decision was made to relocate the parish to Texline. John and Ann Reifers donated land for the new church building, dedicated on June 26, 1983, by Bishop Leroy T. Matthiesen.

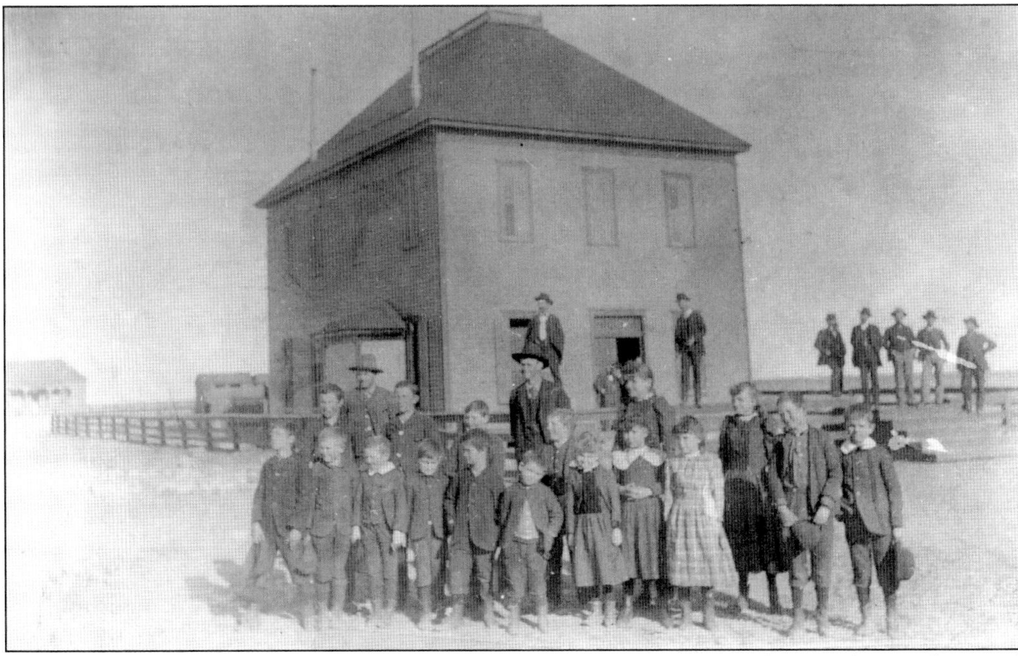

The city of Texline was the county seat for Dallam County from 1891 until 1903 when Dalhart took over that distinction. Texline derived its name from its location as the last city in the northwest corner of Texas, on the state line with New Mexico. Land was purchased by the Fort Worth and Denver City Railway for a division point in 1888. By the end of that same year, Texline had its first post office. Other early businesses included a depot and hotel. Railroad shops also sprang up. The first Dallam County Courthouse was located in Texline and is pictured here in 1890. The courthouse was also used for school; schoolchildren are shown here posing for the photograph.

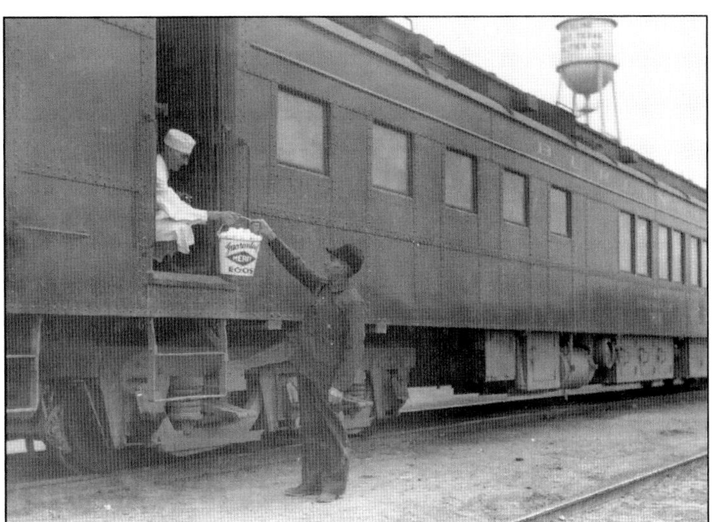

The city of Texline sits on just 1.01 square miles, 38 miles northwest of Dalhart. It was home to Dallam County's first school, which opened in 1892. Although Dalhart sprang up and incorporated in just a couple of years, Texline did not incorporate until 1916. In this photograph, eggs are being delivered to Texline on the Burlington Northern Train, on the line that once carried the Fort Worth and Denver City Railway.

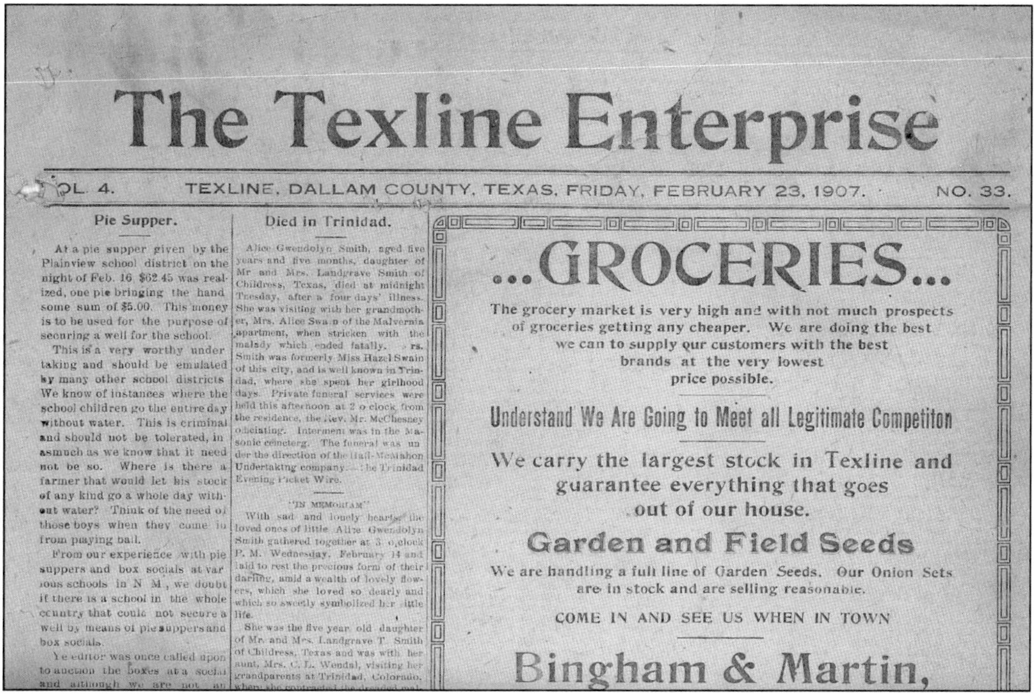

The Texline Enterprise

VOL. 4. TEXLINE, DALLAM COUNTY, TEXAS, FRIDAY, FEBRUARY 23, 1907. NO. 33.

Pie Supper.

At a pie supper given by the Plainview school district on the night of Feb. 16 $62.45 was realized, one pie bringing the handsome sum of $5.00. This money is to be used for the purpose of securing a well for the school.

This is a very worthy undertaking and should be emulated by many other school districts. We know of instances where the school children go the entire day without water. This is criminal and should not be tolerated, inasmuch as we know that it need not be so. Where is there a farmer that would let his stock of any kind go a whole day without water? Think of the need of those boys when they come in from playing ball.

From our experience with pie suppers and box socials at various schools in N. M., we doubt if there is a school in the whole country that could not secure a well by means of pie suppers and box socials.

Ye editor was once called upon to auction the boxes at a social and although we are not an

Died in Trinidad.

Alice Gwendolyn Smith, aged five years and five months, daughter of Mr and Mrs. Landgrave Smith of Childress, Texas, died at midnight Tuesday, after a four days' illness. She was visiting with her grandmother, Mrs. Alice Swain of the Malvernia apartment, when stricken with the malady which ended fatally. Mrs. Smith was formerly Miss Hazel Swain of this city, and is well known in Trinidad, where she spent her girlhood days. Private funeral services were held this afternoon at 2 o clock from the residence, the Rev. Mr. McChesney officiating. Interment was in the Masonic cemetery. The funeral was under the direction of the Hall-McMahon Undertaking company.—The Trinidad Evening Picket Wire.

"IN MEMORIAM"

With sad and lonely hearts the loved ones of little Alice Gwendolyn Smith gathered together at 3 o'clock P. M. Wednesday, February 14 and laid to rest the precious form of their darling, amid a wealth of lovely flowers, which she loved so dearly and which so sweetly symbolized her little life.

She was the five year old daughter of Mr. and Mrs. Landgrave T. Smith of Childress, Texas and was with her aunt, Mrs. C. L. Wendal, visiting her grandparents at Trinidad, Colorado, when she contracted the dreaded mal-

...GROCERIES...

The grocery market is very high and with not much prospects of groceries getting any cheaper. We are doing the best we can to supply our customers with the best brands at the very lowest price possible.

Understand We Are Going to Meet all Legitimate Competiton

We carry the largest stock in Texline and guarantee everything that goes out of our house.

Garden and Field Seeds

We are handling a full line of Garden Seeds. Our Onion Sets are in stock and are selling reasonable.

COME IN AND SEE US WHEN IN TOWN

Bingham & Martin,

The February 23, 1907, edition of the *Texline Enterprise* included advertising for groceries and Folger's coffee on the front page and a banner article about a pie supper held on February 16 that brought in $62.45, with one pie going for a whopping $5. The money was raised "for the purpose of securing a well for the school."

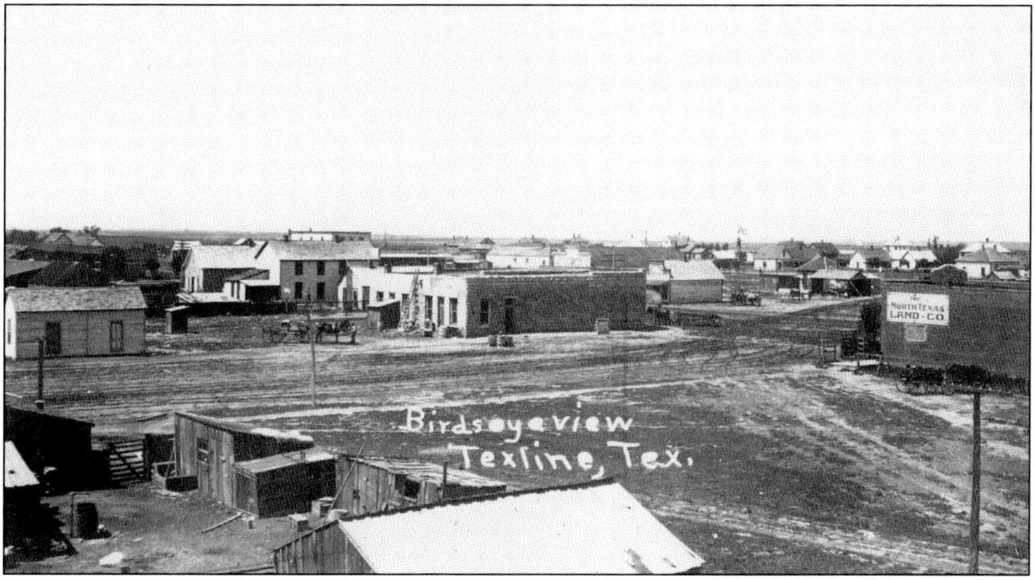

This bird's-eye view of Texline in 1912 was captured on a post card, which was sent to Mrs. Frankie Feaster of Dalhart on October 15, 1912, at a cost of 1¢. The address for Mrs. Feaster was shown only as "Dalhart, Texas." The card's sender, George, wrote, "I arrived in Texline about 4:15 a.m." George noted that he arrived sleepy and with a headache and commented, "My, isn't this a fine day, make me feel like good."

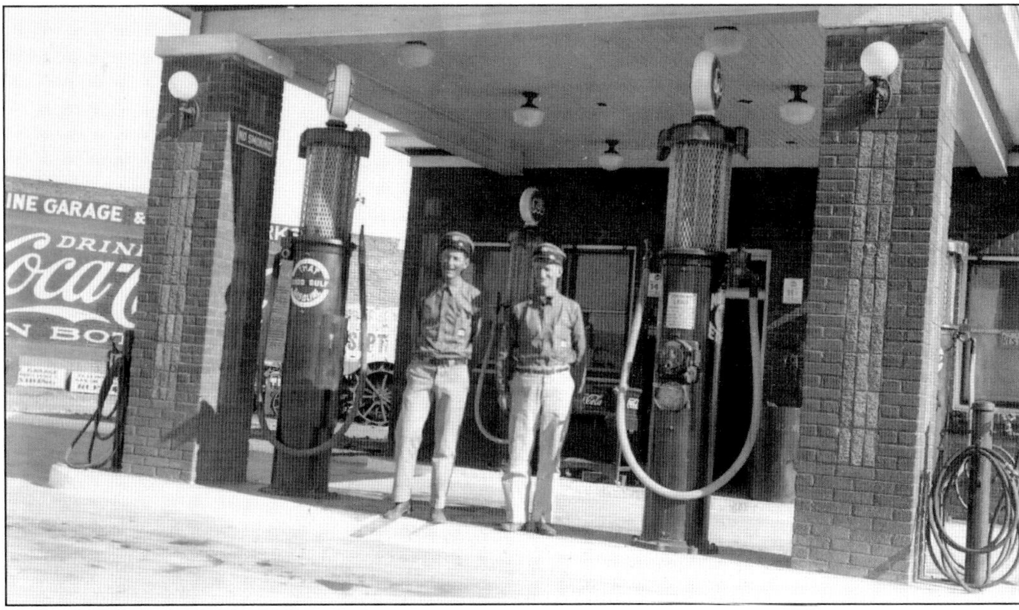

One of Texline's first gas stations was the Gulf service station, seen here in 1940. As seen at many other Dallam County businesses, Coca-Cola has an advertisement in the background here. W.S. "Bill" Wilson and C.F. Wilson are seen here in their uniforms by Autry's Studio in Dalhart. A sign on the building shows the price of gas as 11¢.

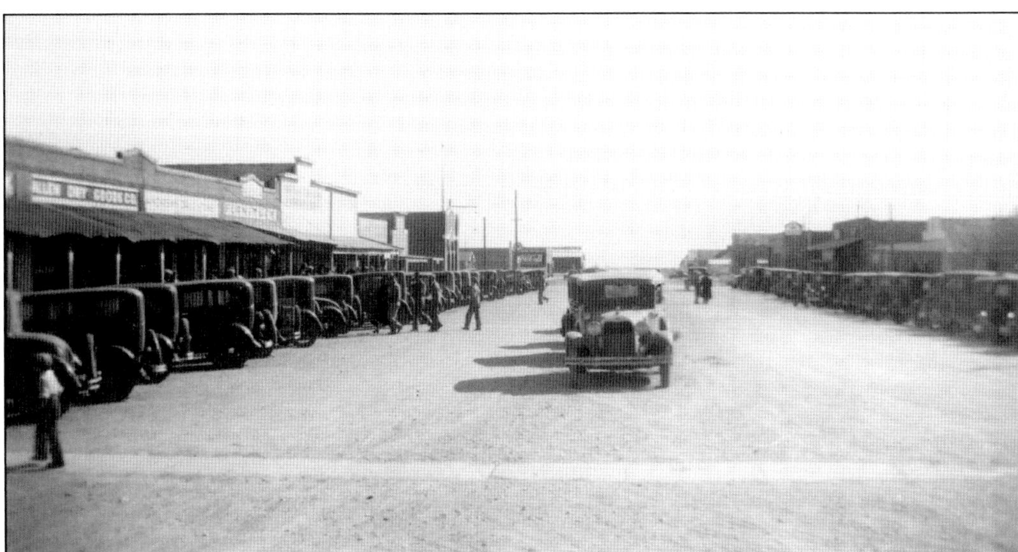

This image shows Texline's downtown scene in the 1920s with vehicles that line the street and appear eerily similar to one another. When the railroad closed its shops in 1923, the population in Texline dropped significantly, and by 1940, it was just 385. In the 1980s, 100 years after its establishment, Texline had a population of approximately 477. Today, Texline and the surrounding area have approximately 500 residents.

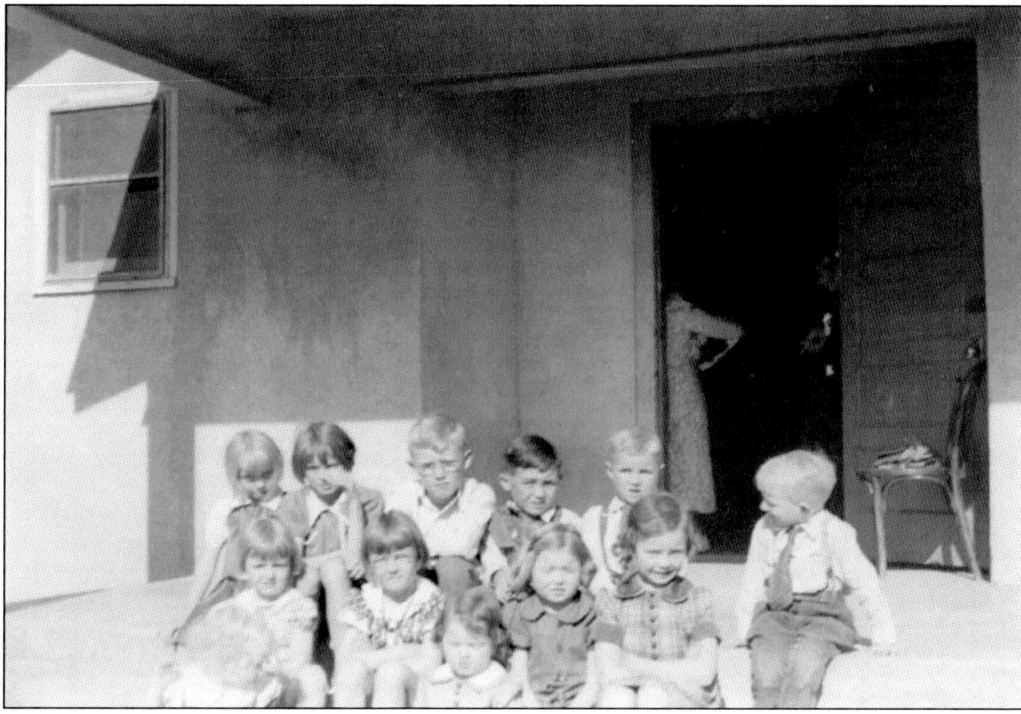

The community of Wilco is about 14 miles due east of Dalhart on Farm Road 2577 and Farm Road 296. Wilco sits in the far northeast corner of Hartley County and was founded in 1909 by James Edward Wilson and Frank B. Wilson, brothers from Effingham, Kansas. The brothers were ranchers and land developers. Wilco had a mercantile store and a combination school and church near the Wilson Ranch headquarters. The brothers laid out a park and planted trees and were successful in selling several town lots. When plans to run the railroad tracks from Enid, Ochiltree, and Western Railroad Line through Wilco fell through, growth ceased. By the 1940s, only the schoolhouse remained. (Courtesy of Martha Hurtt Coble.)

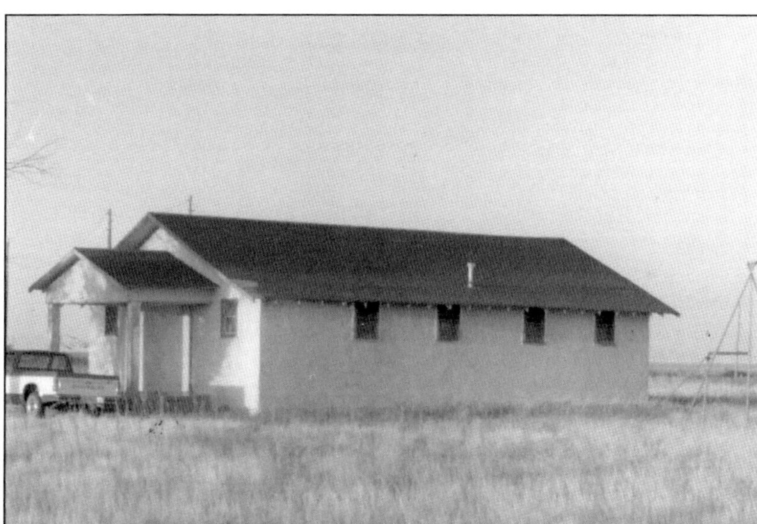

The Wilco School was built in 1920 for the children of the Wilco community. The building was often used for community events. The old schoolhouse in Wilco sits abandoned next to the C.R. Webb farm, also abandoned. (Photograph courtesy of the XIT Museum in Dalhart.)

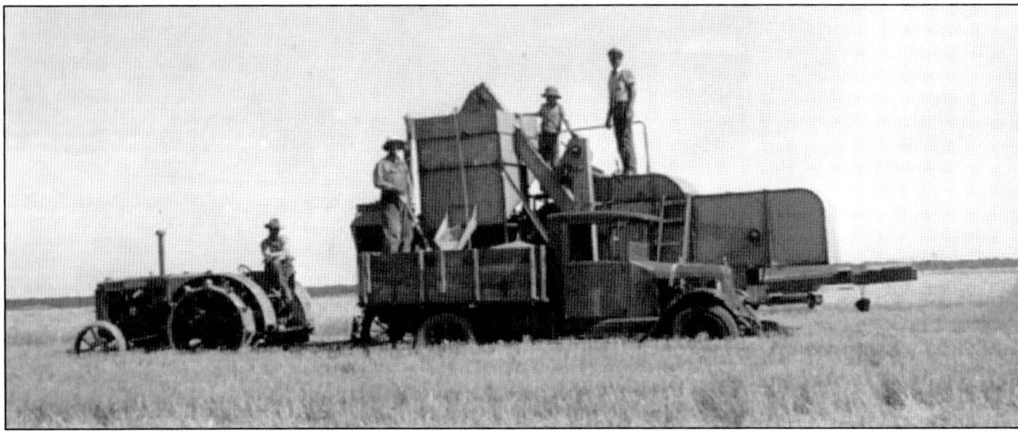

Another family that settled in Wilco in 1930 farmed as well. C.R. and Gertrude Webb arrived with their daughter, Laura, and her husband, William Edgar Hurtt Sr. The Hurtts had three children, William Edgar Jr., Mary, and Martha. Martha, who now resides in Dalhart, recalls that the Wilco School was only used for community events. She attended school in Hartley through the seventh grade. (Courtesy of Martha Hurtt Coble.)

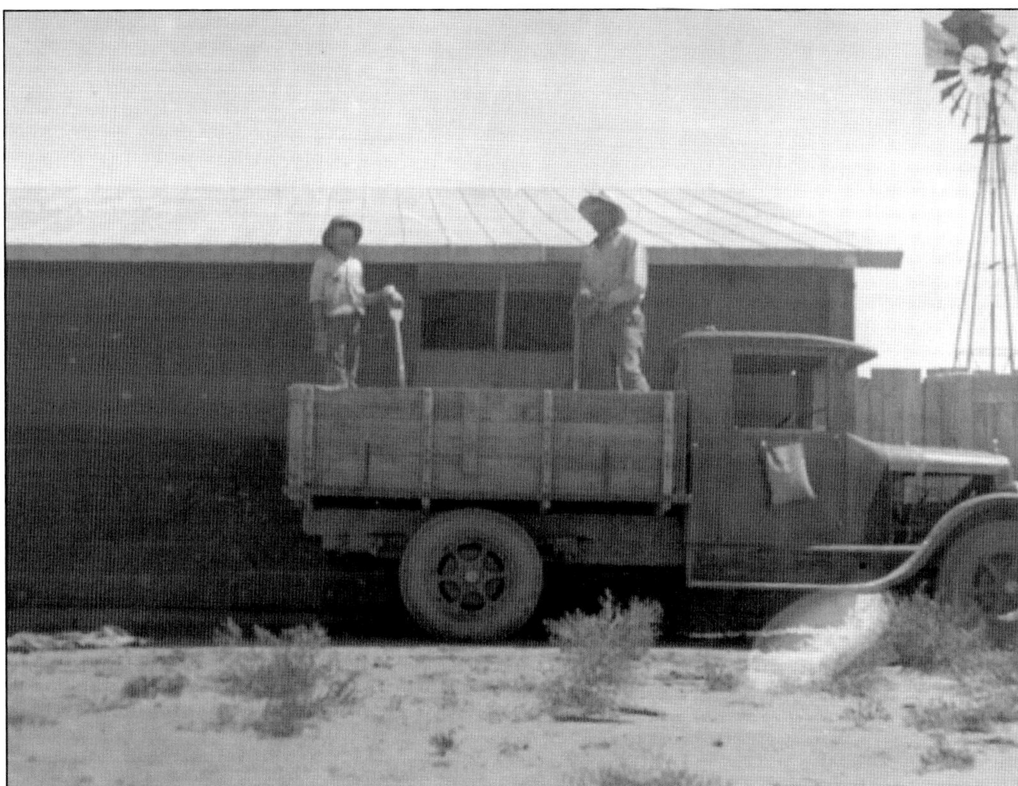

The Webb and Hurtt families farmed in Wilco until William Sr.'s untimely death in 1945 at the age of 45. Laura and her two daughters, Mary and Martha, moved into Dalhart when Martha was in the eighth grade. She transferred from the Hartley School to Dalhart and graduated from Dalhart High School in 1952. Martha married Milton Coble in 1953. Like her own father, Martha's husband died unexpectedly at a young age in 1973. (Courtesy of Martha Hurtt Coble.)

Eight

Lake Rita Blanca

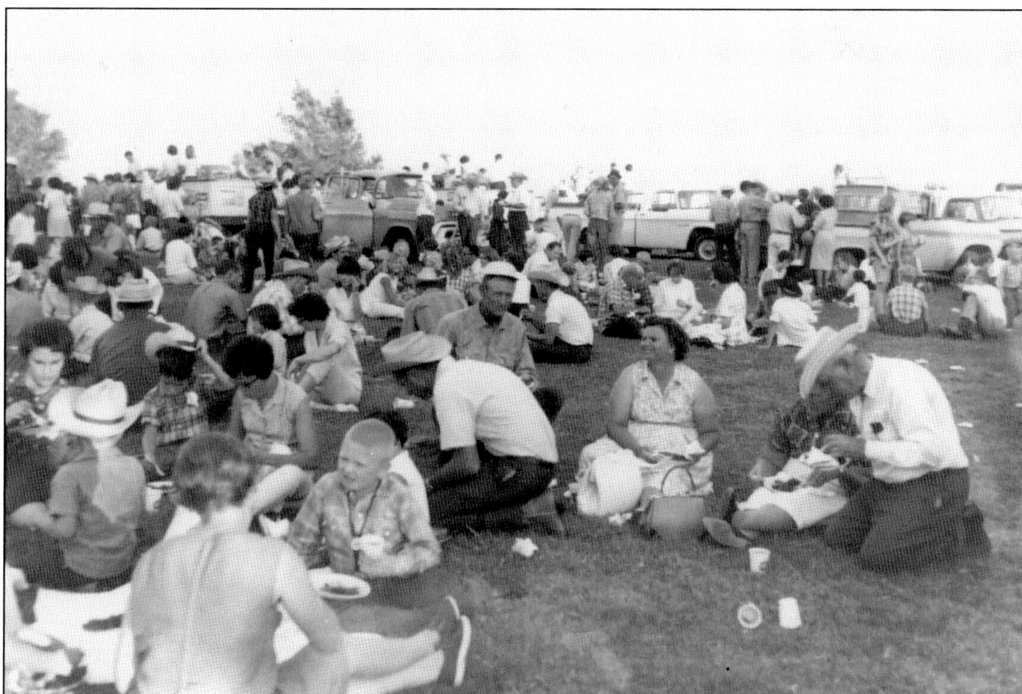

Just south of Dalhart sits the Rita Blanca Canyon and Lake Rita Blanca State Park, a 1,668-acre park that now includes more than eight miles of walking and hiking trials. The park not only provides a place for fun and recreation, but it has become the second-most important wintering area for migratory birds in the United States. An estimated 100,000 geese make the Lake Rita Blanca area their home during the winter months, and their characteristic squawk signals the onset of the winter season. The park is the northernmost park in the state of Texas, and since August 2002, it has been maintained by the City of Dalhart. In this photograph, area residents enjoy a barbecue out at the lake during the 1950 XIT Rodeo and Reunion.

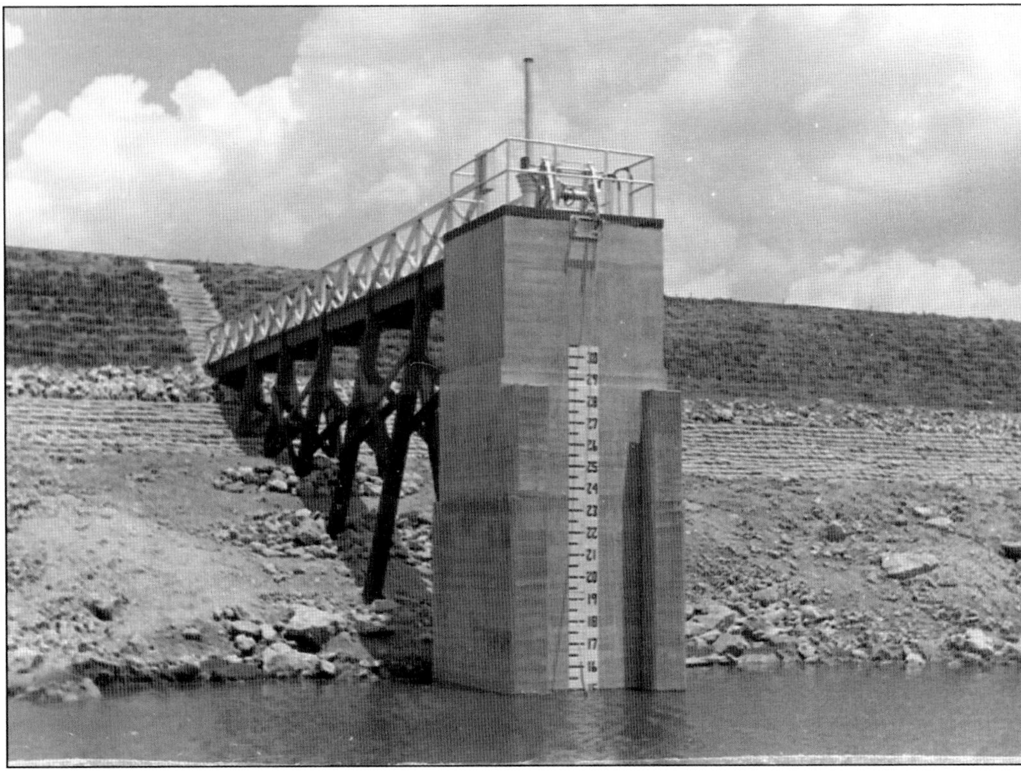

The tower at Lake Rita Blanca still stands today, but the walkway was taken down many years ago. In this photograph, the water level is at 15 feet. Today, in this same location, the water level is between three and five feet, making the tower look much bigger.

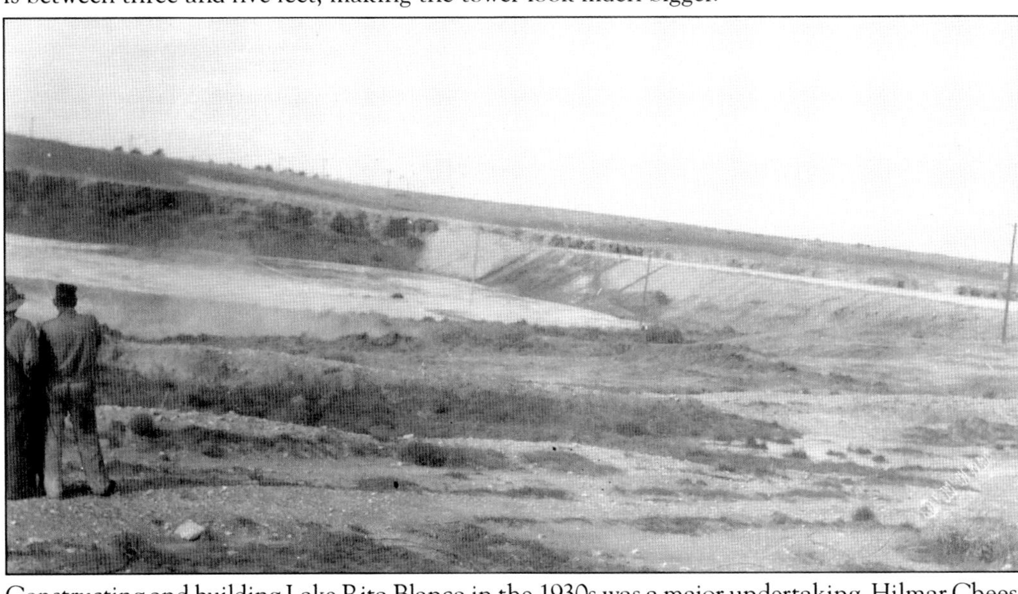

Constructing and building Lake Rita Blanca in the 1930s was a major undertaking. Hilmar Cheese Company, located in Dalhart, provided the funds for trail materials to lengthen the trails from 3.5 miles to 5 miles in 2009. A 2010 project further extended the walking and biking trails at the lake from 5 miles to 8.5 miles.

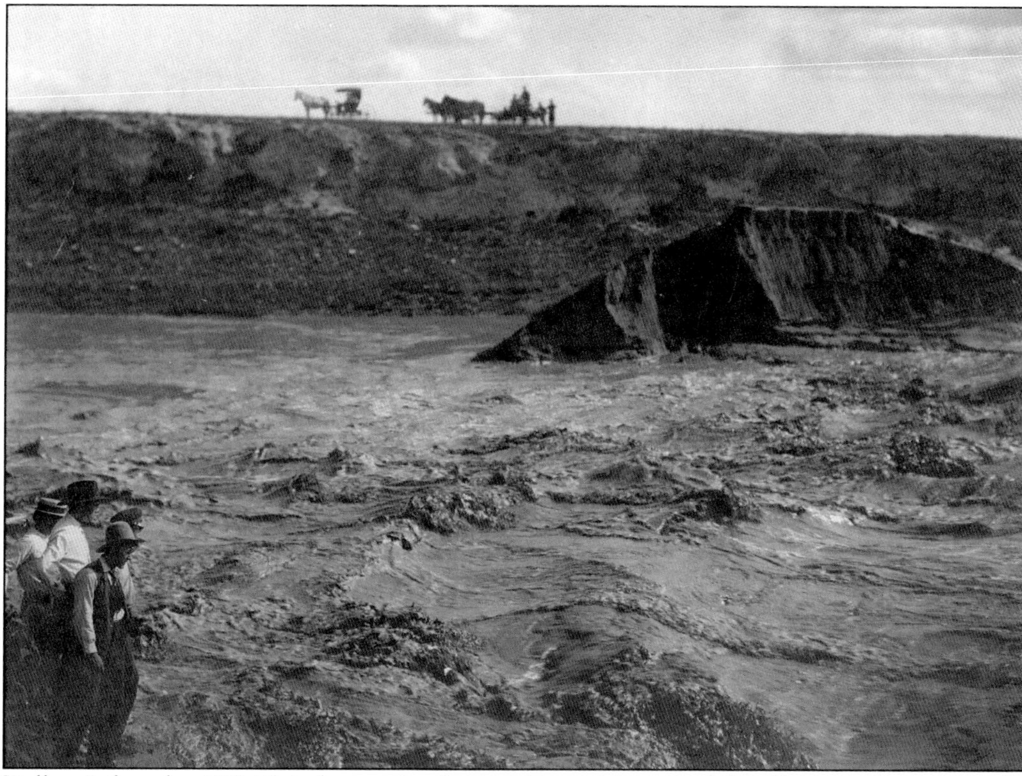

Dalhart's founder, W.J. Blair, began the dam project to make the lake. He moved his zoo to the lake, where he also kept a herd of buffalo. He had great expectations for the lake area, envisioning a tram that would take people from the lake to a picnic area, but the dam was washed out in 1905 in an unprecedented flood. After the dam washed out, much of the interest in maintaining it ended. Another big rain filled the lake within a few days. The *Dalhart Texan* editor Albert Law reported on September 1, 1934, "The rain will fill the lake by nightfall."

Lake Rita Blanca means "Little White River," a name given by the Spanish in the 1800s. The park has two playgrounds and a fishing pond. One playground has a rock-climbing wall for the adventurer. Campers may stay in the park overnight for a nominal fee. Many area residents regularly hike down into the canyon surrounding the lake for a nature walk.

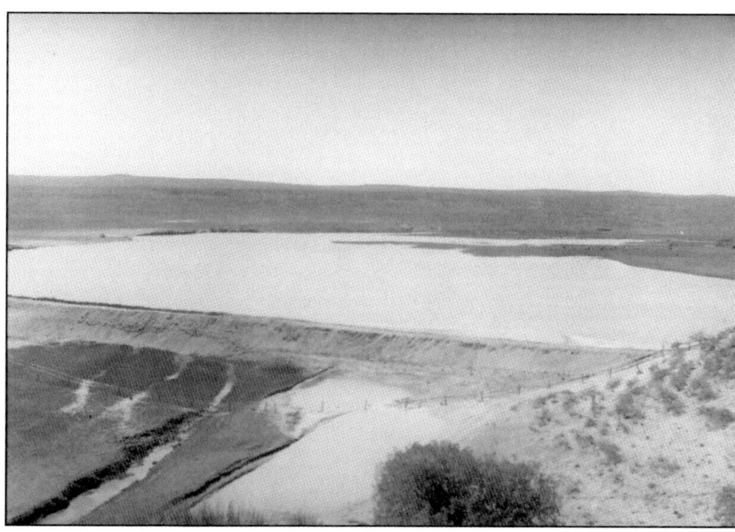

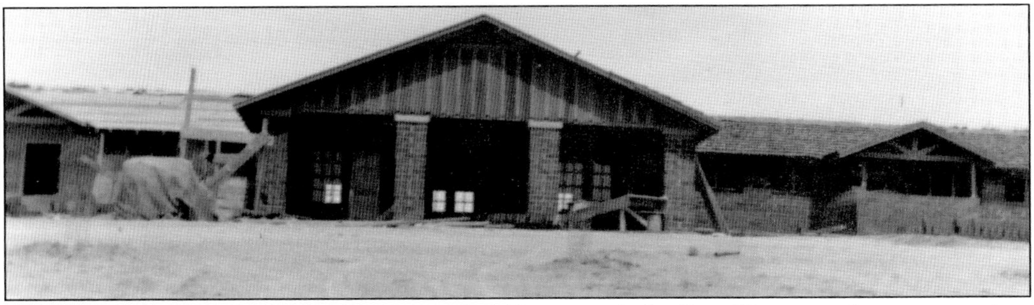

This photograph shows the bathhouse and clubhouse at Lake Rita Blanca under construction. Many improvements to the park have been made since its inception in 1903. A large pavilion is available for community activities and private use and is a great spot for enjoying wildlife. In the evenings, the parking lot at the pavilion is an excellent place to view the amazing sunsets of the Texas Panhandle.

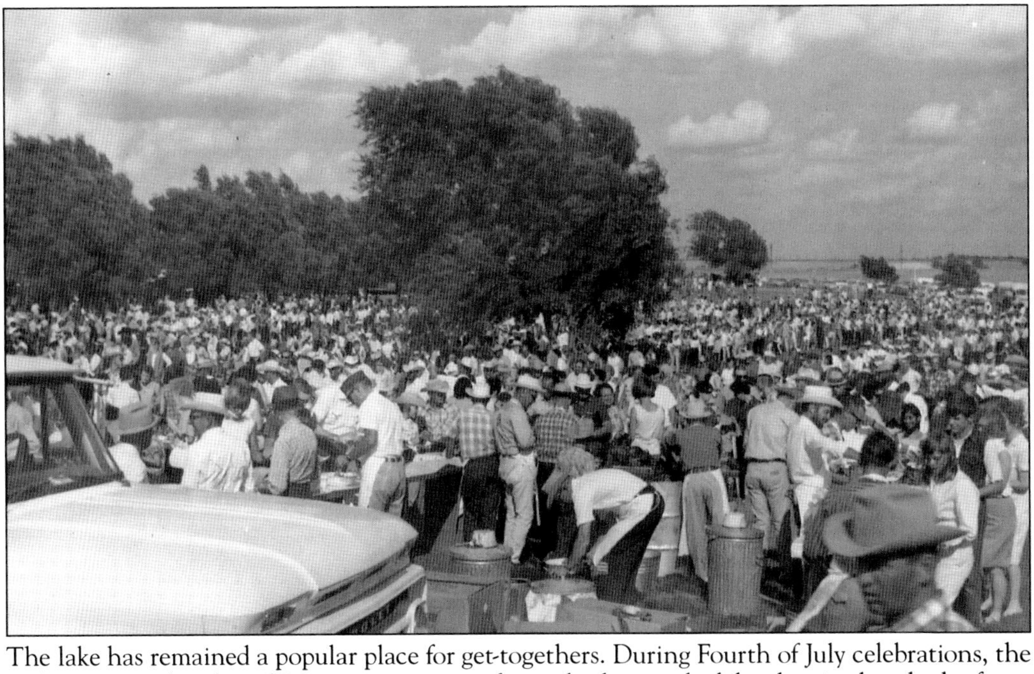

The lake has remained a popular place for get-togethers. During Fourth of July celebrations, the Dalhart Area Chamber of Commerce puts on a fireworks show at the lake, drawing hundreds of area residents. At one time, a picnic and carnival lasted all day long before the fireworks were lit.

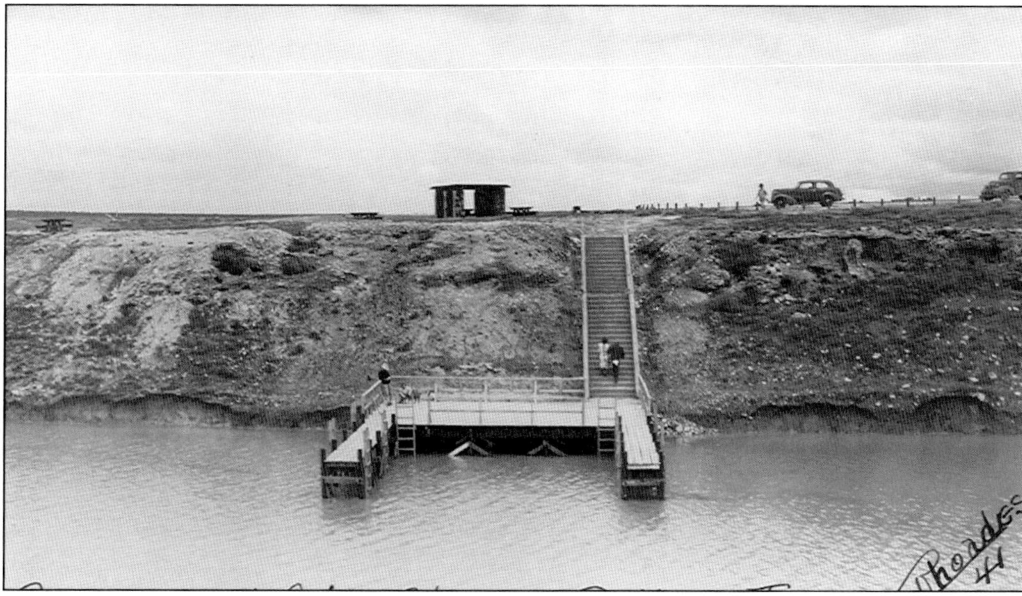

When the lake was first created, a dam helped to fill it to capacity. In the early years, area residents enjoyed all sorts of water sports, including skiing, fishing, swimming, and even ice-skating in the winter. The lake included a boat dock and boat ramp, now gone due to the lake's low water level. Pictured is the boat dock at Lake Rita Blanca in 1941.

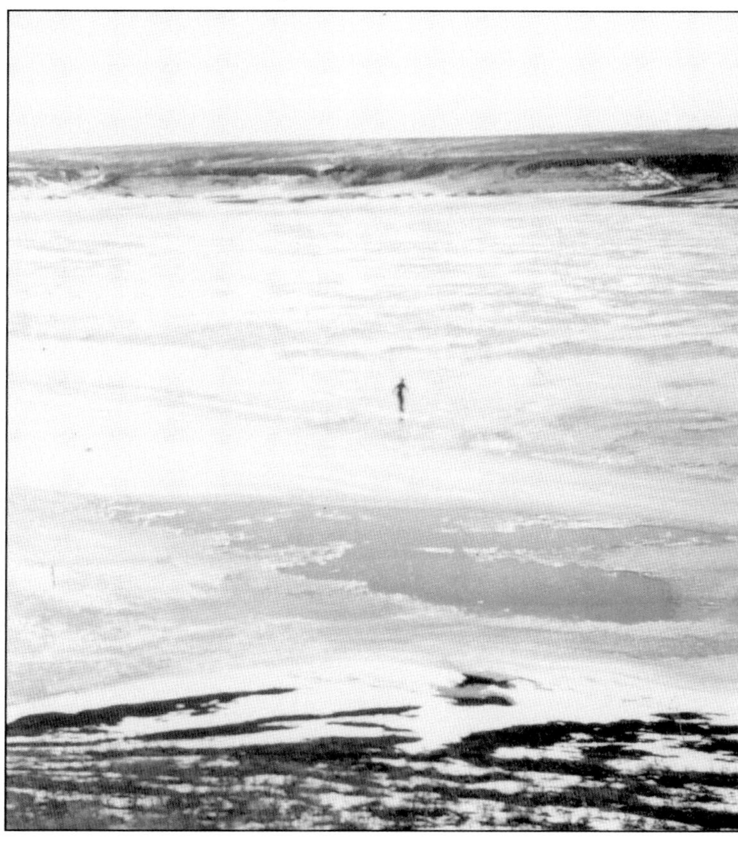

With temperatures in the Texas Panhandle dipping below freezing during winter, ice on the lake was common and became another source for entertainment. The temperature does not often stay below freezing for more than a couple of days in a row, so the ice building enough for this lone skater to enjoy in January 1947 was a rarity.

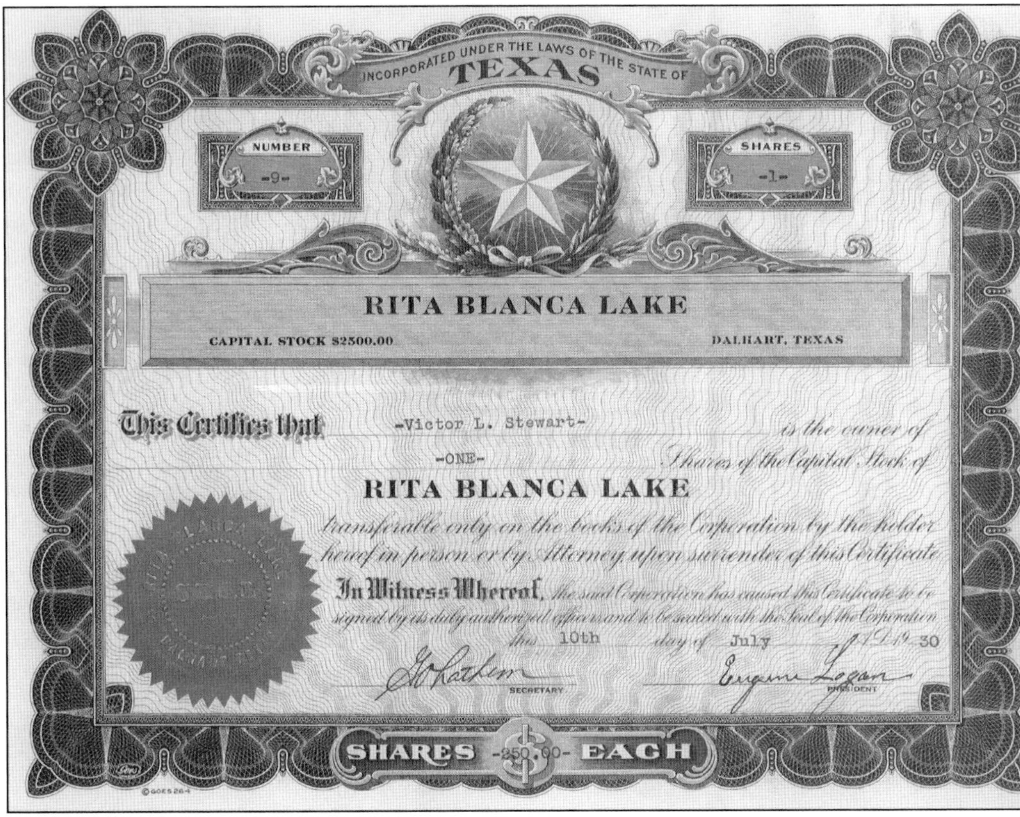

INCORPORATED UNDER THE LAWS OF THE STATE OF TEXAS

NUMBER -9-

SHARES -1-

RITA BLANCA LAKE

CAPITAL STOCK $2500.00

DALHART, TEXAS

This Certifies that -Victor L. Stewart- is the owner of -ONE- Shares of the Capital Stock of

RITA BLANCA LAKE

transferable only on the books of the Corporation by the holder hereof in person or by Attorney upon surrender of this Certificate

In Witness Whereof, the said Corporation has caused this Certificate to be signed by its duly authorized officers and to be sealed with the Seal of the Corporation this 10th day of July A.D. 1930

SECRETARY

PRESIDENT

SHARES -250.00- EACH

Stock in the lake was sold and the certificate shown here was granted to Victor L. Steward on July 10, 1930. The capital share of stock in Lake Rita Blanca had a value of $25,000. The certificate was signed by President Eugene Logan.

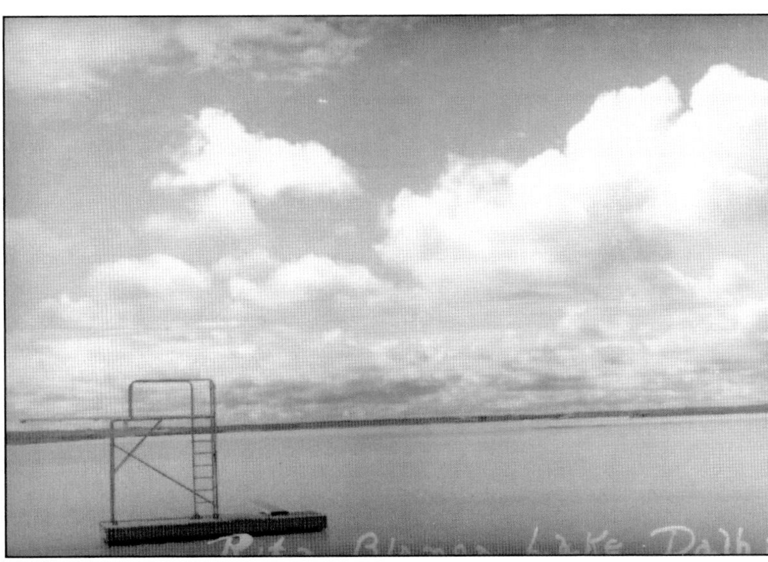

The diving platform at Lake Rita Blanca is long gone due to the low level of the water, but it once was a-bustle with divers enjoying a day of swimming in the lake. Area residents who remember what the lake was once like recall that a day at the lake including picnicking and swimming.

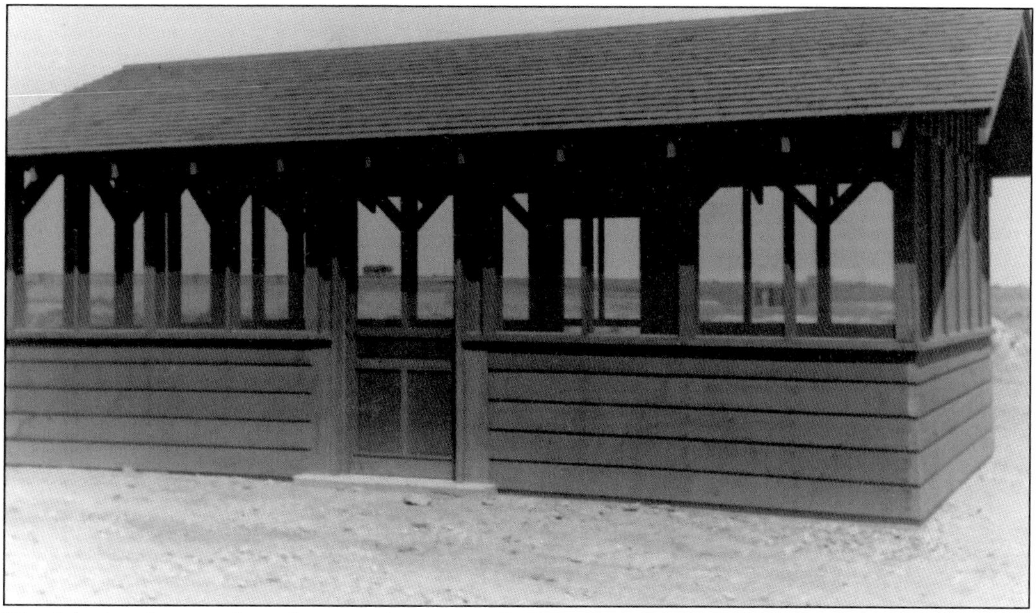

The lake has been a place for picnicking since Dalhart became settled. The pavilion shown here was a place to relax, eat a meal, and enjoy fellowship with friends and family. The pavilion at the lake today seats more than 100 people and is often used for family reunions, company picnics, school picnics, and even wedding receptions.

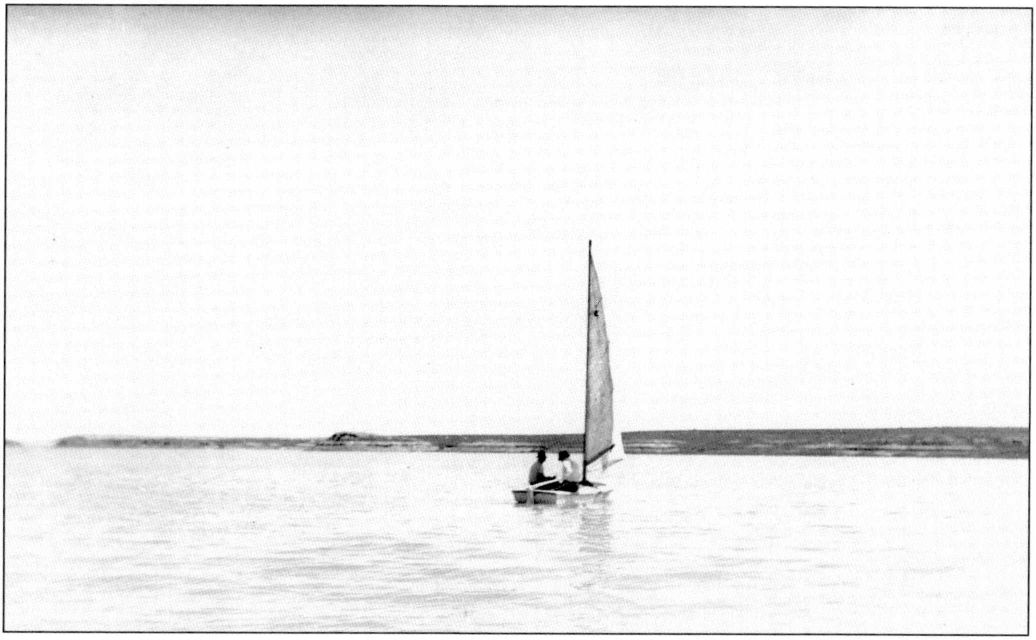

Boaters are shown here enjoying a day of sailing on Lake Rita Blanca. Due to the low water level, boats are no longer allowed on the lake. The water is so shallow that algae easily grows, which prohibits fish from surviving. The lake is home to 100,000 geese each winter, but no fish.

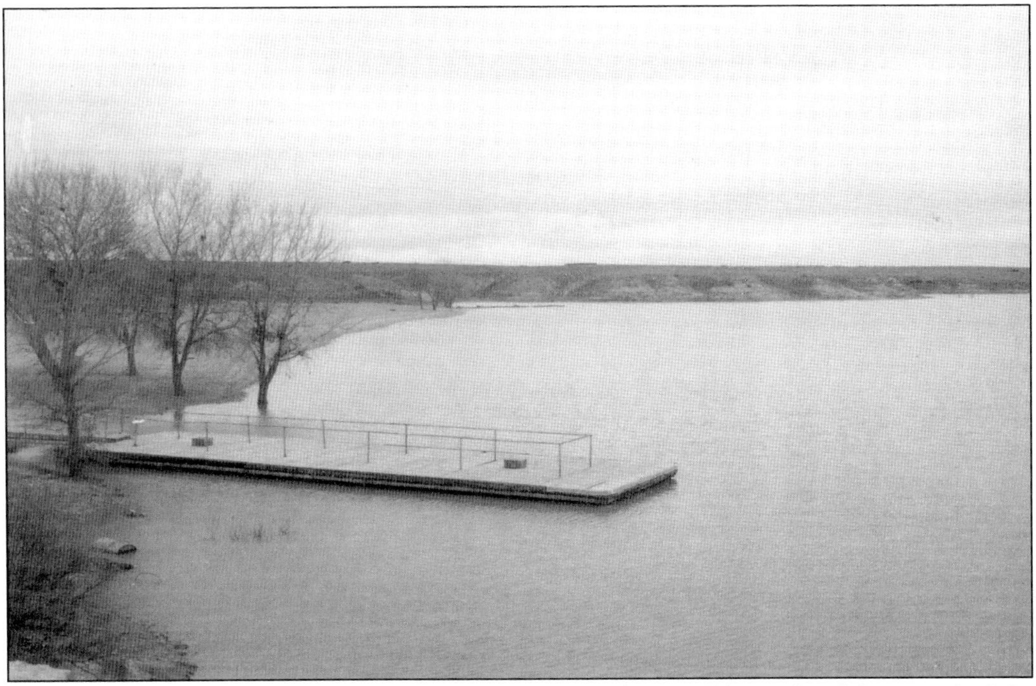

People still enjoy the catch-and-release fishing pond at Lake Rita Blanca, but fishing in the lake itself is futile. The pond has a small fishing dock and the water remains clear and is very pure, being fed from an underground stream. Pictured here is the fishing dock at Lake Rita Blanca.

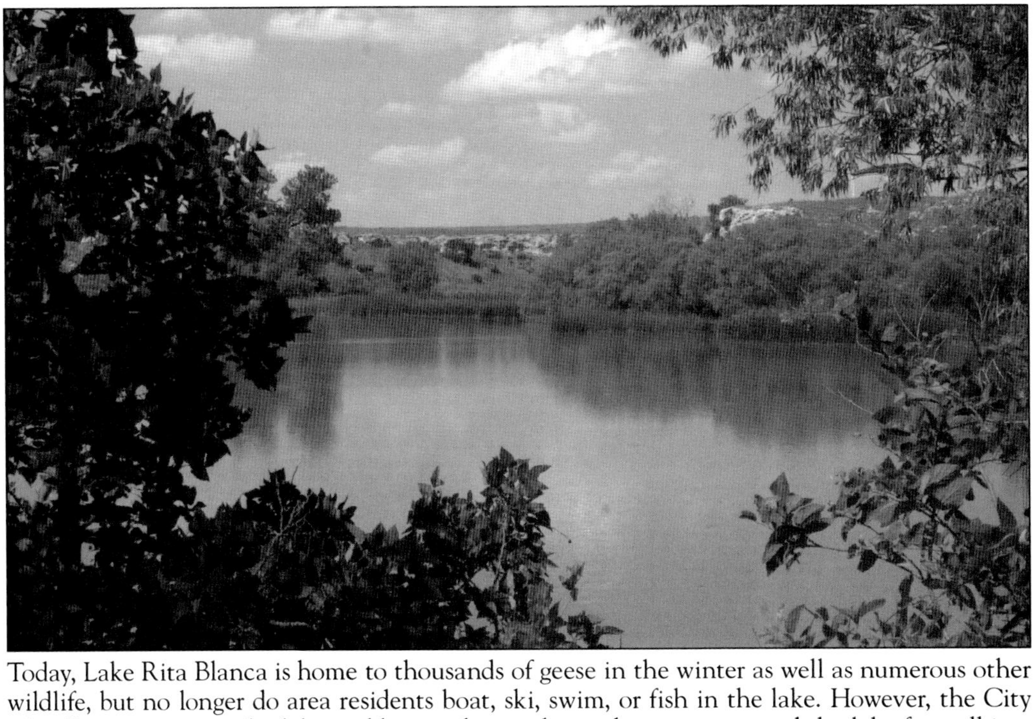

Today, Lake Rita Blanca is home to thousands of geese in the winter as well as numerous other wildlife, but no longer do area residents boat, ski, swim, or fish in the lake. However, the City of Dalhart maintains the lake and has made a pathway that wraps around the lake for walking, hiking, and enjoying the lake's beauty. (Courtesy of Robin Scott.)

Nine

Dalhart Army Air Base

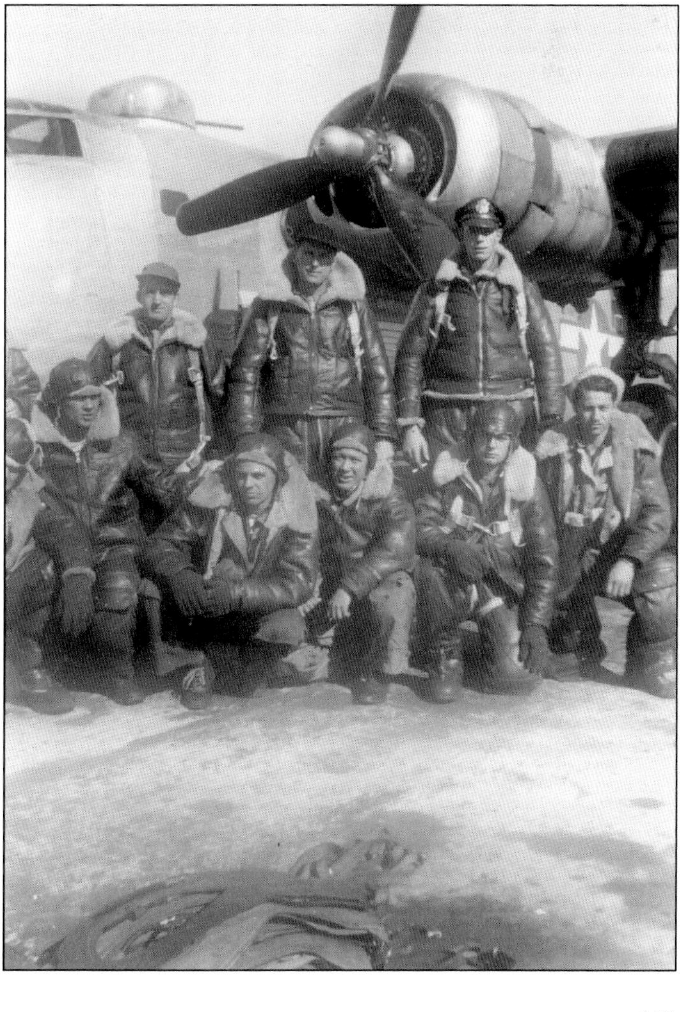

During World War II, many pilots began their training in Dalhart at the 3,000-acre Dalhart Army Air Field. Originally used to train glider pilots, the field was later home to B-17 and B-29 bombers. The base remained open from 1942 through 1946. After the war, the airfield was acquired by the City of Dalhart and is now the Dalhart Municipal Airport. The runway can handle anything from a single-engine airplane to a large jet, and is regularly used by the Hilmar Cheese Company to land its private jet in Dalhart. (Courtesy of the XIT Museum and Mary Pat Powers.)

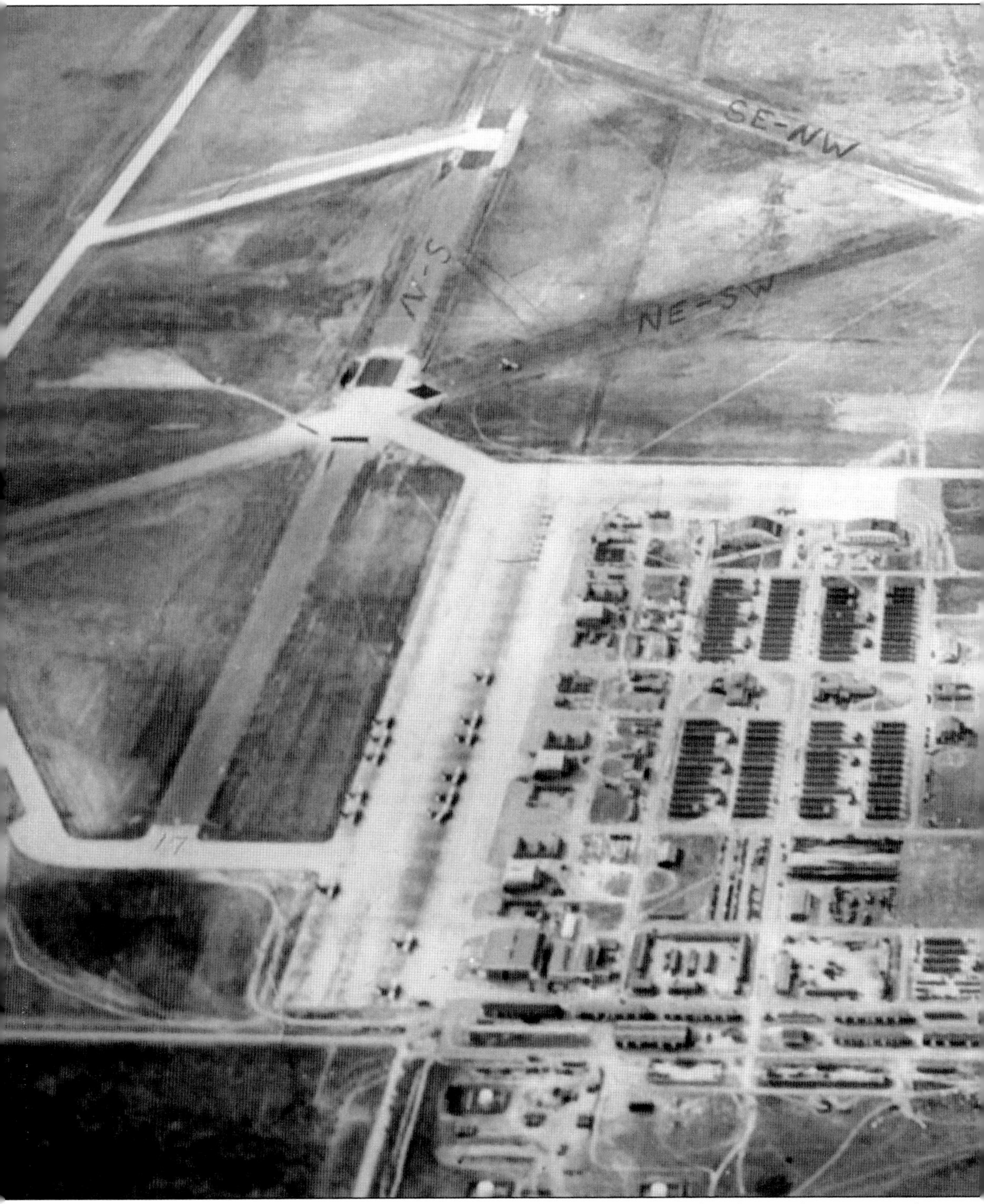

Dalhart Army Air Field, two miles southwest of Dalhart, was activated in September 1942, with an airfield and two auxiliary fields that were added later. Though originally intended for glider training, the field came to be used for B-17 and B-29 training and for fighter planes to be used

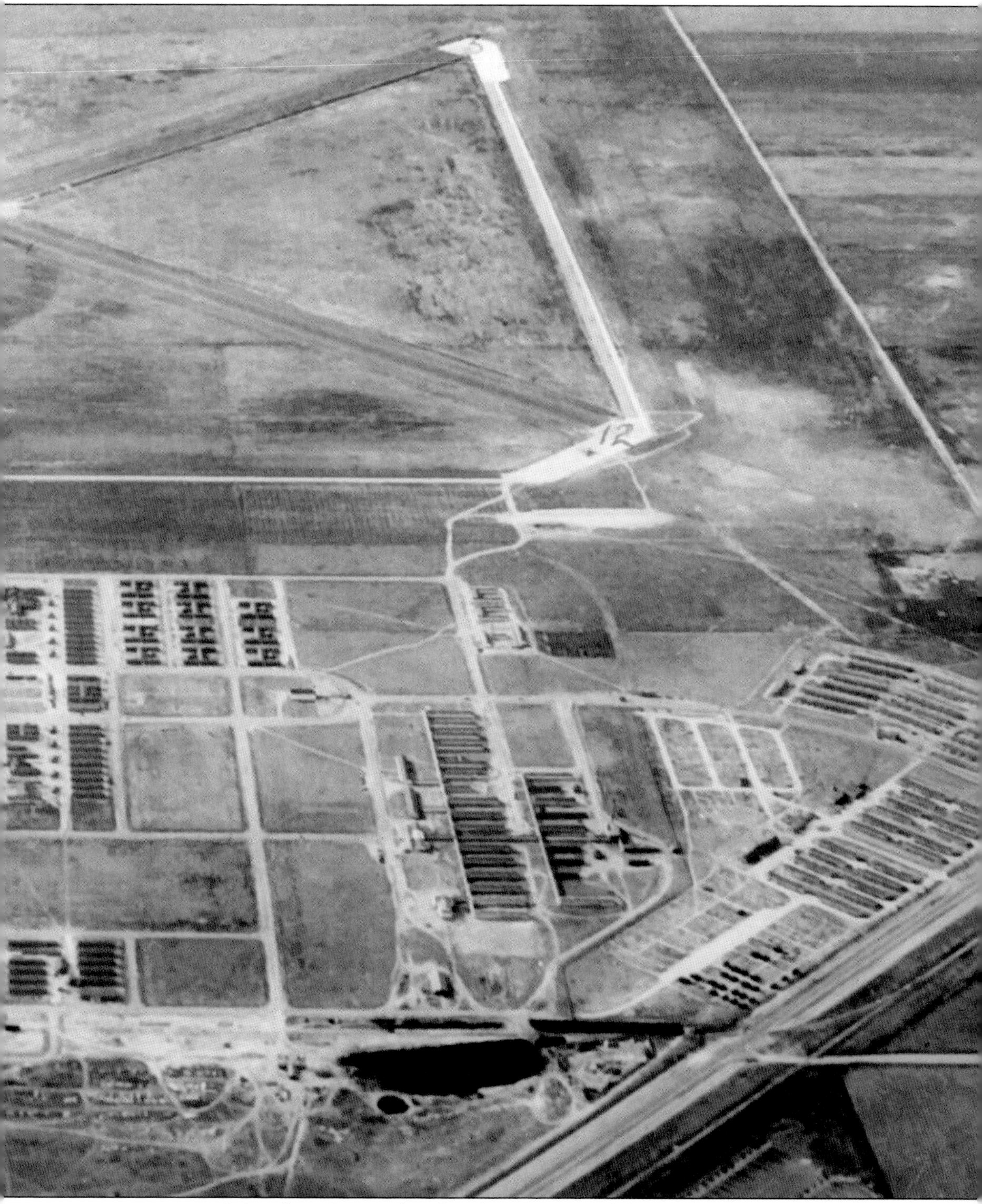

in conjunction with bombers. It was closed early in 1946, and the property went to the city of Dalhart. Since that time, several of the remaining buildings have been used as the Dalhart Municipal Airport.

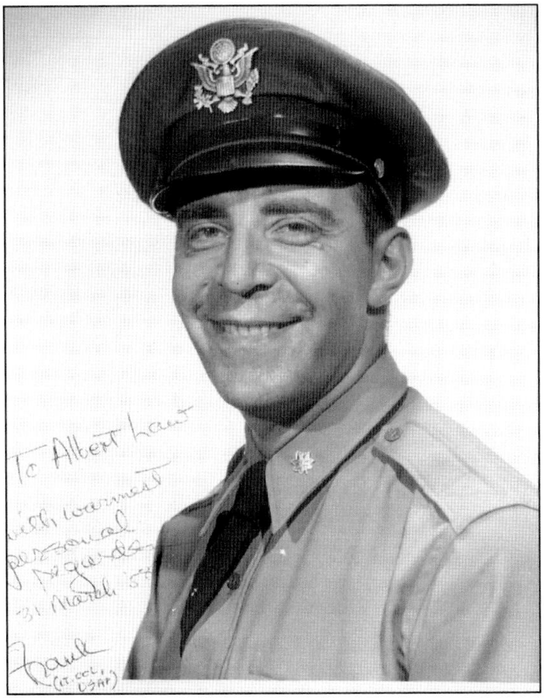

During his time as editor for the *Dalhart Texan*, Albert Law received many letters and photographs from members of the Dalhart community and abroad. This photograph to Albert Law from "Frank," was signed on March 31, 1958, "With warmest personal regards." (Courtesy of the XIT Museum and Zelda Beth Lang.)

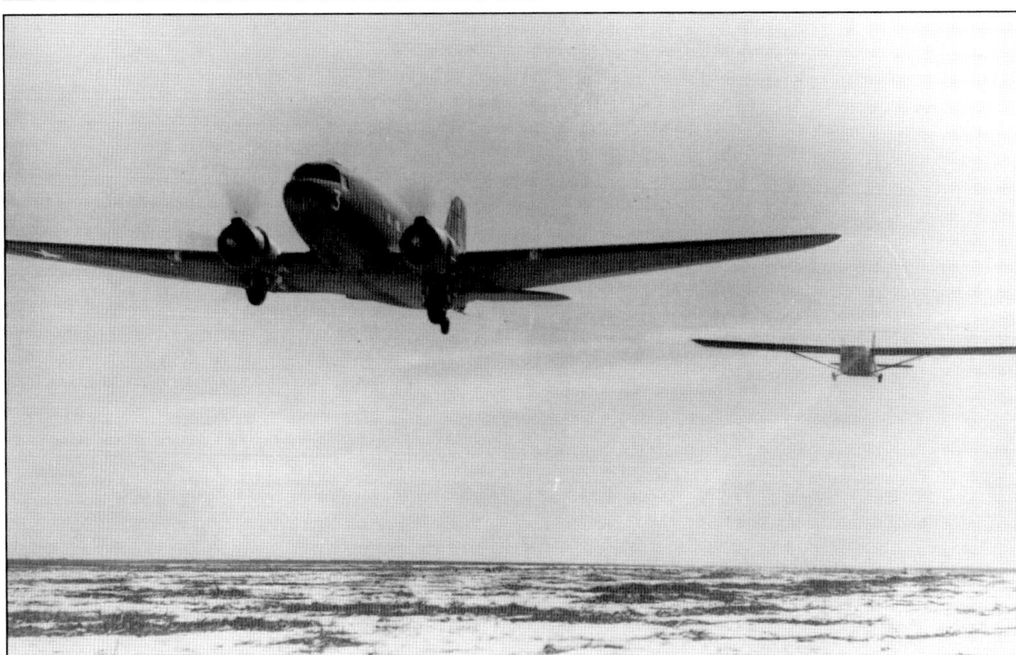

In a November 27, 2002, oral history interview with Nick Olson of the XIT Museum, Charles "Chuck" L. Harruff talked about the glider school and stated that when he first flew to Dalhart from Ohio, he had to follow the railroad as his only reference. He said that in order to figure out what town he was flying over, he would have to dive down and read the name off of the train station, then pull back up and go on to the next town. Harruff flew the C-47 planes that carried the gliders up and released them in flight.

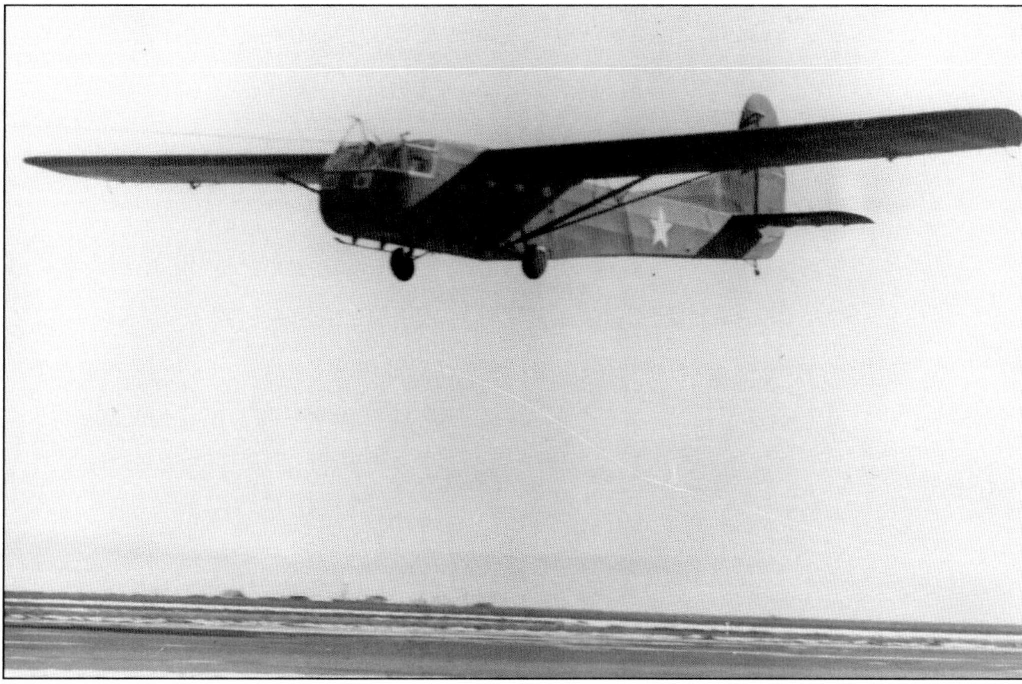

Chuck Harruff reported that gliders were used mainly at night so as not to be shot down by the enemy. The gliders would be towed by a C-47 until the glider pilot learned how to fly the glider. Once away from the air base, the C-47 pilot would cut the glider loose, and the pilot would fly the glider back for a landing. Once, Harruff took off during a bad dust storm. The receptacle on the tail end of his airplane held a long towrope to pull the gliders. On this, his first night flight, when he got only about 400 feet above the ground, the cable came off, and the glider crashed into a concrete building, killing all eight pilots aboard.

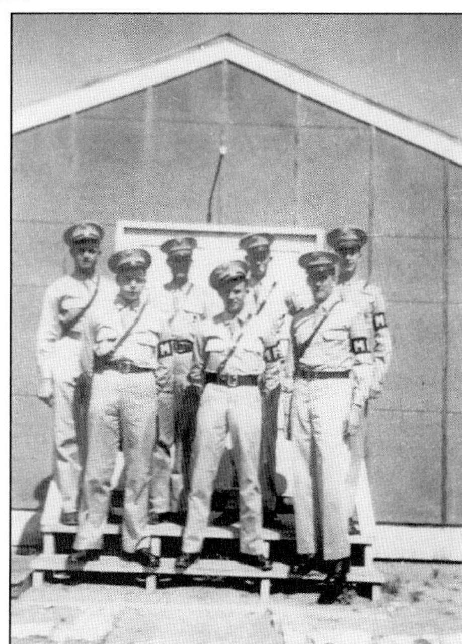

Members of the Military Police (MPs) gather for a photograph in front of the barracks at Dalhart's Army Air Base in 1943. The base had a variety of personnel, not just pilots. The MPs helped keep order and maintain the high level of security the base required.

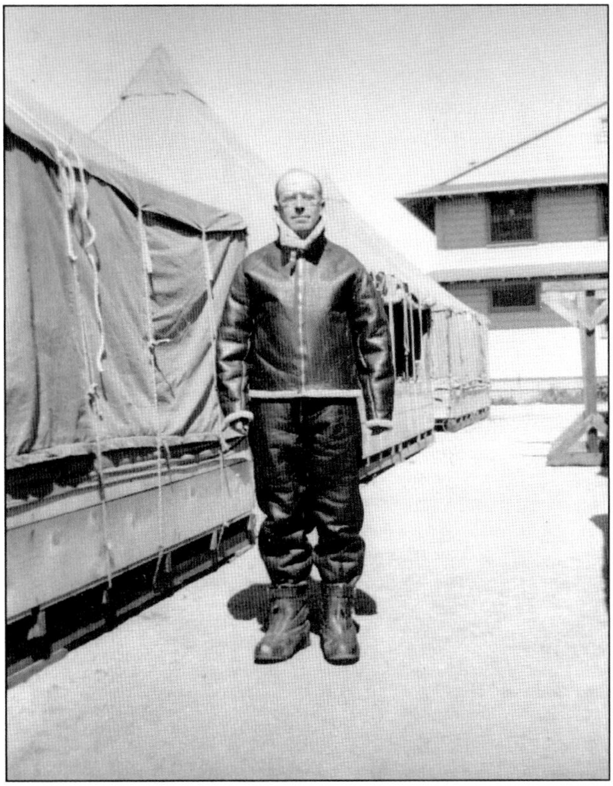

Personnel at the air base lived in chicken coops, garages, or anywhere they could find a spot. Many Dalhart residents took servicemen into their homes. Airmen wore sheepskin-lined clothing to bear the brunt of the cold experienced while flying. Lt. Fred Fleishmann sent this photograph to his sister and wrote, "Wish I could have had this sheepskin-lined suit and shoes to wear on the motorcycle. Boy am I hot in that picture!" Fleishmann was a bombardier for a bomber training in Dalhart. He and his crewmembers were killed when their plane crashed.

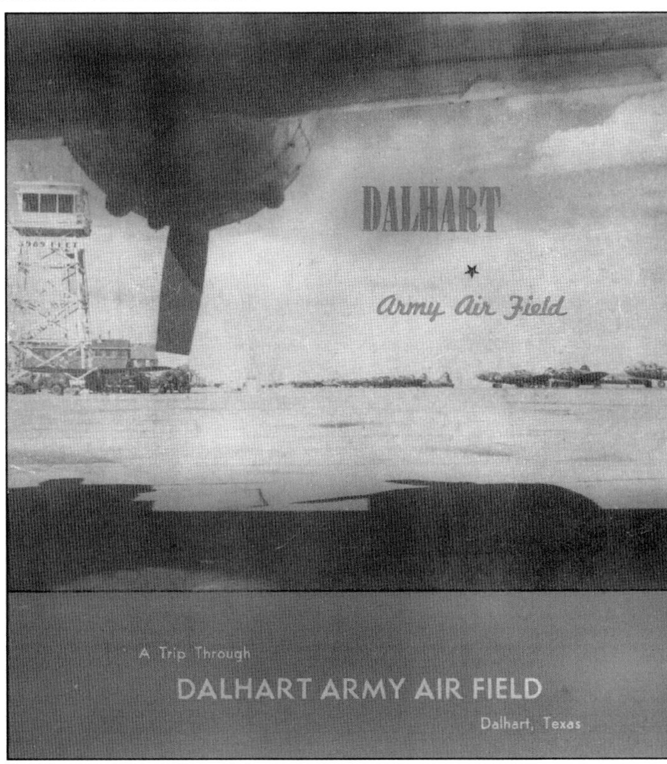

The Dalhart Army Air Field Public Relations Office published *Dalhart Army Air Field: A Trip Through Dalhart Army Air Field, Dalhart, Texas,* in 1942. The publication is a pictorial trip through the air base. The commanding officer of the base was Col. George E. Lovell Jr. In order for the glider school to make its home in Dalhart, residents had to vote on a $60,000 bond issue for the purchase of the 3,040 acres needed for the school. The book stated, "The mission of the base was to receive, organize, and process, and give ground training to such heavy groups and squadrons as will be necessary to the carrying out of the B-29 development program of the Second Air Force."

Ten

Thriving Businesses

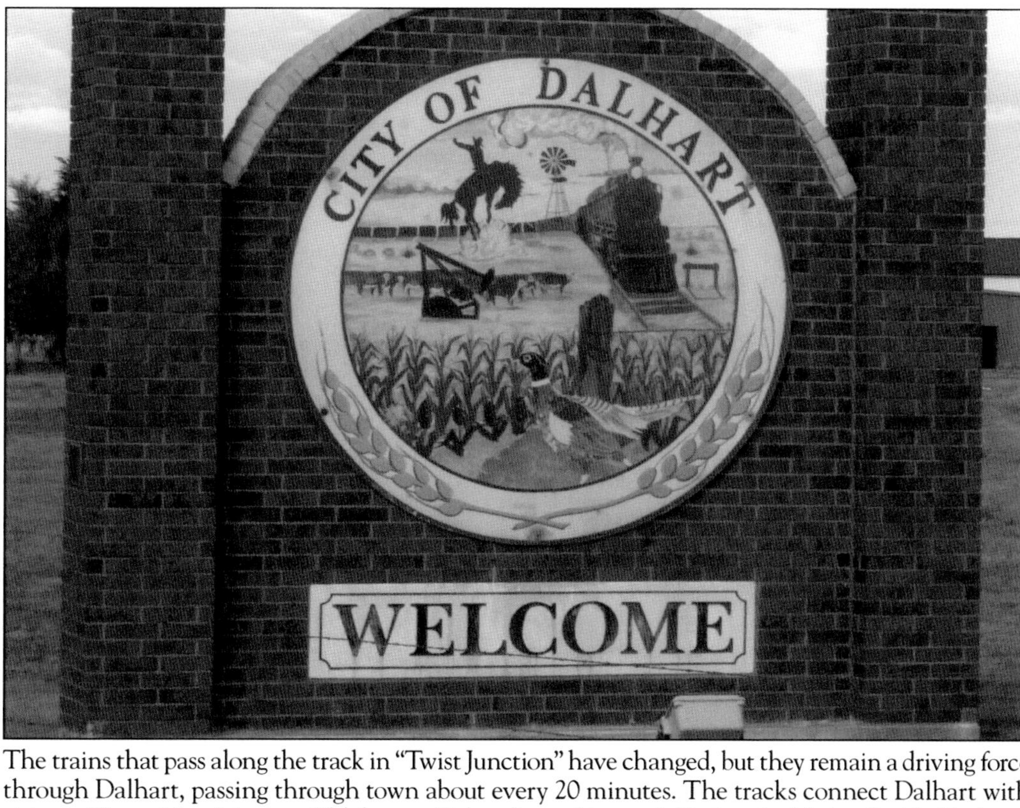

The trains that pass along the track in "Twist Junction" have changed, but they remain a driving force through Dalhart, passing through town about every 20 minutes. The tracks connect Dalhart with cities in Texas, New Mexico, Oklahoma, Colorado, and beyond. Today, the Union Pacific Railroad occupies the tracks that the Rock Island once dominated, and the Burlington Northern and Santa Fe has long since replaced the Fort Worth and Denver Railway. The two railroad companies continue as a driving force in Dalhart's economy. Regular stops in Dalhart are the feed elevators that store grain from local farms until they are shipped abroad. Many other businesses have made a name in Dalhart, some new and some that have stood the test of time. (Courtesy of Nick Olson.)

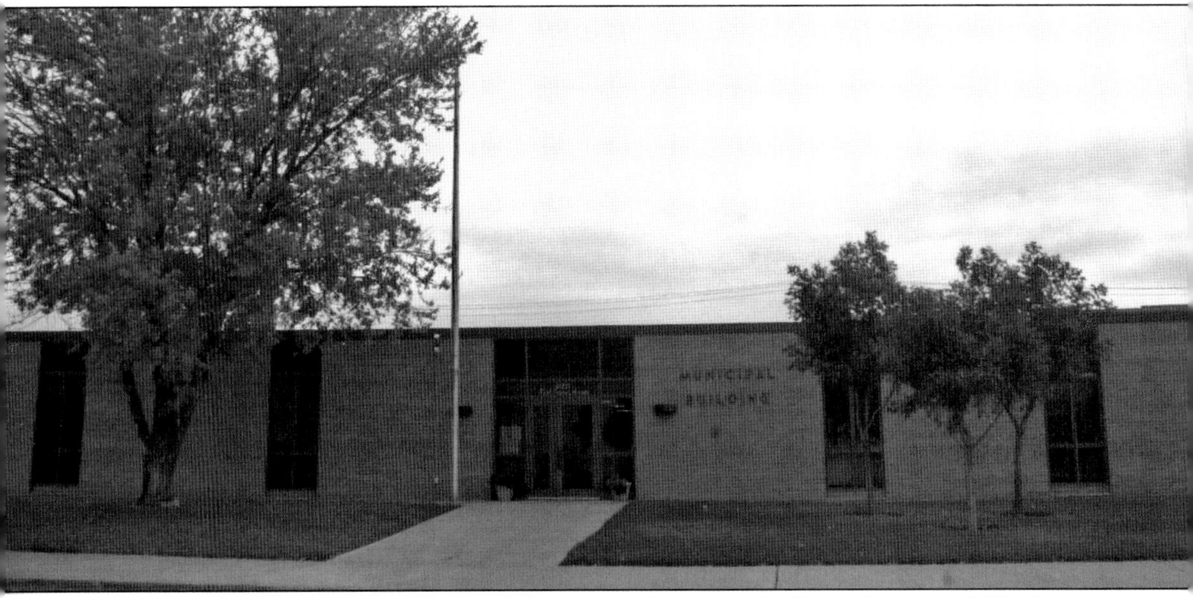

The City of Dalhart is one of Dalhart's largest employers, with 59 employees in 2010. Services that the city provides include water, sewage, street, sanitation, a municipal garage, city parks, Dalhart Memorial Cemetery, Lake Rita Blanca, the Rita Blanca Coliseum, a police department, fire department, animal control, city swimming pool, municipal airport, code enforcement, building inspection, and administration. In 2010, the goals that the city was working toward included infrastructure improvements, street paving, water line upgrades, and painting Dalhart's water towers. The Dalhart Economic Development Commission is a seven-member board that uses funds to improve quality of life, such as maintaining the city swimming pool and helping fund the library-expansion project. The city also administers 40 Celo Jenkins Scholarships each year and the Bonnie DeJarnett Scholarships, the Community Development Fund, and the Motel Occupancy Fund. The Motel Occupancy Fund, or "bed tax" helps to fund the XIT Museum each year as well as the Dalhart Area Chamber of Commerce and many other local endeavors. (Courtesy of Robin Scott.)

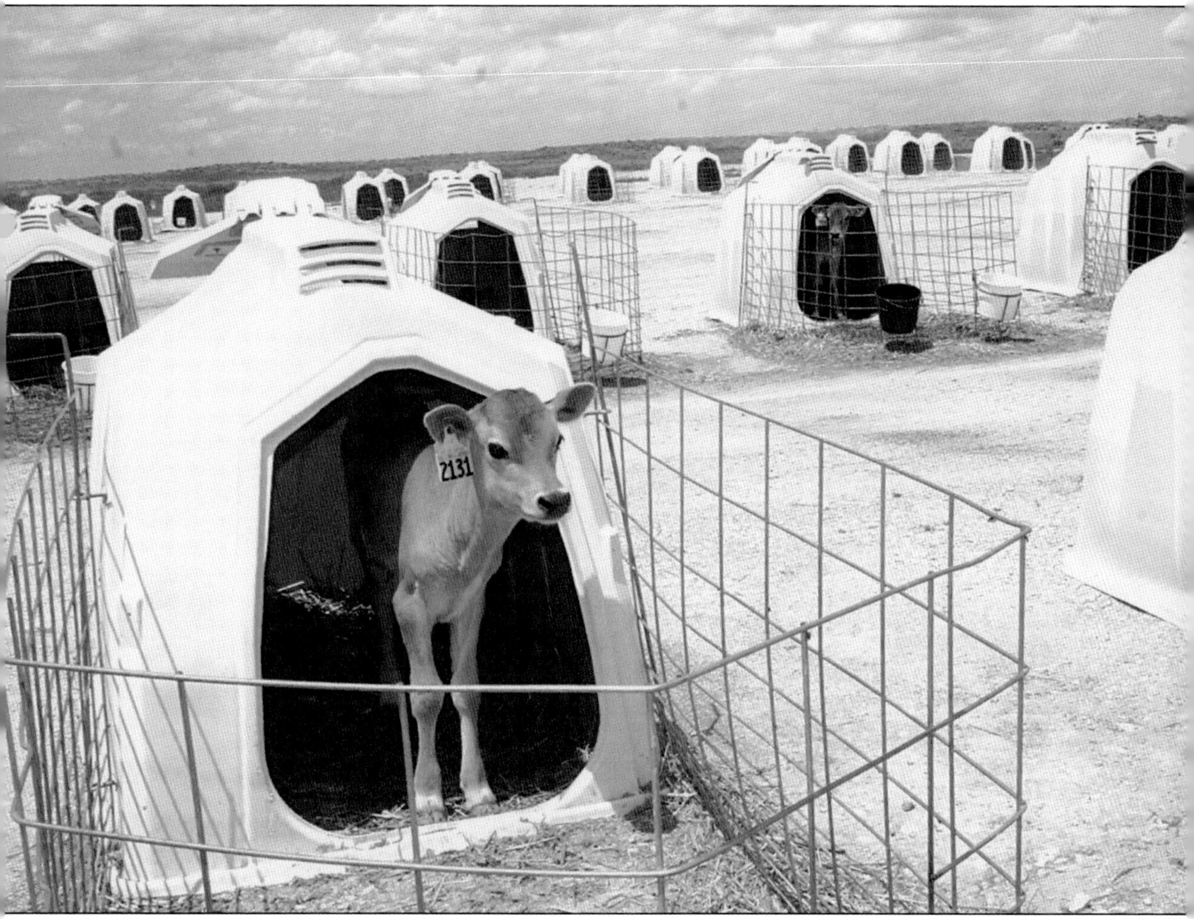

Full Circle Jerseys in Dalhart has proven that even the cows love Dalhart. The company began operations in October 2007 with Tom Mellema's vision to milk Jersey cows even before Hilmar Cheese thought about coming to Dalhart. The dairy milks 2,000 cows with 2,200 others on the premises. All of the cows milked at the dairy were also raised at the dairy and each cow averages 60 pounds of milk per day. Full Circle owner Seito Mellema has found a way to run the company more efficiently by growing all of the feed necessary to keep the cows fed. The Mellemas began farming in 1979, and Full Circle now has 26 employees. A 2010 expansion increased the milking capacity to 3,600 cows. (Courtesy of Robin Scott.)

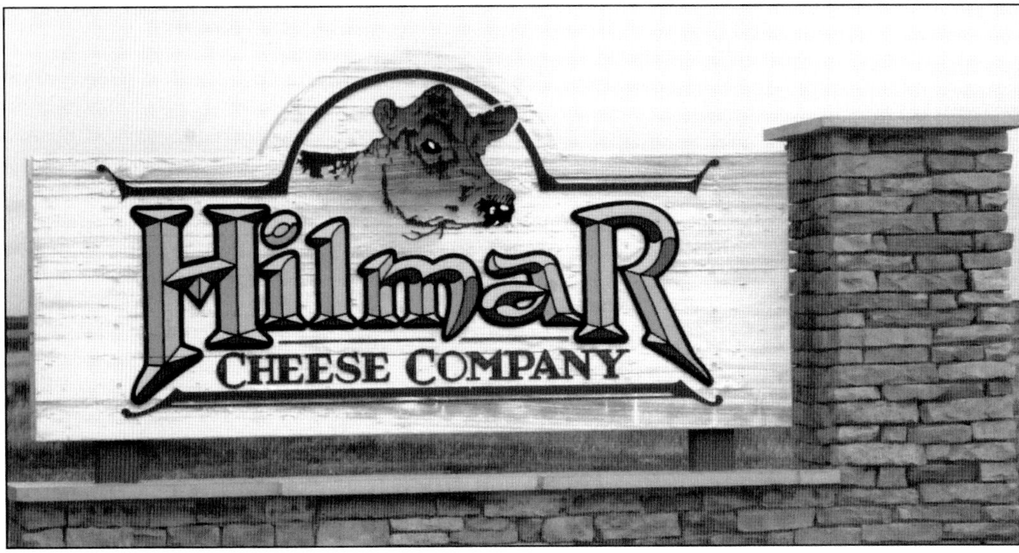

Founded in 1984 by 12 Central California dairy families who owned Jersey cows, Hilmar Cheese Company has grown to include a second manufacturing site in Dalhart. Hilmar Ingredients, created in 2004, is the company's whey protein and lactose products division. Still privately held, the total organization employs almost 1,000. The company is committed to continuous improvement and innovation with a mission to produce high quality products within a framework of environmental sustainability. In addition to caring for its customers and the environment, Hilmar Cheese Company is committed to improving the communities in which it operates through support for education, community activities, and food-bank programs. The benefit to the Dalhart area from the company is nearly immeasurable. One fun benefit is the cheese, which Hilmar regularly donates for community events. (Courtesy of Robin Scott.)

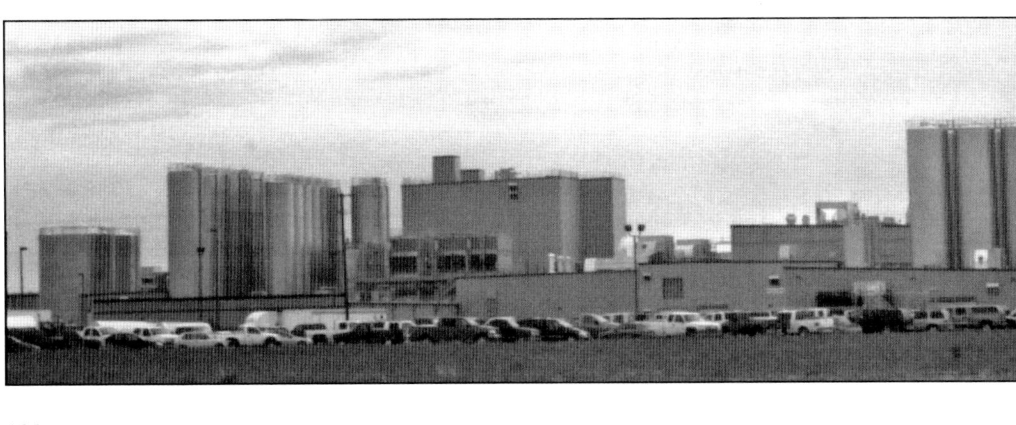

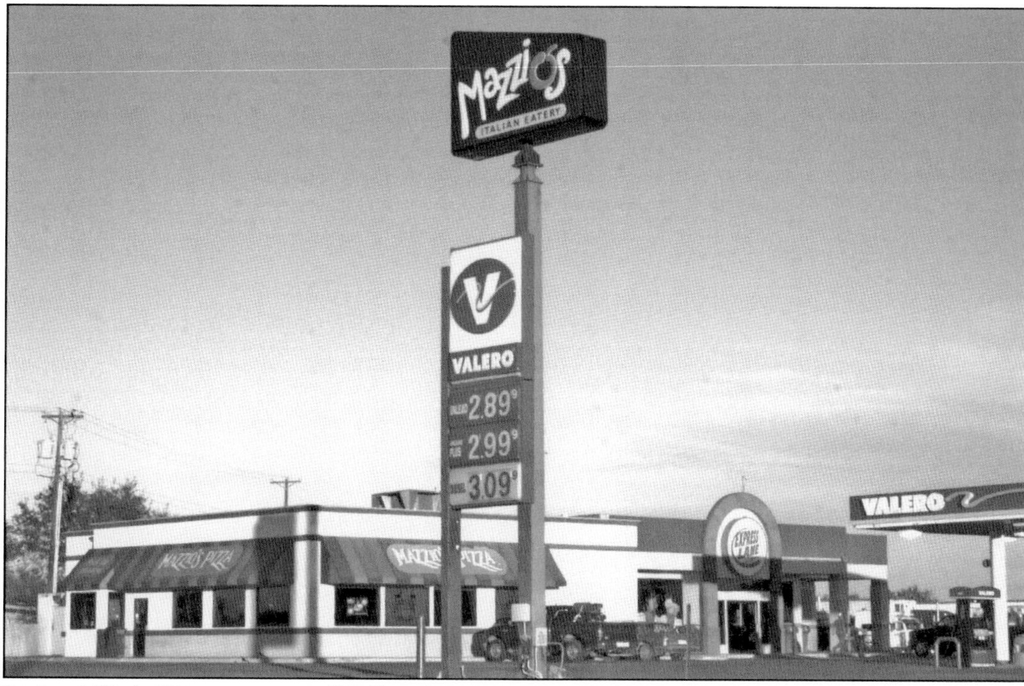

Richard "Dyke" Rogers is one of Dalhart's most prominent businessmen. His businesses are devoted to tourism, agriculture, and real estate. The tourism business includes 18 Express Lane stores with five in Dalhart, employing 135 people and selling convenience items and petroleum products. The tourism business also includes Mazzio's Pizza, an Italian eatery that employs 12 people, and Juan's Burrito's Mexican Grille, which opened in 2011. Dyke's agricultural business includes Frontier Fuel Company, an existing business that he purchased in 1970, selling petroleum products to farmers, dairies, and commercial accounts. The business has grown from $1.2 million to $140 million in annual sales and is one of the largest-volume Pioneer Brand Corn seed distributors in America. The farm management company owns and/or manages over 30,000 acres of irrigated farmland, raising corn, cotton, wheat, and grain sorghum. The Real Estate Brokerage office opened in Dalhart in 2003, specializing in farm, ranch, and dairy sales, and is one of the leading realtors in the United States in its field, based upon sales volume, and advertises around the world with clients in several nations and many states. The businesses are at the center of Dalhart's economy, primarily based on agriculture and secondarily on tourism. Dyke, a 1970 graduate of West Texas A&M University, has noted that Dalhart is a unique place and one of the most progressive agricultural communities in the world, but without enough people to take advantage of the opportunities provided by that culture. He has called Dalhart the "land of milk and honey agriculturally," and a great place to live and prosper. (Courtesy of Robin Scott.)

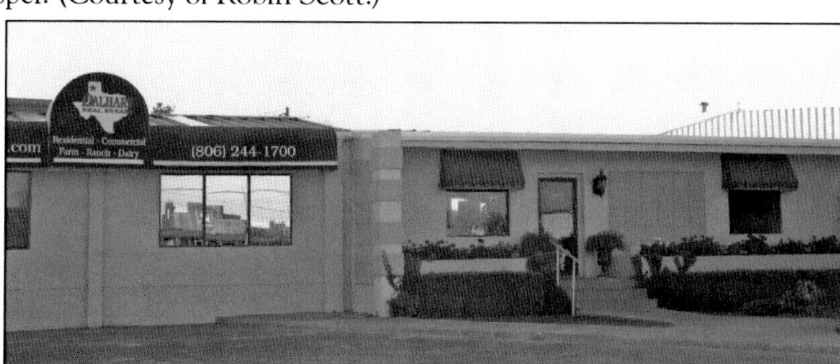

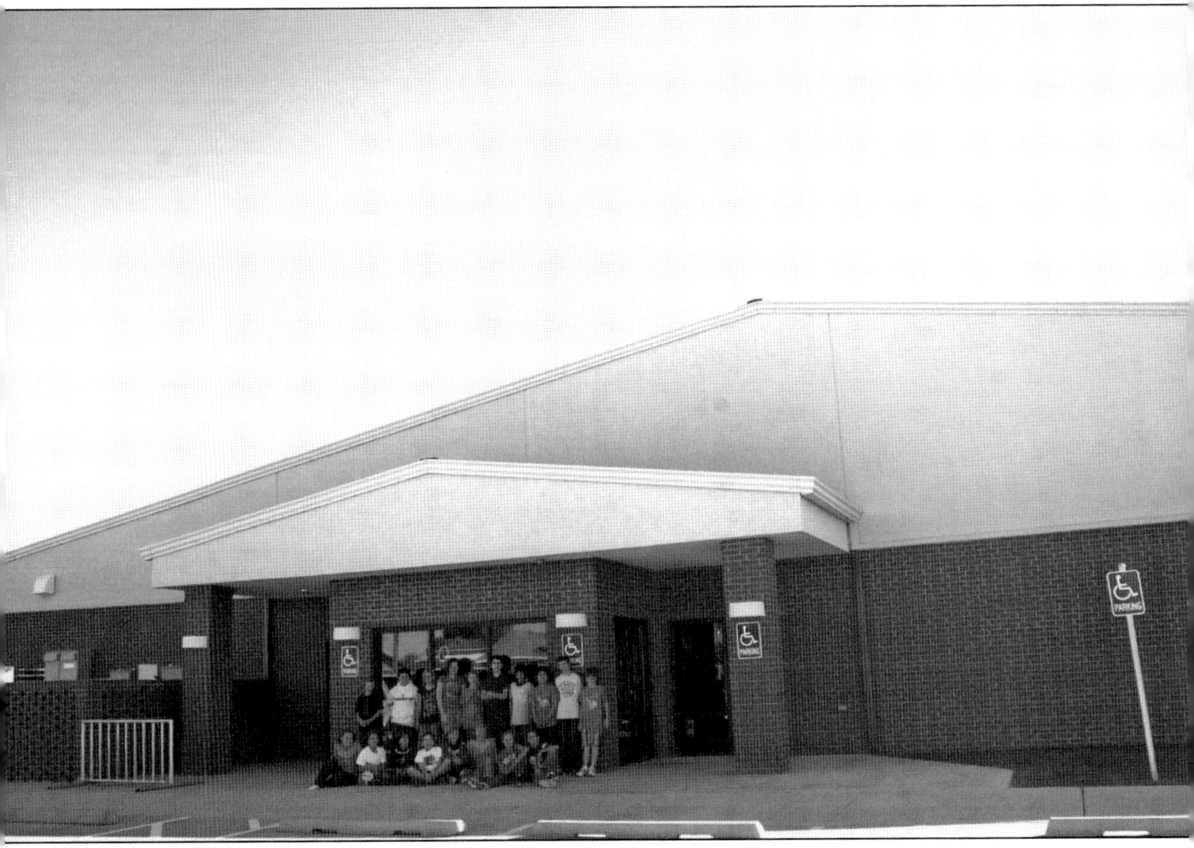

The Recreation Outreach Center, fondly referred to as the ROC, caters to area residents in numerous ways. The need for the ROC has been demonstrated many times over. In 2009, just after it opened its doors for the first time, it became the refuge in the storm for 160 motorists stranded in the blizzard of March 26. In 2010, forty-five Boy Scouts stayed for several hours enjoying the center's many indoor games after their bus caught fire on their way home to Houston from New Mexico. Several college students riding bikes across America have camped out in the spacious gymnasium on cots supplied by the City of Dalhart. The ROC also serves as a safe place for schoolchildren every afternoon, Monday through Friday, with 50 to 100 kids spending their afterschool hours at the ROC. A vacation bible school for 230 area children is another use for the facility, which has a gym with basketball and volleyball courts, a gaming area for ping-pong, air hockey, Foosball, and board games. The ROC also has a full-service kitchen where meals are regularly made for various events. (Courtesy of Robin Scott.)

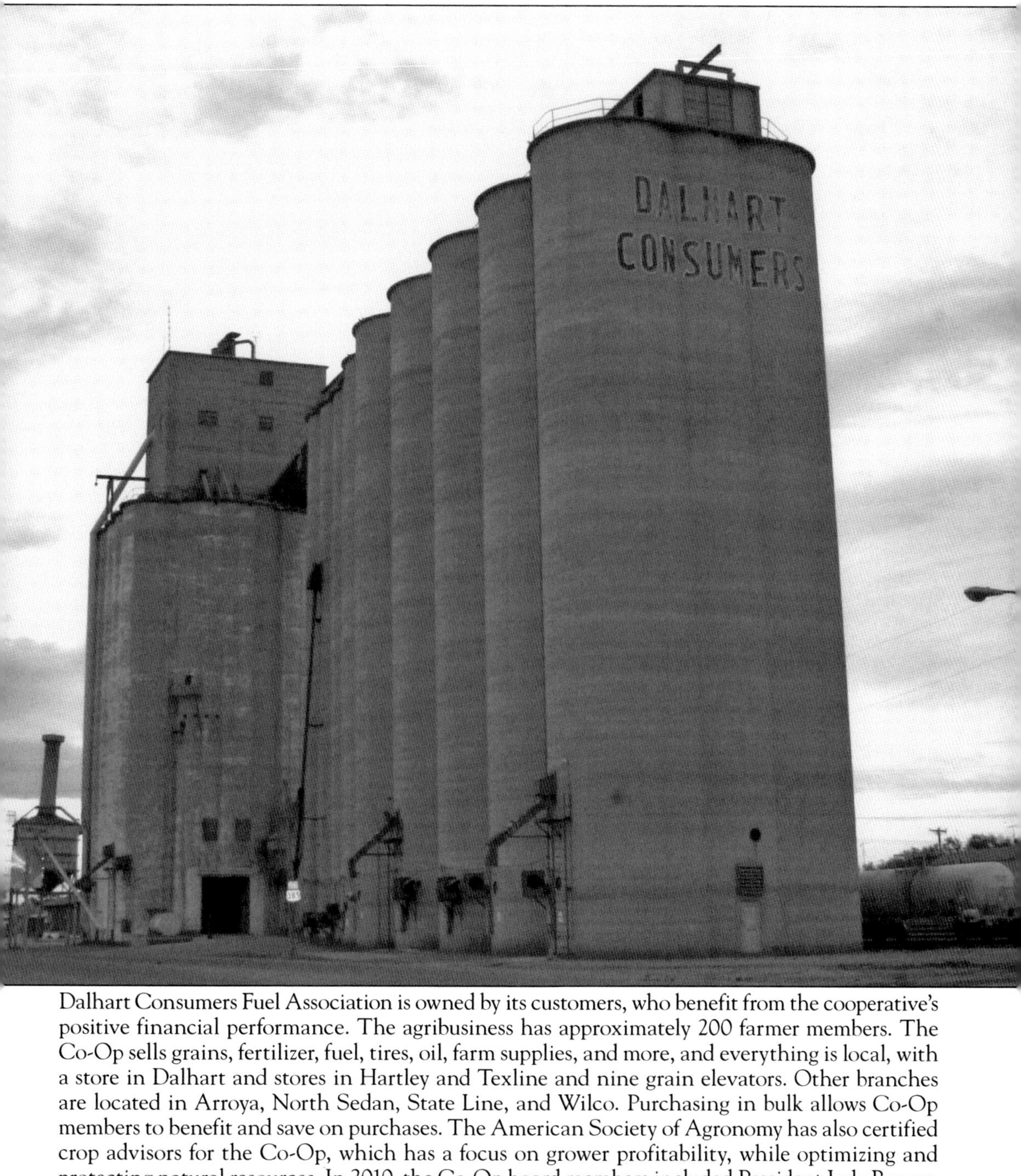

Dalhart Consumers Fuel Association is owned by its customers, who benefit from the cooperative's positive financial performance. The agribusiness has approximately 200 farmer members. The Co-Op sells grains, fertilizer, fuel, tires, oil, farm supplies, and more, and everything is local, with a store in Dalhart and stores in Hartley and Texline and nine grain elevators. Other branches are located in Arroya, North Sedan, State Line, and Wilco. Purchasing in bulk allows Co-Op members to benefit and save on purchases. The American Society of Agronomy has also certified crop advisors for the Co-Op, which has a focus on grower profitability, while optimizing and protecting natural resources. In 2010, the Co-Op board members included President Jody Bezner, Vice President Bud Snead, Secretary Kyle Kemp, Floyd Franklin, Chad Strafuss, Steve Yoder, and Doug Lathem. The company's general manager was Jim Turner. Although the tire shop caught fire in July 2010, the business quickly rebounded to serve the community, even as it rebuilt its main offices and shop. (Courtesy of Robin Scott.)

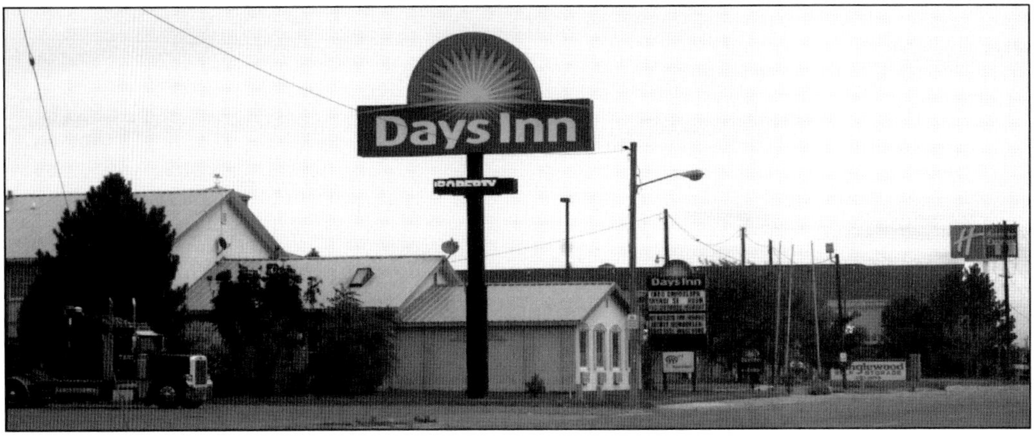

Dalhart's unique location at the intersection of Highways 87, 54, and 385 makes it a place where many travelers stop to eat and stay for the night. Dalhart is less than 50 miles from New Mexico and Oklahoma, and not much farther from Colorado. On the highways leading into Dalhart, there are few hotel accommodations, making Dalhart the perfect place to stop and rest for the night. In 2010, Dalhart had 11 hotels, including the Best Western, Budget Inn, Days Inn, Econo Lodge, Holiday Inn Express, Rodeway Inn, Sands, Super 8, Tri-State Motel, Western Skies, and the XIT Ranch Motel. Each time a visitor spends the night in a Dalhart lodging, he or she pays a hotel-occupancy tax, the "bed tax" that provides much-needed support for area businesses such as the Dalhart Area Chamber of Commerce and the XIT Museum. Although the population of Dalhart is relatively small, its tourism gives it a bigger-town feel, with many Dalhart businesses catering to the traveler. (Courtesy of Robin Scott.)

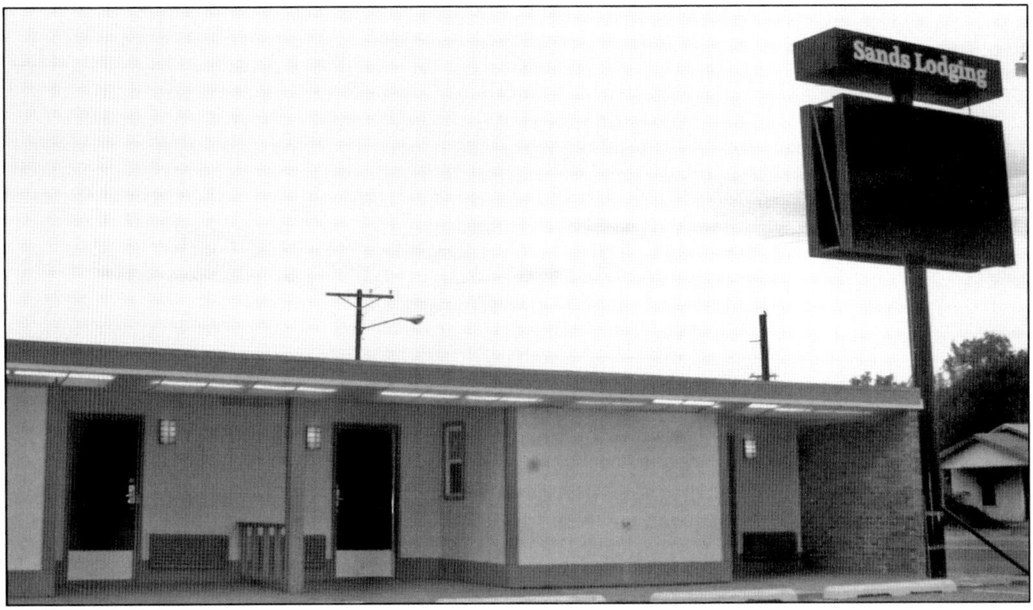

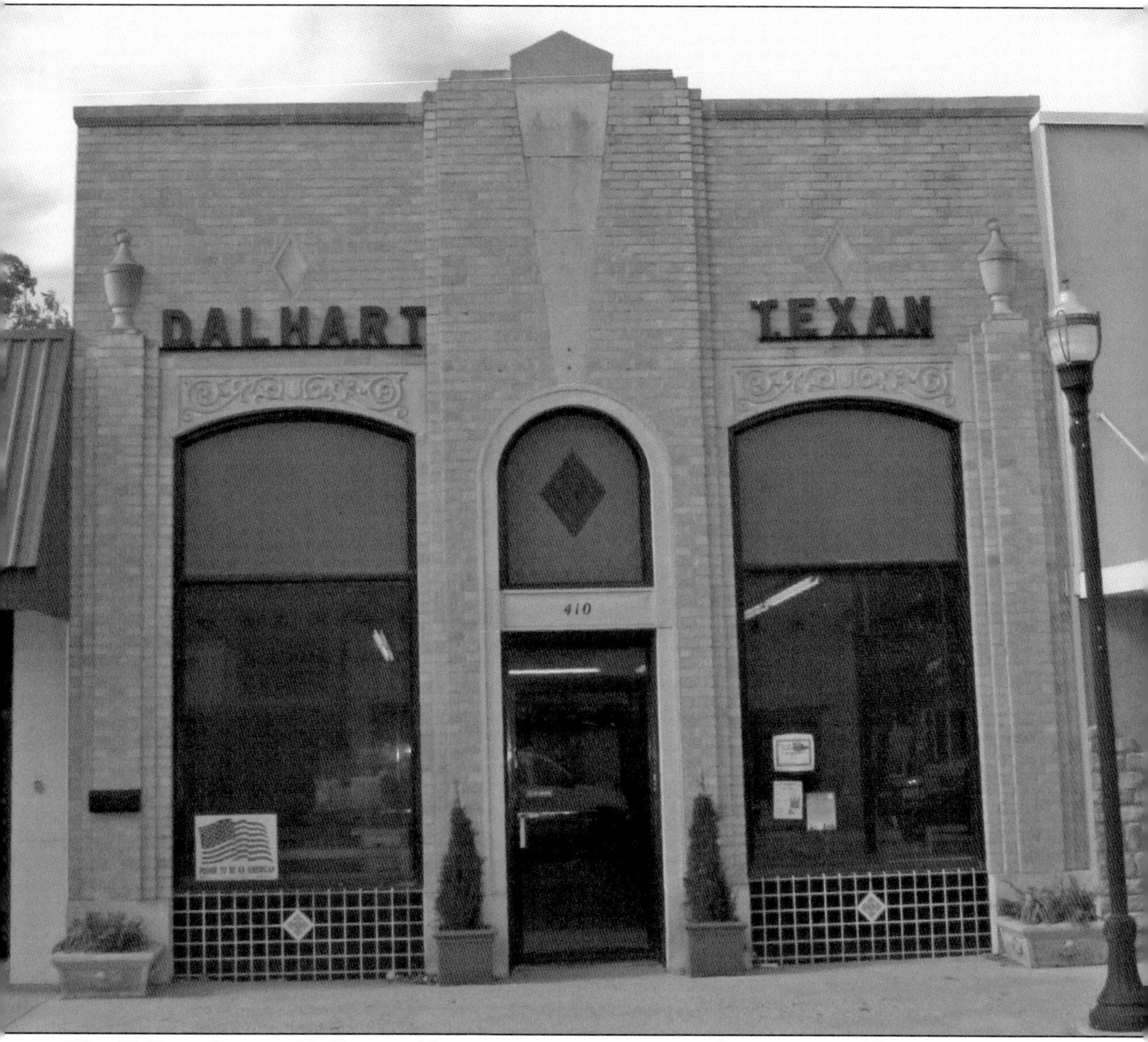

The *Dalhart Texan* is Dalhart's oldest continuously running business, established in 1901 by newsman Robert B. Edgell. Herbert Walker was owner during much of Dalhart's early development, and in 1929, Wilbur C. Hawk, Gene Howe, and John McCarty acquired the paper from Walker. McCarty was editor from 1929 until he left for the *Amarillo Globe News* in 1936, and is credited with encouraging residents to stay in Dalhart during the Dust Bowl years. From 1947 to 1989, Kenneth Hogue published the newspaper. In 1989, he turned the reins over to his daughter, Susan Hogue Clay. Under Clay's direction, the newspaper has gone from predominantly national news to local news, and she ensures that area businesses, organizations, social groups, and schoolchildren are highlighted in every edition, while still keeping area residents connected to the outside world. Over the years, the newspaper has earned many awards, including the Golden Nail Award for its support of the fine arts. In 2010, the newspaper earned top honors in photography and special sections from the Panhandle Press Association. (Courtesy of Robin Scott.)

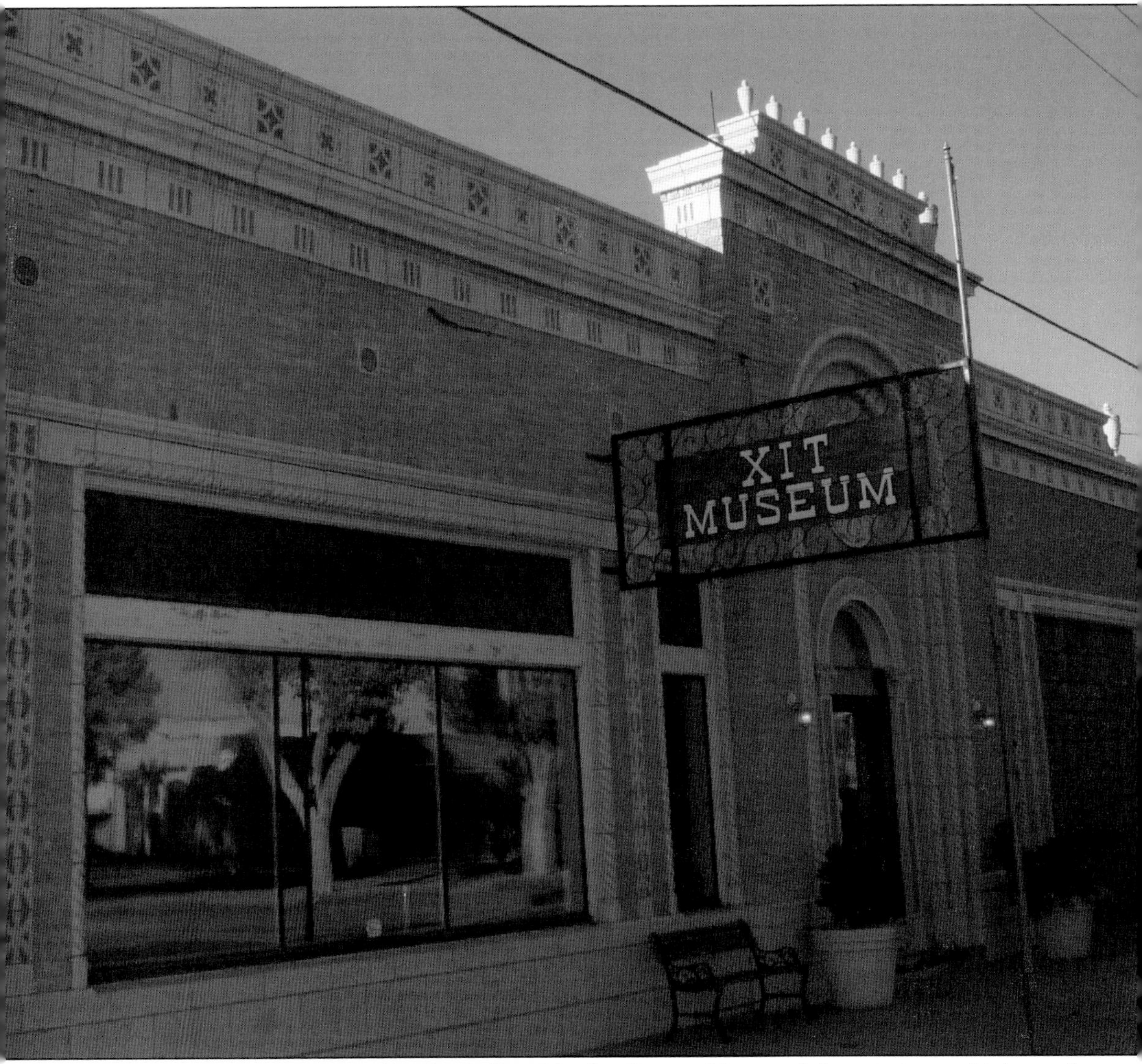

The XIT Museum is operated by the Dallam-Hartley County Historical Association and is located in downtown Dalhart, across the street from the Dallam County Courthouse. The museum opened in 1975. Visitors to the museum have access to a vast amount of historical photographs, artifacts, and documents that chronicle Dalhart's 110-year history as well as that of the people, places, and things of the Texas Panhandle, the XIT Ranch, and outlying communities beyond Dallam and Hartley Counties. Each year, the museum is host to area schoolchildren who learn about indigenous wildlife and habitats. During the summer, children also have an opportunity to hear from an Indian storyteller, participate in wildlife walks at Lake Rita Blanca Canyon, and make arts and crafts. The museum also hosts several special exhibits and open houses each year, celebrating the talents of area children and local artists. The museum's current curator, Nick Olson, has been serving since 1993. (Courtesy of Robin Scott.)

BIBLIOGRAPHY

Blodgett, Jan. *Land of Bright Promise: Advertising the Texas Panhandle and South Plains 1870–1917.* Austin, Texas: University of Texas Press, 1988.

Cantrell, Liz. *Accent West.* August 1997.

Cates, Ivan. *The XIT Ranch: A Texas Legacy.* Channing, Texas: Hafabanana Press, 2008.

Dawson, John C. *High Plains Yesterdays: From XIT Days Through Drought and Depression.* Austin, Texas: Eakin Press, 1985.

Duke, Cordia Sloan, and Joe B. Frantz. *6,000 Miles of Fence: Life on the XIT Ranch.* Austin, Texas: The University of Texas Press, 1961.

Finch, Orville H. Jr. *A Family Named Finch: Volume II.* Amarillo, Texas: Trafton Printing, Inc., 1993.

Haley, J. Evetts. *The XIT Ranch of Texas and the Early Days of the Llano Estacado.* Norman, Oklahoma: University of Oklahoma Press, 1929.

Haley, James L. *Texas: An Album of History.* Garden City, New York: Doubleday & Company, Inc., 1985.

Harruff, Charles. Oral Interview. November 27, 2002.

Hunter, Lillie Mae. *The Book of Years: A History of Dallam and Hartley Counties.* Hereford, Texas: Pioneer Book Publishers, Inc., 1969.

Jones, Eddie. Oral Interview. December 17, 2002.

Panhandle-Plains Historical Review. Canyon, Texas: Panhandle-Plains Historical Society, 1999.

The *Dalhart Daily Texan.* Dalhart, Texas: The Dalhart Publishing Company, 1902–2005.

The *Dalhart Texan.* Dalhart, Texas: The Dalhart Publishing Company, 2005 to present.